D0385813

PELICAN BOOKS

A646

FREEDOM, THE INDIVIDUAL
AND THE LAW

H. STREET

Professor Harry Street was born in 1919. He was educated at Farnworth Grammar School and Manchester University, where he gained his LL.B in 1938. He qualified as a solicitor in 1940, but during the war served as a Flight Lieutenant in the R.A.F. Since 1946 he has been a university teacher. He was Professor of Law at Nottingham University from 1952 to 1956. Since then he has occupied the same position in his own university at Manchester. In 1957–8 he was Visiting Professor at Harvard Law School, U.S.A. He has published several books on legal subjects, and contributed articles to numerous English, Canadian, and American journals. He is married, and has three children.

H. STREET

FREEDOM
THE INDIVIDUAL
AND THE LAW

PENGUIN BOOKS

Penguin Books Ltd, Harmondsworth, Middlesex
U.S.A.: Penguin Books Inc., 3300 Clipper Mill Road, Baltimore 11, Md
AUSTRALIA: Penguin Books Pty Ltd, 762 Whitehorse Road,
Mitcham, Victoria

—

First published 1963

—

Copyright © H. Street, 1963

Made and printed in Great Britain
by C. Nicholls & Company Ltd
Set in Monotype Baskerville

CONTENTS

PREFACE

The purpose of this book is to provide a survey of the present content of civil liberties in England. No book has previously attempted such an account of the legal and administrative basis of the various executive interferences with the citizen's liberty. It is hoped that, besides satisfying the demands of the general reader for a guide to his freedoms, the student of constitutional law or government, whether in university, technical college, or sixth form, will find it useful.

Mr John D. Jump, Reader in English Literature in my University, has read the whole of the manuscript; I am deeply indebted to him for his efforts to make the text as intelligible and free from legal jargon as possible. Mr David Williams, Fellow of Keble College, Oxford, has brought his great knowledge of twentieth-century constitutional law to bear in the course of reading the entire book: I have benefited greatly from his suggestions. I am grateful to the publishers for their guidance and help at every stage in the writing of the book.

September 1963   HARRY STREET

INTRODUCTION

ENGLISHMEN pride themselves on the freedoms which they enjoy. In no one place, however, can they find an account of those freedoms. This book is an attempt to fill that gap. Each of the fundamental liberties will be looked at in turn with a view to ascertaining what the law (whether laid down by Parliament or the Courts) and practice have to say about their content. By the time the reader has finished he will know (to mention a few matters) just what are the relations between himself and the police, what freedom he has to organize meetings, how much censorship there is in Britain, how far the law recognizes his freedom to work, and what restrictions have been imposed on freedom in the interests of national security. One large topic which may be thought relevant has been excluded: the growth of delegated legislation and administrative justice, Crichel Down and so on. That is the one topic which has received adequate coverage in books intended for laymen. In a sense that subject is plainly severable from other aspects of civil liberties, and to include it in this book with proportionately the same detail as for the remainder of the contents would have been greatly to expand the book without perhaps greatly adding to the fund of knowledge readily available at present.

Civil liberties are a fluid subject: almost every day the newspapers report some new development, whether it be the intended deportation of Soblen or Carmen Bryan, or the Fascist meetings and their incitement to racial prejudice, or the satirical attacks of the B.B.C.'s *That Was The Week That Was*. The list is endless, but every effort is made in what follows to keep track of the most recent legal and administrative trends.

We shall see that any evaluation of the limits on our

liberties must always balance the competing interests at stake. Nowhere is this better illustrated than in the recent discussion of the treatment of the reporters, Foster and Mulholland. The Press has used all its power to protest at their imprisonment: it has made telling points in contrasting the privilege of solicitors with the rightlessness of journalists; it has represented the affair as an interference with the freedom of the Press and as another triumph for bureaucracy against the individual. Against all this, other factors must be weighed. Traditionally, freedom of the Press means freedom to *publish* – this case effected no interference with that – not license for the Press to *acquire* news as it thinks fit, immune from the restraints of the law as it does so. The Lord Chief Justice is not preaching totalitarian doctrine merely because he recognizes that in some circumstances closely and directly affecting national security the need for a Court to know the source of a journalist's information in order to test possible leaks in our security outweighs the freedom of a journalist not to reveal the sources of his news. This is how English law goes about its job of defining limits on our freedoms. The citizen may do as he likes unless he clashes with some specific restriction on his freedom. The law does not say: 'You can do that'; it says 'You cannot do this,' which means that you can do everything else except that which it says you cannot do. Whenever such a prohibition is made, the reason will be that some other interest is rated more important than that freedom on which it impinges. The reader will make up his own mind as he progresses whether the line has always been drawn at the right point, but first let him acquaint himself with the present law, which is hard enough to ascertain in many instances. Many decisions will inevitably be seen as compromises; some, it will be contended, have paid excessive regard to the claims of the state.

What is distinctive in form about the English arrangements is that the citizen will not find his freedoms set out in any written constitution. This is in contrast not only with the historic American and French Constitutions but also with twentieth-century trends. As members of the Commonwealth secure their independence they tend to have written constitutions; India, for example. On the international scene, also, the pressure is for statements of principle such as the Declaration of Human Rights. As the reader progresses through the book, it will be no bad thing for him to consider whether we are better off without a constitution, relying on the ordinary Courts to minimize as much as is reasonable any specific encroachments on our freedom. Does the practical, piecemeal improvisation suit us better than the formal high-sounding manifesto? Or do we pay too high a price in more uncertainty about the precise limits of our freedom?

In the United States, for example, there are hundreds of books dealing with civil liberties. So far as is known, this is the first book which attempts to survey comprehensively the state of civil liberties in Britain. One reason for this striking difference is that it is easier to expound a written constitution than to grub in the law reports, Hansard, and newspaper files, to inquire in Whitehall and of the various 'fringe' bodies like the British Board of Film Censors and the Independent Television Authority, whose activities raise issues concerning our liberties. It is in the belief that our liberties will be the more firmly established the better their extent and limitations are appreciated, that the following survey is attempted.

CHAPTER I

PERSONAL FREEDOM AND
POLICE POWERS

In England, the policeman's main task is to detect and catch people suspected of crime so that the Courts may try them for the acts which they are alleged to have done. What powers, in carrying out that task, do the police enjoy and how are they exercised? Does the Englishman's cherished idea that he does not live in a police state match up to reality? Are police powers hedged around with adequate protection for the citizen? This opening chapter considers personal liberty, our most vaunted freedom, against the realities of police behaviour, and follows the police from their powers of arrest to the restrictions imposed on the searching and entering of premises, to police questioning, then to bail and *habeas corpus*, and finally to an extended discussion of the controversial powers of telephone tapping and intercepting mail.

The reader will be constantly reminded that somehow two public interests must be balanced: the need to ensure that criminals are caught on the one hand, and on the other the right of the citizen to go about his business without unnecessary interference.

ARREST

English law recognizes (and rightly so) that a policeman needs greater powers than the rest of us. It is a sensible provision that a policeman who believes a certain person to have committed a crime can make a sworn statement before a justice of the peace or other judicial officer, whereupon the justice may at his discretion issue the policeman with a warrant which authorizes him to arrest the person named. A policeman who arrests that person on the authority of the warrant is fully protected by the law even though it turns out that the man arrested was innocent. Warrants are not issued to the ordinary citizen.

There is not always time to seek out a magistrate before making an arrest. Here again we see the difference between the powers of a policeman and the rest of us. Shops with open counters have many of their goods stolen and frequently employ store detectives (who are merely employees of the shop, not policemen, and therefore have the same powers as other private citizens) to protect them against shoplifting. The shop detective who believes that somebody in the shop has stolen goods may arrest him, provided that he takes him to the police station or before a justice within a reasonable time in order to be charged with the offence. But he makes the arrest at his peril; if either the goods have not been stolen or they have been stolen but a reasonable man would not in the circumstances have suspected the man arrested of being the thief, the shop employee and his employer will both be liable for false imprisonment to the person arrested. For instance,[1] W. H. Smith & Son Ltd thought that one Walters was in the habit of stealing books from their bookstall at King's Cross railway station; their employee challenged Walters while in possession of one of their books and took him to the police station. Walters was charged with stealing and found not guilty by a jury who accepted his plea that he did not intend to steal. Walters was able to recover damages from W. H. Smith & Son Ltd for the false arrest although the Court found that they had reasonable grounds for believing Walters guilty, because the book had not in fact been stolen by Walters or anyone else. This may seem harsh on the company, but an alternative course of action had been open to them. They could have reported the facts to a policeman and left him to charge Walters, whereupon they would not have been answerable for false imprisonment, and the policeman would have been protected as long as he acted on reasonable suspicion, even though no crime had actually been committed by anyone.

Stealing is one of those more serious offences known as felonies. It is only for a felony that the common law gives a citizen this power to arrest on reasonable suspicion that the person arrested is the one who has committed the offence, and gives a policeman the power to arrest on reasonable suspicion that the felony has been committed by the person arrested. For lesser crimes, misdemeanours and summary offences tried only before magistrates, private citizens cannot arrest, and policemen may do so only in the exceptional cases where an Act of Parliament authorizes it. If, therefore, a policeman on the beat sees a pedal cyclist riding by without lights after lighting-up time, and orders him to stop for the purpose of 'booking' him for this offence, the cyclist is legally free to ignore the order. This is a summary offence for which there is no power to arrest. The policeman cannot here invoke the powers which he is given by road traffic legislation when he is controlling traffic, or the power to halt mechanically propelled vehicles for a check of driving licences: he merely has power to charge the cyclist with the offence if he can discover his identity, but the man is under no obligation to give his name and address. The astute policeman might justify any arrest by asserting a reasonable suspicion of stealing, but he will have to think of this one quickly, as the following case shows:

Leachinsky was a dealer in rags or waste who bought supplies from time to time from Michaelson in Leicester.[2] In August 1942, he bought three bales of waste, and in picking them up he asked Michaelson if he had any remnants from which he might make a dress for his wife. Michaelson said he had, and Leachinsky bought a considerable number of remnants and had them packed in a single bale. The four bales were shipped to Leachinsky's warehouse in Liverpool and they were all described as waste. At the time of the purchase of the remnants war-rationing restrictions on the purchase and sale of cloth were in effect.

When the goods arrived in Liverpool the police, being

suspicious, examined the goods and discovered that one of the bales contained cloth and not waste. When Leachinsky started to unload the bales, he himself set aside the bale of cloth. Christie and Morris, police officers, then questioned Leachinsky about a bale of cloth and the latter professed to know nothing about such cloth. The officers, not satisfied with the explanation, arrested Leachinsky under the provisions of the Liverpool Corporation Act, 1921. This Act provided that if a person's name and address were unknown, he could be arrested and brought before the Court to give an explanation of his possession of goods believed to have been stolen by someone, although not necessarily by the person arrested – the charge usually referred to as 'unlawful possession'. The two police officers knew Leachinsky's name and address and later, in evidence, Christie admitted that he knew that he had no power to arrest under the Liverpool Corporation Act and that he had made the arrest in this way simply because it was 'more convenient'.

Leachinsky was charged in the police Court with 'unlawful possession' and after spending a night in gaol was brought before a magistrate on 1 September, when a remand of one week in custody was granted. During this period the police saw Michaelson in Leicester and the latter denied that he had sold the goods to Leachinsky and claimed that they had been taken from him without his authority. When Leachinsky was brought before the magistrate on 8 September, a further remand was granted of one week, under bail, and at the hearing on 15 September the police withdrew the charge of unlawful possession and Leachinsky was discharged. Before he could leave the Court he was re-arrested for theft of the remnants. At his subsequent trial, he was acquitted and Michaelson was proved to have been lying. Leachinsky sued Michaelson for libel and recovered £250. Leachinsky then brought an action for false imprisonment against Christie and Morris: anyone, whether policeman or citizen, who arrests another when he has no authority at law to do so, commits this wrong of false imprisonment and is liable to pay heavy damages to the person whom he unlawfully arrests.

At the trial before Mr Justice Stable the defendants obtained judgement, the trial judge taking the view that the two police officers had reasonable grounds for suspecting Leachinsky of theft, and although the arrest on the 'unlawful possession' charge was improper, they could justify the arrest by their state of mind at the time of the arrest. As he put it, 'Why did they arrest him? If they arrested him because they believed he had committed a felony and there were reasonable grounds for so believing, they do not lose the protection of the law.' The Court of Appeal reversed this judgement, and the House of Lords affirmed the award of damages for false imprisonment made in the Court of Appeal. The House of Lords held that even though the policemen had valid grounds for arresting Leachinsky on reasonable suspicion of stealing, they chose to arrest him for an offence under the Liverpool Corporation Act, which did not in the circumstances authorize the arrest. Viscount Simon said:

(1) If a policeman arrests without warrant upon reasonable suspicion of felony, or of other crime of a sort which does not require a warrant, he must in ordinary circumstances inform the person arrested of the true ground of arrest. He is not entitled to keep the reason to himself or to give a reason which is not the true reason. In other words a citizen is entitled to know on what charge or on suspicion of what crime he is seized. (2) If the citizen is not so informed but is nevertheless seized, the policeman, apart from certain exceptions, is liable for false imprisonment. (3) The requirement that the person arrested should be informed of the reason why he is seized naturally does not exist if the circumstances are such that he must know the general nature of the alleged offence for which he is detained. (4) The requirement that he should be so informed does not mean that technical or precise language need be used. The matter is a matter of substance, and turns on the elementary proposition that in this country a person is, prima facie, entitled to his freedom and is only required to submit to restraints on his freedom if he knows in substance the

reason why it is claimed that this restraint should be imposed. (5) The person arrested cannot complain that he has not been supplied with the above information as and when he should be, if he himself produces the situation which makes it practically impossible to inform him, e.g., by immediate counter-attack or by running away. There may well be other exceptions to the general rule in addition to those I have indicated, and the above propositions are not intended to constitute a formal or complete code, but to indicate the general principles of our law on a very important matter. These principles equally apply to a private person who arrests on suspicion.

Who pays the damages awarded against a policeman who falsely arrests somebody? Only the policeman can be sued, neither the Crown nor the local authority which appoints him is answerable for his false arrests: he is exercising the independent discretion cast upon him as a constable, and not acting as somebody else's servant, so that the ordinary rule that the employer can be sued for the employee's wrongdoing does not apply. Does this mean that the policeman has to find damages and both parties' legal costs (which might very well exceed the damages) out of his own pocket? Mr Butler, as Home Secretary, dealing with the payment of damages to the motorist who offered to help with evidence Brian Rix, the actor, when a P.C. Eastmond was summoning him for a traffic offence, and whom Eastmond allegedly assaulted for his pains, said in the House of Commons that the usual practice was for the police authority to meet the constable's damages and costs.[3] No doubt Mr Butler was right in saying that this is the usual practice, but there is no legal authority for local authorities paying damages awarded against policemen in such cases. An interested ratepayer, in order to prevent an illegal drain on public funds, could seek the levy of a surcharge against councillors who approved such payments in council meeting.

What happens when the person arrested is ultimately acquitted of the charge for which he was arrested? He can ask the Court to make him a grant towards the legal costs he has incurred in defending himself. Only in comparatively rare instances when the Court feels that the charge should never have been brought is the Court likely to make any grant towards his costs. When a person acquitted can establish that the prosecution was instituted out of spite or for some purpose other than bringing him to justice, and that there was no reasonable and probable cause for believing him guilty, he may after his acquittal sue his prosecutor in damages for malicious prosecution. In practice it is so difficult to prove all these essentials of this wrong that those acquitted very rarely succeed in obtaining damages for this; the reader will see from a House of Lords case described a few pages later that there are particular difficulties in suing the police for malicious prosecution.

TAKING A SUSPECT TO THE POLICE STATION

The detective story and the daily press regularly tell us that the police detain citizens for questioning. When the B.B.C. put on a programme about police practices a former Scotland Yard superintendent vouched in the *Radio Times* that the programme would be accurate in every detail,[4] and at the end of the programme an assistant chief constable of a large city stressed that the actions of the police were authentic. In the programme a man was told by a policeman that the policeman would have to detain him pending inquiries, although no charge was then preferred against him. Occasionally, it emerges in the course of a trial that the accused was detained against his will before being charged and without having been arrested. There is much more similar evidence that it is the practice of the police to take a suspected person to the police station in order to question him with a view to ascertaining whether he is to be charged with some offence. Yet Courts from the House of Lords downwards have frequently had to make it clear that the police have no power to require a person to go to the police station in order to answer questions. This direction to the jury by Mr Justice Devlin (as he then was) is typical:

'You may sometimes read in novels and detective stories, perhaps written by people not familar with police procedure, that persons are sometimes taken into custody for questioning. There is no such power in this country. A man cannot be detained unless he is arrested.'

If, then, a policeman is to compel a citizen to accompany him to the police station, he must arrest him, and, as we have seen, inform him of the reason for the arrest. If he takes him to the station, or detains him there, against his will, this is the wrong of false imprisonment for which the victim can recover damages from the policeman. Still less, of course, can a policeman lawfully insist that a witness visit the station in order to make a statement or to answer questions, or indeed that he make a statement anywhere. The citizen can be served with a subpoena ordering him to attend as a witness when the case comes into Court for hearing, but that is all. And it is the Court, not the police or the prosecution, who alone can issue a subpoena.

What then happens in practice? It may be supposed that the police experience little difficulty in securing the attendance at the police station of those whose presence they require. No doubt the first reaction of the Englishman, if not of the Irishman, is to do as a policeman asks. One distinguished judge has recently attributed this readiness, rightly or wrongly, to 'the Englishman's tolerance of, and indeed affection for, the unwritten rule; his natural instinct is to act according to what he believes to be the general understanding among his fellows as to how he should behave rather than to look for a rule permitting or prohibiting what he proposes to do and to study its terms'. The witness will recognize his public duty to aid detection of crime by giving the police all possible assistance. The innocent suspect will welcome the chance to clear himself. Even the guilty may see some advantage in trying to convince the police of his innocence; and in due course the jury may draw unfavourable conclusions from the accused's refusal to give a statement to the police. It may be doubted, too, whether the average citizen realizes that the police have no compulsive power; and one can hardly expect the police to make their task harder by prefacing every invitation to come to the station with the express intimation that the citizen may please himself whether he accepts. If he should complain of this 'detention for questioning' he will of course succeed in an action for false imprisonment unless the police prove that he consented to the detention. A citizen who complied without protest with the request to accompany the officer to the station, under the mistaken impression that he had to go, would be deemed to have consented. If, however, the policeman by his statements or conduct led him to believe that he was compelled to go, the policeman would have no defence. We read of persons being detained in police stations for hours, sometimes days, without being charged, while they 'assist the police in their inquiries'. Theoretically, these persons are free to leave at any time, and certainly they can sue if they are prevented from leaving. The difficulty here is of course largely one of proof. Who will be believed, the policeman who states that the man wished to remain in the station, or the man who says that they refused to let him go until he answered their questions? The burden of proof is on the policeman: unless the Court is satisfied by a preponderance of evidence that the man did stay of his own free will, he can recover damages from the policeman who detained him.

SEARCH

No English case has conclusively decided the point, but probably a policeman may search a person whom he lawfully arrests and take and detain property found in his possession which will form material evidence on his prosecution for the crime for which he has been arrested. The law has long imposed serious restrictions on the claims of the police to search private premises. A series of cases in the seventeen-sixties followed the issuing by the government of the day of general warrants to search premises, i.e. warrants in which either the person or the property is not specified. In the great case of *Entick* v. *Carrington*[5] the Secretary of State issued a general warrant to officers who broke into the house of Entick, who was suspected of editing a seditious publication, *The British Freeholder,* and seized his books and papers. The Lord Chief Justice of the day castigated the government's conduct severely and awarded Entick £300 damages for trespass. John Wilkes was awarded £1,000 damages against an Under-Secretary of State who entered his house and seized papers under a warrant to arrest the (unnamed) authors, printers, and publishers of the *North Briton.*[6] The Courts firmly established the rule that no state official or policeman may enter a citizen's premises unless he has authority of law. This authority may derive from a search warrant issued by a magistrate under powers conferred by one of the many statutes which authorize search for particular offences, e.g., the Official Secrets Acts, or the Larceny Act, 1916. In *Elias* v. *Pasmore* (1934)[7] Pasmore had a warrant for the arrest of one Hannington, who was an official of the National Unemployed Workers Movement. Pasmore entered the premises of the Movement in order to arrest Hannington, and, in addition to arresting him, seized a number of documents and removed them to Scotland Yard. Elias was the lessee of the premises and was also charged with an offence. The police retained many of the seized documents even after the trial of Hannington and Elias. Elias sued Pasmore for trespass to his premises and the return of the documents and damages for their detention. It is unfortunate that a case which raised such important points for the first time in English law went no further than the judge at first instance. This judge held that Pasmore acted illegally in refusing to return the documents at the conclusion of the trial. He also held that Pasmore was entitled to seize documents which were evidence of a crime committed by anyone, whether it be of the person arrested, or of the owner of the premises where the arrest of another took place, or of anybody else. His reasoning rested on the laconic observation that 'the interests of the state' excused the seizure, a view quite out of harmony with the leading case of *Entick* v. *Carrington*. His decision has been strongly criticized, and may not be followed when the matter again comes up for decision. It would be extraordinary if English law permitted a policeman to delay arrest until a suspect visited some premises other than his own which the policeman wanted to search for purposes wholly unconnected with the crime allegedly committed by the person arrested – such exploratory searches are certainly illegal in the United States. The 1929 Royal Commission on Police Powers and Procedure[8] reported that it was the practice of the police, even when arresting without a warrant, to search the premises where the person was arrested and to seize documents.

When the Home Secretary was questioned by Sir Stafford Cripps in the House of Commons about the search of the premises where Hannington was arrested (before the law suit), he answered that the practice of searching the premises of a person arrested was well established, that he was satisfied that Pasmore's conduct was proper, and that this conduct 'has constantly been brought to the notice of the Courts and was recognized as necessary and proper by the Royal Commission'.[9] Police practice had not changed by 1961. The wife of a Nottingham University lecturer was charged with shoplifting. Despite her protestations of innocence and her explanation, the police visited her home and searched it upon the pretext that it was the usual practice. When dismissing the case for lack of evidence the Nottingham Court expressed its disapproval by awarding her 100 guineas costs.

There is no doubt that the practice is illegal. The police may be made liable in damages for trespass, unless they can satisfy the Court that the owners freely consented: the contention of the Home Office that the practice has become law through tacit approval of the Courts is plainly erroneous.

A recent House of Lords case[10] cast incidental light on police practices. McIver, a police sergeant at Scotland Yard, had been making inquiries about one Glinski in connexion with a conspiracy to defraud. Glinski was arrested on 13

September but was released and not charged on that occasion. Nine days later, Glinski was a witness for Jack Comer of Soho when the latter was on trial at the Old Bailey. Comer was acquitted and the police suspected Glinski of perjury and wanted to know more about him. The officer in charge of the perjury investigation consulted McIver, who re-arrested Glinski on the conspiracy charge in his room in Paddington. With Sgt McIver was a detective concerned in the perjury investigation who went to search for any material that might be of use in it. Notice that Glinski was not arrested for perjury. He was tried and acquitted of conspiracy and then sued McIver for malicious prosecution. At this trial Glinski gave evidence that when McIver arrested him, McIver told him that he was a fool to give evidence for Comer, and that he would not have been charged with conspiracy if he had not given evidence. The jury presumably believed Glinski's evidence, for they found that McIver was actuated by malice. They awarded Glinski £2,500 damages against McIver. On appeal, the House of Lords reversed this verdict, although they did not upset the finding of malice, on the ground that Glinski had failed to prove that McIver, in addition to being malicious, had no reasonable cause for instituting proceedings.

The case raised another important point. Although McIver actually laid the charge, he sought to defend himself on the ground that he merely acted on superior orders. The House of Lords was equally divided on the validity of this defence. It raises a serious point. So long as English law requires all charges to be made by individuals, whether police officers or otherwise, and there can be no question of Scotland Yard being vicariously liable, it would be most unfortunate if victims of malicious prosecutions were left remediless because the policeman prosecuted could shelter behind unnamed senior officers who had not themselves been willing to take personal responsibility for charging the citizen.

ENTERING PREMISES

Another case illustrates the restrictions on the power of the police to enter premises.[11] A policeman noticed a lorry which he believed to be obstructing the highway. Shortly afterwards, he observed that it had been moved into a nearby garage for repair. He entered the garage in order to make inquiries, and was promptly ordered by the owner to leave. Instead, he began to pull out of his pocket a document proving that he was a police officer, whereupon the owner had to commit an assault and battery on him in order to remove him from the premises. The policeman prosecuted the owner for assault on him in the execution of his duty: the owner was found not guilty because the policeman had no lawful authority to remain when ordered to leave and could indeed have been successfully sued by the owner in trespass. On the other hand, if the police believe on reasonable grounds that a breach of the peace is likely to occur, they are justified in attending a public meeting on private premises even though the organizers ask them to leave; in the garage case above, the crime involved was not breach of the peace, but merely obstruction of the highway.

POLICE QUESTIONING

So far we have dealt with police conduct in connexion with criminal investigation outside the police station. Next we must consider what happens when the suspect is brought to the police station.

Our concern shifts to the questioning of suspects, which is controlled in two ways. The judges have formulated rules which are intended to regulate the way in which police make investigations. These Judges' Rules do not have the force of law, but whenever a statement has been taken from a man in disregard of any of the rules, the judge at the subsequent trial may at his discretion refuse to admit the statement in evidence. Secondly, the law excludes evidence of confessions which have been made involuntarily: the prisoner is entitled to demand as of right the rejection of an involuntary confession. This matter is of great importance because statements made to the police constitute the most important evidence in criminal detection – a fact which may disappoint readers and viewers of detective stories, who have been encouraged to expect something less humdrum.

The Judges' Rules recognize that where a police officer is trying to discover the author of a crime, there is no objection to his putting questions to any person, whether suspected or not, from whom he thinks that useful information can be obtained. This rule applies whether the questions are being asked in the police station or elsewhere. The rule seems essential if the police are not to be hampered in their task of detecting criminals, although of course the police cannot insist on an answer to any of their questions. Once a person has refused to make a statement or, having made one, declines to say any more, he must not again be asked to make a statement.

When the police officer has made up his mind to *charge* a person with a crime, he must first caution him that he is not obliged to say anything unless he wishes to do so, but that whatever he does say will be taken down in writing and may be given in evidence. But the sensible recommendation of the 1929 Royal Commission on Police Powers that the police should *always* issue a preliminary caution before questioning has been ignored. This rule about suspects who voluntarily attend for questioning is obviously very difficult to enforce. Suppose that the police have already learned enough to justify charging, but believe that further questioning will elicit information sufficient to ensure conviction. Is it not asking too much of human nature to expect the police to cease the questioning and to deliver the caution? If they are challenged later, who is to contradict them when they assert that they had not then made up their mind to charge?

The Judges' Rules provide that a person *in custody* is not to be questioned at all on the subject of the crime for which he is in custody. If, therefore, the police have decided to charge somebody but have not arrested him they may question him after caution – this distinction between charge and custody might seem shadowy, but there it is in the Judges' Rules. The Rules do not clearly define custody, but where a man has been brought to the police station against his will he is in custody for the present purpose, although, as we have seen, he would not have been lawfully arrested. Thus in one case[12] a man was invited to attend the police station for questioning and during the interview he confessed without having been cautioned. Cross-examination of the police elicited that the man would not have been allowed to leave if he had asked to do so. The Court held that he was in custody, and had therefore been questioned in breach of the Judges' Rules. Of course he was fortunate in having a policeman so responsive to cross-examination. The Royal Commission recommended that as soon as a person is in custody he should be told of his right to consult a lawyer, but the police do not follow this recommendation.

With regard to the rule about confessions, unless the prosecution can prove that the statement was not obtained from the accused either by fear of prejudice or by hope of advantage exercised or held out by the police or other person in authority, the confession will not be admitted in evidence at the trial. If the Court finds that the police told him that it would be better for him to confess – for example, that he would get a lighter sentence, or that the police would not oppose an application for bail – or that they put pressure on him to make a statement, the police will not be allowed to give evidence of the confession. The Courts are motivated by two considerations: the exclusion of confessions likely to be false and the regulating of fair police practices. The second of these is furthered by removing the temptation to the police to extract a confession in the hope that it will eventually be admitted in evidence. These then are the rules about police questioning. What happens in practice? Casual reading of newspapers is enough to indicate that persons who eventually are charged are often taken to the police station and remain there for many hours, sometimes a day or two, having no contact with the outside world, before they are charged on the basis of what they have told the police. The Royal Commission of 1929 found no reliable evidence of confessions obtained by violence, but they found considerable evidence that the police used such devices as keeping the suspect waiting for long periods (the Director of Public Prosecutions of the time defended this practice of detention in his evidence), constant repetition of the same suggestion, bluffing assertion that the police knew all the facts anyway and that a clean breast would make things easier at the trial, and so on. Much more skilful methods have been evolved since then as psychology has developed, and presumably the police have a similar tendency today to press inquiry hard against the man whom they genuinely believe to be guilty. A recent American legal text book quotes a letter from an English policeman written to an American friend in 1950:

Though the judges fondly imagine that their Rules are carried out to the letter they in fact very rarely are. All sorts of avoiding action are taken or otherwise the percentage of detections would be more than halved. You may have gathered that the said avoidance causes policemen to commit no little perjury in the box, and that would be a true assessment. ... The ignorance of the Great British Public neutralizes the Judges' Rules. When we deal with an educated man who knows his rights, we have had it, unless we have outside evidence enough.

One often reads even in responsible newspapers that the suspect has one safeguard: that the police have only twenty-four hours from when he first enters the station in which to secure a statement. This is a myth: there is no such time limit for questioning a man. The only limit imposed is that once the man has been *charged* he must be brought before a magistrate within twenty-four hours, and that, if this is impracticable, the station officer must ordinarily release him on bail except for serious crimes.

The mere fact that a confession is obtained by persistent and prolonged questioning of somebody under great emotional distress does not thereby render it inadmissible. But, even though there is no suggestion that violence has been used, it may be asked whether suspects should be allowed to be interrogated when suffering from lack of food or sleep, and whether they should be denied the opportunity to have their solicitor present before statements are made. The suspect who wishes to complain of unfair treatment by the police is often in this predicament: if he has previous convictions, there is a rule of evidence that by cross-examining police witnesses about their treatment of him, he may make it possible for them to do what otherwise they could not do, viz., give evidence of his previous convictions, which may of course greatly prejudice the jury against him.

To set against these considerations is the overwhelming public importance of ensuring that guilty persons are detected and punished. Take *R.* v. *Voisin*,[13] for example: on the body of the murdered woman was a label with the words 'Bladie Belgiam' on it. Without a caution, the suspect was asked to write 'Bloody Belgian', which he did in the same spelling as on the label, and thereby ensured his conviction. It is arguable that confessions are likely to be true, and that the Court can make up its mind on the point at trial. How can the police pursue their common technique of summoning all the professional criminals whose methods resemble those used in the crime under investigation to an identification parade before witnesses of that crime, if they have no power to 'detain for questioning'? If a suspect is to be informed of his right to consult a lawyer, the police will get no statement, for any lawyer will counsel silence on the part of his client. Similar objections apply to the proposal that interrogation should take place only before a magistrate. Do we want rules which enable guilty men to stay free and unpunished for their crimes?

There is the further problem of the mode of recording statements. It is the practice of the police to interview in pairs at least and to compose their notes of the suspect's statements soon after the interview has ended. Doubts often arise whether the notes are genuine. Attempts sometimes appear to have been made to conceal that questions have been asked even though questions are permitted to elucidate the suspect's statements and two policemen will purport to have made independently identical notes of a long interview. The policeman will not often admit the slightest deviation from the drill manual.

There is undoubtedly much professional and public concern about police questioning. The Government sensibly yielded at last in 1962 to the public demand for an examination of the problem, after having refused a little earlier to allow the Royal Commission on the Police then sitting to consider the matter, on the ground that police powers had previously been investigated as recently as 1929. The Judges' Rules are obviously far from perfect, and possible improvements in methods of recording statements deserve consideration. If methods which frustrate subsequent tampering with the tape can be evolved the case for tape-recording statements to the police would be strong. Perhaps in any event contemporaneous recording by the police of statements made to them should normally be insisted on. The rule subjecting the accused to cross-examination of his character if he challenges the methods of police witnesses should be abolished. It is also worth asking whether the custody-after-charge protection of the Judges' Rules should be extended to all questioning. The *Podola* case[14] (where a man was in such a physical state after being detained in a police station for murder of a policeman that he had to be taken to hospital for a considerable period before he was fit to stand trial) raises doubts whether suspects should be left in police cells, as distinct from prisons (which are free from police control), especially where serious crimes against policemen have been committed.

Another aspect of police investigation is not protected by the Judges' Rules. The police make every attempt to conduct a medical examination of persons whom they suspect of drunken driving. They have no duty to caution the suspect before inviting him to be tested, although of course they have no power to make him submit to the examination and tests. Scottish Courts refuse to admit such evidence unless the accused consents to be examined after having been informed that the examination may be used in evidence at his trial, and that he cannot be compelled to submit to an examination at all. It is to be regretted that the English Courts do not afford similar protection.

It is always important that innocent persons be not convicted, but especially so in Britain. For we are one of the few countries in the Western world which provides no remedy in the Courts against the State by way of damages for a person who is subsequently shown to have been convicted and sent to prison for a crime which he did not commit. All he can hope for is that the Government will make him an *ex gratia* payment. Parliamentary questions have elicited that the Home Secretary has due regard to precedents in fixing the amount of compensation.[15] Major Lloyd-George (now Lord Tenby) stated in the House that £300 was a normal payment to an innocent man who had been wrongly imprisoned for an offence of causing grievous bodily harm which he did not commit and who had served years of his sentence before being released with a free pardon. Indeed the Home Secretary described the amount as generous. This rate is no more than a small fraction of the rate at which Courts would award damages in actions for false imprisonment, as members of Parliament told Major Lloyd-George.

English law may appear inconsistent in another respect. We have seen that confessions obtained by threats or inducement are not admissible in evidence at all. On the other hand, if a policeman obtains evidence by an illegal search, e.g., if he discovers ammunition on the person searched, he is not prevented from putting this in evidence. Contrast this with the rule in United States Federal Courts, that evidence obtained by illegal seizure is excluded. In a Californian case one Rochin was suspected of trading in narcotics. When police broke into his room, they saw him swallow some capsules. They promptly handcuffed him and rushed him to hospital where a doctor forced him by means of a stomach pump to vomit. The Supreme Court of the United States refused to admit in evidence two capsules containing morphine which were found in the vomit: in England the evidence would be admissible.[16] In support of the English position it may be argued that if a policeman acts illegally the remedy lies in an action against him for damages which English law affords. Real evidence in the shape of bullets or morphine capsules cannot lie, and there is no sense in letting a guilty man go scot-free because the evidence has been obtained unlawfully. The case of confessions can be readily distinguished in that the illegality, i.e. the coercion, affects the truth of the evidence; the truth of the real evidence obtained by illegal means remains notwithstanding the illegal way in which it was obtained. On the other hand Americans maintain that to tolerate this kind of police behaviour is to set course for the Police State in the worst sense. Such invasions of a citizen's privacy must be stopped. There is one way to stop them: to make it no longer worth while for the police to get evidence in such ways by forbidding them to use it when they have got it.

BAIL

Inevitably, there is a considerable interval in the ordinary course of things between charge and trial. If the criminal process is commenced by summons, the accused remains at liberty until trial: this is the normal procedure for minor offences, e.g., most road traffic offences. We have seen that when the accused has been arrested, he must be brought before a magistrate within twenty-four hours if he remains in custody. The machinery of bail operates to allow many accused persons liberty pending trial. The police have power to grant bail, and so have the magistrates. If the magistrates refuse bail, the accused can appeal to a High Court judge, and a notice in all prison cells reminds him of that right. Hundreds do appeal yearly, and from five to ten per cent are granted bail on this appeal.

The accused must enter into a recognizance to surrender for trial when called upon, or to forfeit the sum named in the recognizance, which may be anything from £10 to say £5,000 depending on the circumstances. Often one or two other sureties in named sums will be required. The behaviour of the police with respect to bail is impartial; they will investigate the standing of suggested sureties, and will give evidence of their attitude to the request for bail. If the accused absconds, the accused and the sureties must pay to the Court that proportion of the amount in the bond which the Court decides in the particular case, and normally it will be the whole or most of that sum. Prisoners cannot have insurance companies or other paid bodies act as bondsmen. Conditions are sometimes imposed, e.g., surrender of passports, or reporting at police stations daily.

Except for murder and treason, there is a discretion whether to grant bail. Is the accused likely to abscond, will he commit other crimes (the professional housebreaker who wishes to accumulate some savings whereby to maintain his family while he is in prison), will he subject witnesses for the prosecution to undue pressure, does he need his freedom to prepare his defence, what delay before trial is expected either in the light of the Court calendar or of the time which the prosecution will take to complete their inquiries, are there grounds of personal hardship such as close relatives who are sick or unable to maintain themselves without his earnings, how clear-cut does the prosecution's case appear? These are the main factors which must be taken into account in deciding whether to grant bail. It is believed that the system works well.

HABEAS CORPUS

It is curious that the most famous of all the Englishman's symbols of liberty should bear a Latin name: *habeas corpus*. It is a direction by a judge to anybody who has a person in custody to bring that person before the judge so that he can investigate the legality of the detention. It represents a vital

link in the subjection of officialdom to the law. Its significance cannot be measured by the frequency with which
men are set free by it. What counts is that police and others
are aware that it is immediately available to prevent illegal
imprisonment. The slave brought by ship into British
territorial waters en route elsewhere;[17] the demobilized
army officer pulled from his civilian bed for alleged military
crimes over which the Army no longer has jurisdiction;[18] the
Polish seamen who feared punishment for their political
opinions if they were not freed from their ship in the Thames
before it sailed back to Poland;[19] the foreigner who was
being extradited to his own country for a political crime for
which extradition was not available;[20] the inmate of a
mental hospital who was illegally detained there by the
hospital authorities;[21] the woman imprisoned by the Vice-
Chancellor of Cambridge University for 'walking with a
member of the University';[22] all these secured their release
upon a writ of *habeas corpus*. Even the validity of detention by
order of either House of Parliament may be challenged in
this way. An application for *habeas corpus* takes precedence
over all other business before the Court.

Unfortunately, the Administration of Justice Act, 1960,
has restricted the liberty conferred by *habeas corpus*. Previously, once a Court had ordered the gaoler to set the man
free, that decision was final. Now, the custodian can with
leave appeal from the Divisional Court of the Queen's
Bench Division straight to the House of Lords against the
grant of *habeas corpus*. If therefore a man is ordered to be set
free by a Divisional Court in a criminal matter, he may
find himself remaining a prisoner because the House of
Lords reverses the decision of the lower Court. In civil
matters a released person is not re-imprisoned – the object
of giving the custodian a right of appeal is to enable him to
raise points of law before the higher Court. It seems that the
Government introduced these restrictions by way of
retaliation for the fact that they felt constrained to release in
the nineteen-fifties over three thousand mental patients after
a decision of the Queen's Bench Division had established

that the detention of one inmate was illegal. At one time it used to be thought that a person who failed to secure release from one judge could apply successively to all the other judges. The Act of 1960, not unreasonably, prevents more than one application unless new evidence is adduced. A person whose release is refused may always appeal.

Valuable though *habeas corpus* is, its limits must be noted. It operates only where the tribunal or person had no *jurisdiction* to detain. If some tribunal acting within its jurisdiction erroneously ordered detention, *habeas corpus* would not secure release. It is no protection against that kind of honest mistake in the course of legal administration.

TELEPHONE TAPPING AND INTERCEPTING MAIL

In 1956 the Bar Council were investigating a complaint of unprofessional conduct on the part of a barrister called Marrinan. They asked the police if they could provide any evidence. The police had been intercepting all telephone calls to and from a criminal suspect, Mr Billy Hill, without his permission or knowledge, and in this way had acquired details of telephone calls between Hill and Marrinan. Even though Marrinan had not been under suspicion, the police handed over to the Bar Council's secretary transcripts of the tapped telephone conversations. The Home Secretary authorized the handing over and the disclosure of the contents to all members of the Bar Council involved in the investigation of the complaint against Marrinan. In due course Marrinan was disbarred after the Bar Council's committee had made its findings. In 1957, when these matters came to light, the Home Secretary reacted to the public concern at this revelation of wire tapping by setting up a Committee of Privy Councillors (Lord Birkett, Sir Walter Monckton, and Mr Patrick Gordon Walker)

to consider and report upon the exercise by the Secretary of State of the executive power to intercept communications, and, in particular, under what authority, to what extent, and for what purposes this power has been exercised and to what use information so obtained has been put; and to recommend whether, how, and subject to what safeguards, this power should be exercised and in what circumstances information obtained by such means should be properly used or disclosed.[23]

These terms of reference have that degree of obscurity which is usual when Governmental inquiries are initiated. Presumably, the terms were drawn up so as to prevent the committee from reporting on the legality of the power, to confine that part of the inquiry to the authority under which the power had purported to be exercised. It is the usual practice to draw up terms of reference which make the public believe that the inquiry will relate to everything which the public wants to know or about which there is public disquiet, but which in fact exclude whatever the Administration does not wish to be ventilated. The Committee first looked at the practice of intercepting mail, a practice which Lord Campbell, a distinguished nineteenth-century Lord Chancellor, had found to be illegal at common law. Government witnesses pressed the Committee with the argument that these interceptions were made under the authority of the royal prerogative and that they were part of a more general prerogative power to intercept all communications. No decisions of the Courts supporting the existence of such a power could be found; the one classical work of authority, written in the nineteenth century, on the royal prerogative, made no mention of such a power. The extent of the royal prerogative is a question of law, and it is not open to the monarch or government of the day to declare its extent for themselves. The ruling of English law in Entick v. Carrington that an official has no power to interfere with a citizen unless the official can prove affirmatively that the law confers on him such a power will be recalled. In the Crown Proceedings Act, 1947, the Government had found it necessary to make an express provision that the Crown was not to be liable in damages for anything done in relation to letters; when it is considered that the same Act also reserved existing prerogative powers of the Crown, it is difficult to maintain the view that the Crown had such a prerogative power, for, if so, why make the express provision in the Act? The alternative governmental argument was that 'how it arose can only be conjectured because historical records are wanting, but that the power existed and was used permits of no doubt whatever'. This is relevant to the question of what powers were exercised in fact, but it is useless as a legal justification for the exercise of the power unless the Government prove that the law established the power – a person does not ordinarily derive the right to act in a certain way from the mere fact that he has from time to time done so without lawful authority. The next argument was that Parliament had recognized the power to intercept. The Post Office Act, 1953, and earlier Acts, exempted from criminal liability anything done in relation to postal packets and telegrams by post office officials acting on an express warrant in writing under the hand of a Secretary of State. The argument that such Acts validate interception is absurd; they merely state that people who commit such acts are not criminals.

The Committee then considered wire-tapping. Until 1937 the General Post Office acted on the view that anybody could intercept telephone communications, but in that year the Government decided as a matter of policy that a warrant of the Secretary of State should be obtained before a telephone communication was intercepted. Those who maintain the legality of wire-tapping have not even an Act like the Post Office Act on which to rely. If they call in aid the royal prerogative they cannot merely establish a power to intercept letters but must prove a power of interception so general in its terms as to cover forms of communication (like the telephone) unknown when the power was laid down. The only relevant Act is the Telegraph Act, 1868, which made it a misdemeanour for any official, contrary to his duty, to intercept the contents of telegraphic messages, and empowered the Postmaster-General to make regulations to carry out the intention of the section. Naturally, the Committee was unwilling to accept this as proof of the power, for it suggests the unlawfulness rather than the legality of interception. The Committee reached the lame conclusion that 'it is difficult to resist the view that if there is a lawful power to intercept communications in the form of letters and telegrams, then it is wide enough to cover telephone communications as well'.

The Crown has not provided any lawful authority to support the interception of telephone communications. This does not mean that the citizen can obtain damages when his calls are intercepted, because the Government wrote into the Crown Proceedings Act of 1947 a provision which is effective to exempt them from any such liability. The position may well be that the Crown has no power conferred by law to tap telephones but that the citizen has no means of redress if the Crown does authorize tapping of his calls.

The Committee then reported that it had been the practice of the Home Secretary to issue warrants for intercepting telephone calls in order to detect breaches of emergency food regulations, evasions of exchange control, posting of Irish Sweepstake tickets in violation of the Lotteries Acts, sending of letters with obscene contents, and traffic in drugs. These warrants were usually issued to the Metropolitan Police. Warrants were also issued to the Board of Customs and Excise to track smugglers, and to the Security Service. In 1951 the Home Office prepared a memorandum setting out the principles which would guide its issue of warrants. The offence must be serious, normal methods of investigation must have failed or be unlikely to succeed, and the interception must be likely to result in a conviction involving a sentence of at least three years. Customs offences must be of substantial and continuing fraud which would seriously damage the revenue or the economy of the country if unchecked. Warrants to the Security Service were to be only in respect of subversive or espionage activity likely to injure the national interest. The Committee found that the highest number of telephone taps in any one year was 241, and that the power had been exercised scrupulously and effectively.

The majority of the Committee was satisfied with the way in which interceptions were being carried out, and subject to minor changes recommended continuation of the present practice. One member would have preferred restrictions on the exercise of the power much more severe than those outlined in the Home Office memorandum of 1951. The Committee unanimously recommended that transcripts should not be passed on to persons outside the public service and called the Home Secretary's conduct in the *Marrinan* case 'mistaken'. The Government have accepted the Committee's recommendations. On the other hand, the Government will do nothing to prevent police from persuading a telephone subscriber to let them have an extension to his telephone so that they can listen in to his conversations and then hand over the information to some private body investigating complaints of breaches of professional etiquette by the person whose call was, without his knowledge or permission, being overheard. It was in this way that a Dr Fox was removed from the medical register in 1959 for unprofessional relations with a married woman patient. The Government will not regard listening in on an extension, put in by the police for the purpose, as an 'interception', and so such listening in remains free from the restrictions set out above.

The Government has made out a strong case on grounds of expediency for restricted use of wire-tapping. There are, however, many objections to the present arrangements. It is undesirable that governments should indulge in practices for which there appears no lawful authority. Is the Home Secretary the appropriate person to decide when to issue the warrants? The overworked doctrine of ministerial accountability to Parliament does not really strengthen his claim, for no record of the use of the power will be available to the public or to members of Parliament. We have seen that Home Secretaries have misused their powers in the past. Most European countries require the order of a judge before an interception is permitted. Would not a High Court judge be a more suitable person here?

One of the dominant characteristics of British Governments is that they resist any legal restrictions on the exercise
of their powers: at all costs they will do no more than make
ex gratia concessions of no legal effect. So with wire-tapping:
notice that the Government has not agreed to embody in
legislation the restrictions on its use recommended by the
Committee and accepted by it. If its contention that wire-
tapping is lawful be sound, it remains legally free to issue
warrants to anybody to intercept any communications for
any purposes. Things are strikingly different in say,
Australia. The Telephonic Communications (Interception)
Act, 1960, in that country makes it a criminal offence for
anybody to make an unauthorized interception or an
unauthorized disclosure. Interception is permissible only
where the activity threatened would prejudice the security
of the Commonwealth. Moreover, the Attorney-General's
warrant is required. These legal restrictions are greatly to
be preferred to the freedom which British Governments
enjoy. American experience points to other weaknesses in
the British system. Even if the police tap telephones without
a warrant, the evidence will not thereby be rendered
inadmissible: the majority did not endorse the recommendation of one member of the Committee that no intercepted
material should be admissible in evidence. In the United
States, no evidence obtained by wire-tapping, whether by
federal or state officers, is admissible in any Federal Court.
The absence of all these restrictions in England is obviously
calculated to make officials less careful in the exercise of
these powers, which are in principle obnoxious. But British
Governments so systematically avoid the imposition of legal
restrictions upon their powers that it would be rash to expect
them to follow the Australian and American examples.

The discussion so far has centred on wire-tapping on
behalf of the police and other public bodies charged with
crime detection. For technical reasons British telephones
cannot readily be tapped by persons other than Post Office
engineers (who of course tap for the police); we are therefore
largely free from the menace experienced by other countries,

especially the United States, where unauthorized private tapping is practised on a large scale and those who practise it command high fees from the large business corporations which employ them.

In any event, electronic devices have rendered wire-tapping an old-fashioned method of overhearing conversations. Little is known about the extent to which police and others eavesdrop by these new methods: for example, by the use of portable radio equipment which can be hidden in a briefcase or even in a person's premises. One thing is plain: such evidence will not be rendered inadmissible merely because the police have to break into private premises in order to conceal the equipment there. No doubt one day an incident involving such devices will come under public scrutiny, and public concern at the law's failure to restrict their use will show itself, although whether with any legal results is more doubtful.

CHAPTER 2

PUBLIC MEETINGS

HISTORICALLY, the Englishman's right of public meeting has been of great importance. The public meeting has been one of the chief methods of influencing public opinion on big issues, and the key factor in electioneering in particular. Television has greatly reduced the importance of election meetings, but so long as television remains so 'respectable' as to give little expression to the unorthodox or even the provocative or controversial, meetings and especially demonstrations will remain important: the Ban the Bomb campaign is an obvious example. The exposition of the law about meetings and processions, has, however, to start with a negative.

PLACE OF MEETING

Englishmen have no *right* to hold a public meeting any-where: even if they begin to hold public meetings in their own premises they will presumably need town and country planning permission from the local authority for this change in use of the land. There is a popular belief that there is a right of meeting in such places as Speakers Corner at Hyde Park and Trafalgar Square. This is erroneous: the Commissioners of Works have been entrusted by Parliament with control of meetings there, and they make regulations which set out the terms on which they will allow meetings. So also with parks managed by local authorities: a statute empowers local authorities to make by-laws which regulate the use of the parks, and it is usual for them to have specific by-laws about public meetings. If therefore a by-law requires police permission for meetings and forbids the distribution of literature, breaches of the by-law will be criminal offences. Exceptionally, a citizen might persuade a Court that a particular park by-law was so unreasonable as to be void. (Is it reasonable to elevate the need to keep the parks clean above the claims of free expression, so as to prohibit the handing out of literature and pamphlets because many of them will be thrown down when read?) If a particular organization believed that it was being discriminated against in the matter of permission to hold a meeting, it is not clear what legal remedies, as distinct from the obvious political steps of having the matter raised in council and the local press, are available. It is a gap in the law that there is no clear-cut legal process for preventing political discrimination on the part of a local authority in controlling public meetings in its parks and open spaces. The citizen has no right to use premises belonging to local authorities for meetings, except a statutory right to use school or other premises controlled by the local authority upon payment of a reasonable fee for meetings organized by a candidate in connexion with a parliamentary election. Of course, many local authorities habitually let on hire meeting-halls to local associations and societies, but as the law stands this is a purely private business arrangement completely in the discretion of a local authority. A rate-payer could secure the Court's intervention if the local authority charged lower fees to one political body than another, yet it is very doubtful whether he could have any legal remedy if the local authority systematically refused to allow particular associations the use of its premises on payment of the ordinary fee. The citizen's rights seem inadequate here: the rights given in respect of parliamentary elections could well be made of general application. Whereas nobody would contend that there should be a right to hold meetings on the premises of some other private person or body, there ought to be some obligation on public bodies to provide equal facilities for meetings of outside organizations.

We are all familiar with processions and indeed meetings on highways. Is this the exercise of some legal right on the Queen's Highway? We have rights on every highway, but only to pass along it in a reasonable manner. Whoever owns the surface of the highway can sue us in trespass if we use the highway for any other purpose. Local authorities usually own the surface of main roads, so that they could sue in trespass anyone who used those roads for purposes other than that of passage. Other highways are usually owned by the owner of the land fronting the highway. The racehorse trainer who objected to press racing correspondents timing from the highway his horses' practice gallops on his adjoining land[1] and the landed duke whose pheasant shoot was interfered with by somebody deliberately opening and shutting his umbrella on the highway[2] had their remedy in trespass. A landowner can also eject a trespasser with reasonable force after first requesting him to desist from the trespass; whether a local authority could employ its policemen to do this is a nice question. It is a criminal offence to obstruct free passage along a highway, and policemen may arrest offenders without a warrant; the Courts have decided that the offence may be committed although only part of the highway is obstructed, and even though no nuisance is committed. It follows that meetings on highways are unlawful: the owners of the appropriate part of the highway can always have the public removed, and any obstruction will constitute a criminal offence.

A procession will not ordinarily be a trespass to the highway because the highway is merely being used for passage. It may, however, be a criminal obstruction; obstruction is so loose a word that in practice everything turns on how the police interpret it in deciding whether to prosecute, and how the Courts choose to interpret it in the event of a prosecution; certainly there may be a criminal obstruction even though passage is not completely blocked. In short the position is as uncertain, and perhaps as unsatisfactory, as that of the motorist who parks his car under the ever-present threat of prosecution for obstruction. This elasticity of the term 'obstruction' provides the police with a powerful weapon to restrict freedom of public meeting, a weapon which they do not hesitate to use. Further, the Public Order Act, 1936 (which was passed to counter the outbreak of Fascist–Communist strife), empowers a chief officer of police, who reasonably apprehends that a procession may cause serious public disorder, to give directions imposing conditions necessary for public order and to prescribe the route (for example, he may divert the procession from a hostile district): if he thinks the above procedure to be inadequate, he can ask the council of a borough or urban district to make an order prohibiting classes of processions for a maximum period of three months, and such an order by the local authority (or by the Commissioner of the Metropolitan or City of London Police in the London area) is effective when the Home Secretary consents to it. Some have thought during the outburst of Fascist meetings in 1962 that it is regrettable that there is no similar power to prohibit, or to impose conditions as to place of, public meetings in the open air. But this would surely be a dangerously wide new executive power which the Government has wisely refused to assume.

Suppose that the organizers of a public meeting have satisfied all the above requirements about place of meeting. Are they free to go ahead with the meeting, confident that so long as they behave in a peaceable manner they will not fall foul of the law? The answer, perhaps surprisingly, is no. We now have to examine a series of decided cases. Of each of them we shall have to conclude that we do not know exactly what law they lay down. All these cases were decided by a Divisional Court of the Queen's Bench Division. The standard of judgment in that Court is not normally high, but these cases perhaps fall below the usual level. Cases which decide important issues normally go to a Court of higher status, where they are argued at length, and finally adjudicated upon by experienced appellate judges who adjourn the case in order to prepare considered written opinions. Judgments in the cases now to be described were delivered extempore upon conclusion of counsel's argument. Until the Administration of Justice Act, 1960, no appeal was possible from these judgments of the Divisional Court. It follows that important points of law have not been given the considered and authoritative ruling which they require. If similar issues arise in the future, the Act of 1960 creates the possibility of clarification, for it provides for leave to appeal to the House of Lords where the Divisional Court certifies that a point of law of general public importance is involved in the decision.

The first of the cases, *Beatty* v. *Gillbanks* (1882),[3] was a prosecution for the crime of *unlawful assembly*: an assembly of three or more persons with intent either to commit a crime by open force or to carry out any common purpose, lawful or unlawful, in such a manner as to give firm and courageous persons in the neighbourhood of such assembly reasonable grounds to apprehend a breach of the peace in consequence of it. The Salvation Army regularly met in Weston-super-Mare and held processions in the streets. This had excited opposition from a body known as the 'Skeleton Army', and disorder had frequently resulted. Disregarding a notice by magistrates and a direction from the police purporting to prohibit their processions, the Salvation Army held another procession, and commotion ensued. The magistrates convicted members of the Salvation Army of unlawful assembly, but the conviction was reversed on appeal to the Divisional Court. In effect, the Divisional Court appeared to rule that the Salvation Army members did not commit the crime, because the disturbances were caused by other people, whom the Salvation Army did not incite, and not by the accused. The Court did not make clear, however, whether they were laying down a general rule that if others committed the disturbance, those who held the meeting were not guilty, or whether they merely found on the facts of this particular case that the accused did not cause the disturbance because it was not the natural and probable consequence of their procession that the Skeleton Army should create the commotion.

In *Wise* v. *Dunning* (1902)[4] Wise led a Protestant crusade in Liverpool, holding meetings in the streets which Roman Catholics as well as his supporters attended. At these meetings, by his language and gestures Wise insulted the Roman Catholics present, who thereupon committed breaches of the peace. Wise did not himself commit breaches of the peace, and counselled his supporters not to do so, but he declared his intention to continue to hold meetings. The police prosecuted Wise, not for unlawful assembly, but for *disturbing the peace*. The magistrates exercised their power to bind over Wise to keep the peace and to require him to find sureties. The Divisional Court upheld the magistrates. They purported to distinguish *Beatty* v. *Gillbanks* on the ground that the disorder was the natural and probable consequence of Wise's conduct. Perhaps the case may decide that, where the accused is guilty of using insulting and abusive language of a kind likely to provoke others to commit breaches of the peace, he may be bound over to keep the peace. This imposition of *binding over and finding of sureties* can be a severe punishment, as the next case shows. In 1914 George Lansbury, the Socialist leader, speaking at a suffragette meeting, urged that they should continue their policy of militancy.[5] The magistrates required him to enter into a personal recognizance of £1,000 and to find two sureties of £500 each, and ordered that in default he should suffer three months' imprisonment, on the ground that he incited others to commit breaches of the peace. This means that if the accused is, as Lansbury was, unable to provide the recognizance and sureties, he must go to prison. The Divisional Court upheld the award of the magistrates, laying down that it need not be shown that anyone was put in bodily fear; a mere apprehension of a breach of the peace was sufficient.

Duncan v. *Jones* (1936)[6] shows the police making use of a charge which was not available to them in *Beatty* v. *Gillbanks*, that of *obstructing a police officer in the execution of his duty*, which Parliament made a crime for the first time in 1885 by the Prevention of Crime Act. Duncan was told by Jones, a police inspector, that she could only hold her meeting some 175 yards from the proposed place of meeting on the highway. When she indicated her intention to hold it at the original spot she was arrested and charged. Merely to obstruct a police officer is no crime; he must be obstructed in the exercise of his duty – the prosecution must prove that the police officer was entitled to do that which he was prevented from doing. Did he then have the power to forbid Mrs Duncan to hold her meeting where she wanted to hold it? A meeting held by her at the same place fourteen months previously had been followed by a disturbance on the same day in a training centre for unemployed workers, which was across the road. The superintendent of this centre believed that the meeting caused that disturbance, and that further meetings in the same place would have the same result. It was not alleged that she had caused any obstruction, other than by the presence of her box and the crowd around it, or that she or any person at the meeting had caused or provoked a breach of the peace. The Divisional Court held that there was evidence which could support a conviction by the lower Courts. It was also found that she must have known that a disturbance was a probable consequence of her holding the meeting, that she was not unwilling that such consequences should ensue, and that the police inspector reasonably apprehended such a breach of the peace. The Divisional Court held that on these findings she was rightly convicted of obstructing the police officer in the execution of his duty. The case certainly does not decide that whenever a policeman believes a breach of the peace likely a person who refuses to move on commits an offence; if the Court finds that the policeman's belief was an unreasonable one in the circumstances no offence is committed. It is uncertain whether the offence is committed if the accused neither foresaw nor desired that others would create a disturbance. In any event it is plain that the case vests wide powers in the police. It is no wonder that they no longer rely on the crime of unlawful assembly when prosecuting those holding meetings: *Beatty* v. *Gillbanks* and the protection which it conferred is a dead letter. For the same reasons although the law books are full of other crimes like rout, riot, and affray, there is no point in burdening the reader with the subtle differences between them. Our concern is with the weapons in the legal armoury which the police regularly use: and the ones that count are obstructing a policeman in the execution of his duty, and disturbing the peace, with its attendant punishment by way of binding over as an alternative to a fine.

To translate these cases into practical terms: organizers of public meetings are not safe from criminal prosecution merely because they and their supporters will behave themselves. They take a great risk if they do not seek police permission beforehand, for if the police believe that disorder is likely and forbid the meeting, disobedience will be criminal unless the magistrates find that the police's apprehension was unreasonable (and common sense suggests that magistrates are highly unlikely to override the view taken by the police on the spot). The right of public meeting then is dependent almost entirely on the police exercising their discretion in a reasonable manner. The promoter should cooperate with the police in the expectation that they will treat him fairly: if he proceeds in defiance of their wishes, conviction is likely.

THE CONDUCT OF THE MEETING

The police have ample powers to control disorderly behaviour at meetings. They make most use of those given by Section 5 of the Public Order Act, 1936, whereby it is an offence for any person in any public place or at any public meeting to use threatening, abusive, or insulting words or behaviour with intent to provoke a breach of the peace or whereby a breach of the peace is likely to be occasioned. The Fascist meetings in 1962 led to pressure to extend this Section so as also to make it an offence to make speeches calculated to incite racial prejudice. One would hope that Section 5 is already wide enough to cover those speeches which result in public disorder; it would be a false step to make the delivery of a speech criminal merely because of its content. The ruling of the Lord Chief Justice in *Jordan*'s case (1963) that the offence is committed if the words are likely to provoke a breach of peace among the particular audience, even though that audience is an unreasonable one and made up of hooligans whose aim was to prevent the speaker from making an address, confirms the view that the Section needs no extension.7 On the other hand, the increase of the maximum penalties made by the Public Order Act, 1963, is sensible. A constable may arrest without warrant any person reasonably suspected by him of committing this offence.

In 1932 the Home Secretary had stated in Parliament that the police had no lawful right to go to a meeting unless either the promoters asked them or they had reason to believe that a breach of the peace was actually being committed. Yet, three years later, in 1935, there was decided the remarkable case of *Thomas* v. *Sawkins*.8 A meeting was advertised in a hall of a Welsh town for the purpose of protesting against the Incitement to Disaffection Bill, which was then before Parliament, and demanding the dismissal of the Chief Constable of Glamorganshire. The public were admitted without payment. The promoter asked police officers who entered the meeting hall to leave. A constable used force on him because he believed that he was about to remove his superior officer forcibly from the hall. No crime or breach of the peace was alleged to have been committed. The promoter prosecuted the police officer for battery. The Magistrates' Court found that the police had reasonable grounds for believing that if they were not present at the meeting seditious speeches would be made and breaches of the peace would occur. They held that the police had a right to enter and remain in the meeting hall, so that no battery was committed. The promoter appealed unsuccessfully to the Divisional Court. What however did the Divisional Court decide? It will be noted that the police apprehended both sedition and breach of the peace. The case certainly decides, therefore, that the police may enter and remain wherever they apprehend both sedition and breach of the peace. One of the three judges held that they could remain if they apprehended any offence, the second if they apprehended either breach of the peace or sedition, and the third if they apprehended both breach of the peace and sedition. No subsequent case has cleared up these differences of opinion on these important questions of police power to attend public meetings. The other difficulty is whether the case applies to private as well as to public meetings. The Court held that because it was a public meeting the police were entitled to be there. But there can be no doubt that, even though a general invitation is issued, the promoter can turn away particular individuals. Logically, therefore, this case would seem to imply that the police have a right to attend private meetings in private premises where they believe that the appropriate offences are likely to be committed if they are not there.

This case seems to confer tremendous powers of interference upon the police, and there was no precedent for it. Certainly, earlier Irish cases had decided that where the only means of restoring the peace is to use reasonable force, a policeman has a defence to a claim of battery: for example, where a policeman removed an orange lily being worn by a lady who walked through a crowd of Roman Catholics. But *Thomas* v. *Sawkins* goes much further. Suppose the police believe that somebody at a private meeting of a few persons in a private house may say something seditious (and we shall see later how elastic is the legal definition of sedition). Apparently, the police will be entitled to enter the private house without the owner's permission and attend the meeting. They cannot disperse the meeting merely because they believe that some offence will be committed, but they can do so, remember, if they believe that a breach of the peace would otherwise be likely to ensue.

The activities of the anti-bomb demonstrators in 1961 illustrate the workings of this branch of the law. Before the advertised time of the Trafalgar Square meeting Bertrand Russell and other organizers were summoned for inciting members of the public to commit breaches of the peace, and on their refusing to be bound over to keep the peace were sent to prison. Originally, the Home Secretary exercised his power under the Public Order Act, 1936, to ban processions in the Trafalgar Square area. When that ban expired on

17 September the Commissioner of the Metropolitan Police used a power available in London only given to him by the Metropolitan Police Act, 1839: he issued regulations for preventing obstruction for a further twenty-four hours in the same area, and for this, unlike action under the Public Order Act, no consent of the Home Secretary is required. Disobedience of the Commissioner's order is an offence, just like disobedience of the Home Secretary's order under the other Act, though the maximum punishment under the Metropolitan Police Act is smaller.

Does the law strike a fair balance between police and organizers of meetings, between public order and free speech and discussion? If a person is behaving in a peaceable way, should the police be free to take the easy way out and stop the meeting before they have first tried to control the real offenders, the rowdies who are likely to break up the meeting? Does the present law (reinforced by the 1963 decision that the speaker must take his audience as he finds it, and violates the Public Order Act if his insulting words are likely to provoke disorder by the thugs present) not afford undue temptation to a police force, and an under-manned one at that, to put their own convenience ahead of the right of free speech? In answering these questions it must be remembered that the police have a statutory power to arrest and charge those whom they think guilty of insulting or abusive language or behaviour. Those who sponsor unpopular causes from the public platform will commonly excite mutterings and hecklings from their audience; no doubt they commonly exaggerate, vilify, and distort, but should they not, nonetheless, be protected by the police against the threats of their audience? If they do not obtain this protection, and instead the police throw their weight on the side of those who would break up the meetings, do not the police become in effect the new censors of speech? Whatever one's opinions of the views of the Mosley group, one would not want to see their opponents free to break up their meetings or to prevent them from taking place by threats to use violence and thereby prevent those views from being expressed.

We have been discussing the power of the police, not private citizens, to break up meetings. The controversy arising out of the disturbances of the Conservative Party's annual meeting at Blackpool in 1958–9 illustrates the power of private citizens. Apparently Empire Loyalists entered a meeting in the Winter Gardens to which admission was by ticket only without the permission of the Conservative organizers, and when they interrupted speeches by the playing of musical instruments they were forcibly ejected from the building. One would need to know more facts before deciding whether this ejection was lawful. A private occupier of premises may eject trespassers on his premises after first asking them to leave; if they have entered peaceably he may not use force on them until they have failed to comply with his request to leave. We do not know whether the Conservative Party were the occupiers of the premises or whether they merely paid a fee to the owners for permission to use them. If they were not the occupiers they had no power in themselves to eject anybody; in this event, only the owners of the Winter Gardens and those whom they employed to act on their behalf could eject after prior request to leave. If the Conservative Party were the occupiers, then those whom they employed to control the meeting, their stewards, could eject, but not employees of the owners. None of these individuals would have the power to detain and arrest those who interfered with the meeting.

CHAPTER 3

FREEDOM OF EXPRESSION (1): THEATRE, CINEMA, RADIO, AND TELEVISION

IN this and the following chapters the theme is freedom of expression. The law may interfere in two ways. It may prevent expression by imposing restraints before the communication is made: in short, censorship. It may punish as criminals or mulct in damages those who have transgressed by publishing. This division is not clear-cut, nor is it always possible to separate legal and administrative matters. Both here and in Chapter 4 we shall consider censorship of the principal media of communication, and in Chapters 5 and 6 discuss the ways in which the already published word may fall foul of the law.

Theatre

HISTORY OF CENSORSHIP

As early as the fourteenth century a member of the Royal Household, the Master of the Revels, supervised entertainment in the Royal Court. Among other tasks, he looked at the manuscripts of plays submitted for royal presentation. By the sixteenth century appointments to the post were made by royal patent which did not, however, make any reference to any powers outside the circle of the royal court. Both Mary and Elizabeth on their accession issued proclamations asserting their general control of plays, but there is no evidence that they were effective outside the court. By the end of the sixteenth century, after strife between the Royal Household and local authorities, especially the City of London, the royal supervision of all plays was established: for example, the manuscript of

Massinger's *Believe as You List* (1630), with the signed licence of the Master, is in the British Museum. It seems that the motive force was the income which the Master of the Revels could earn from fees for approving manuscripts; for the same reason licences for printing plays were at that time required. The Master's function was to protect royal interests, including the preservation of the social order in its existing form, rather than to act as guardian of morals. William III tightened up the Master of the Revels's instructions by specifically directing him to look for political allusions or satires and lampoons against the court or aristocracy, and by generally authorizing supervision on moral grounds. Soon afterwards the office of Master of the Revels declined in importance, and the Lord Chamberlain, who had always been his superior officer at the royal court, assumed his powers. In 1737 Walpole, irked by stage satires on himself by Fielding, introduced the Theatres Act, which for the first time gave legislative sanction to the Lord Chamberlain's powers. The present censorship powers of the Lord Chamberlain derive from the Theatres Act of 1843 which, although the subject of much comment, including criticism from several Governmental Commissions charged to report on its workings, has remained substantially unchanged since its enactment.

THE PRESENT LAW: THEATRES ACT, 1843

Section 12 of the Act provides that no new stage play or part of a play may be produced and acted for hire at any theatre in Great Britain unless a copy has been sent to the Lord Chamberlain seven days before the performance and he has issued a licence. It is a criminal offence punishable by fine to perform such a play without licence or in a form differing from the authorized script. To the licence the Lord Chamberlain attaches a Memorandum that the licence should be forwarded to the manager of the company performing the play in order that it be produced to the proprietors of theatres at which the play is presented. A theatre manager may be guilty of presenting a play in an unauthorized manner even though he was unaware of the deviation from the authorized script for he is entitled to demand the licensed script of the producer and to compare it with the play as performed. In 1958 the producer and actors of a Theatre Workshop play were convicted of presenting parts of it in a form diverging from that licensed by the Lord Chamberlain. Nor did it avail the producer of a play at Northampton, who was charged with presenting a play with a script altered from the approved one, that he was not present at the performance and had ordered the approved script to be used. There is further sanction against managers of theatres: another licence, either from the Lord Chamberlain or from local authorities or from justices, depending on the area where the theatre is situated, is required before plays can be put on in a particular building by the owner of that building. There is power to revoke this licence if a manager is convicted of presenting a play in breach of the Lord Chamberlain's licence, although the Lord Chamberlain has not revoked any licence in recent times.

A 'new play' means one written after 1843, but the Lord Chamberlain interprets this as including a translation made after that date of any play. A play is defined by the Act as covering every 'tragedy, comedy, farce, opera, burletta, interlude, melodrama, pantomime, or other entertainment of the stage'. The Public Morality Council and others complain from time to time that the Lord Chamberlain is too lax in allowing partial nudity in variety performances and revues. The Act's definition of plays has never been construed by the Courts, but on the view taken by the Lord Chamberlain, these complaints are misconceived because such music hall 'dances' are outside the scope of the Act. He maintains that because the Act speaks of entertainment *of* the stage, as opposed to *on* the stage, it extends only to entertainment which comprises a consecutive train of thought plus physical and manual actions but not necessarily speech. In his view, therefore, variety performances consisting entirely of comedian cross-talk acts, acrobats, dancers, and the like are not stage plays, although a music hall sketch is. This interpretation of a difficult section of the Act seems justifiable. Provided that there is a music and dancing licence in force in respect of the premises no further permission is required for putting on 'nude shows'. On the other hand the Lord Chamberlain rejected a striptease pantomime version of Cinderella in 1960, for that fell within the statutory definition of a 'play'. He will also scrutinize cross-talk and the like which merely forms part of a show which on the whole he interprets to be an 'entertainment of the stage'.

The Act is silent on the grounds for refusal of a licence. Presumably the Lord Chamberlain can refuse a licence for a play on any ground whatever; nor does the Act require him to inform the applicant of his reasons for refusal. It is difficult to see on what grounds the Courts could interfere with his decision, except to reverse his ruling that a performance was a 'stage play' within the meaning of the Act. The Act gives no power to appeal to the Courts or to anybody else against his decisions, and certainly no such right of appeal can be implied.

Section 14 of the Act confers another power on the Lord Chamberlain. He may forbid the performance of any play (not necessarily a new play) anywhere in Great Britain or in such theatres as he shall specify, either absolutely or for such time as he thinks fit, 'whenever he shall be of the opinion that it is fitting for the preservation of good manners, decorum, or of the public peace'. This Section fulfils two purposes. First, it enables the Lord Chamberlain to withdraw a licence from a play. For example, in 1907, the licence of *The Mikado* was withdrawn on the occasion of the state visit of Prince Saluki of Japan because it was thought likely to give offence. Secondly, it gives him control of pre-1837 plays, which can be performed without first obtaining a licence. This Section, unlike the one previously examined, states the grounds on which the power can be exercised. Notice, however, that it operates when *he is of the opinion* that it is fitting for the prescribed reasons that the performance be forbidden. An aggrieved person could not, therefore, ask the Courts to quash the Lord Chamberlain's decision on the ground that the play was fitting; the Act gives him the final say, except that, perhaps, the Courts could interfere if they found that his opinion was so unreasonable that no reasonable person could have held it.

Most people believe that there is one large gap in the Theatres Act. It is argued that if a theatre forms a club and members of the public must join and pay a membership fee in order to see the play, the performance becomes a private one, and the Lord Chamberlain has no jurisdiction over it. This argument is false. First, Section 14 which empowers him to forbid the performance of any play anywhere or in specified theatres may extend to these club performances: only if one could construe the word 'anywhere' to be restricted to 'theatres' could it be argued that club performances are outside the Section. The view that plays at such theatres do not have to be submitted in advance under Section 12 presumably rests on the argument that such a play is not being produced 'for hire' within the Section. It seems very unlikely that those words can be given a meaning which excludes theatre clubs, especially as the restriction to 'public' performances which is contained in the earlier section about licensing of theatres is not reproduced in this section. Moreover, the Act provides expressly that an actor shall be deemed to be acting for hire if money or other reward is taken and charged directly or indirectly, or if 'distilled or fermented exciseable liquor' is sold on the premises. In practice these clubs do not submit their plays to him, and the Lord Chamberlain does not invoke the Act in respect of them. There is only one explanation. The Lord Chamberlain deliberately refrains from exercising his powers of censorship over these clubs because he is anxious to foster advanced or experimental drama. No doubt if powerful theatrical interests were to exploit successfully the private theatre for banned plays he would intervene.

THE LORD CHAMBERLAIN

The Lord Chamberlain is the senior officer of the Royal Household, whose main duties are concerned with ceremonial matters affecting the royal family. There is a widespread misconception that his appointment is a political one. This misconception arises from the fact that it used to be a political appointment, and was one at the time when the last of the Committee reports on censorship in the theatre was published. The change took place in the following way. The Macdonald Government wanted political appointments in the Royal Household to cease, but the Conservative opposition disagreed, presumably on the ground that this would restrict the power to dispose of political failures by 'kicking them upstairs'. A compromise was reached. By this, certain appointments, including that of the Lord Chamberlain, were to be filled at the Sovereign's own discretion, subject to an undertaking by those chosen that they would not take part in parliamentary votes or proceedings, and other appointments, such as that of Lord in Waiting, were to be the responsibility of the Prime Minister. The appointment of the Lord Chamberlain is, then, personal to the sovereign and, indeed, terminates upon the sovereign's death; it is always made from the peerage. The salary is included in the Civil List estimates, which, as with the judges, has the effect of preventing questions from being asked in the House of Commons about the Lord Chamberlain's discharge of his duties; he is not accountable to either the House of Commons or the House of Lords, and no Minister assumes responsibility for him.

Conceding then that the Lord Chamberlain is largely free from either legal or political accountability, what means has the theatrical world of knowing the principles by which he will be guided in examining plays? The only official source is to be found in Regulations endorsed on all licences issued by him, which Regulations have not been changed for more than fifty years. A memorandum attached to the licence makes the following sensible provision:

Any proposed alteration or addition to this Play must be submitted for the Lord Chamberlain's approval. *Failure to observe this Regulation may endanger the continuation of the performance of the Play.*

On the back of the licence it is stated:

Mem. The particular attention of the Management is called to the following Regulations, which refer to all Stage Plays licensed by the Lord Chamberlain. The strict observance of these Regulations is to be considered as the condition upon which the Licence is signed.

Any change of title must be submitted for the Lord Chamberlain's approval.

No profanity or impropriety of language to be permitted on the Stage.

No indecency of dress, dance or gesture to be permitted on the Stage.

No objectionable personalities to be permitted on the Stage, nor anything calculated to produce riot or breach of the peace.

No offensive representations of living persons to be permitted on the Stage.

It must not be assumed that these are the only requirements of the Lord Chamberlain. They are described as conditions upon which the licence is granted, and, although this is not explicit, it seems that they are intended to control matters which a mere production of the written script would not reach; they relate to the manner in which an approved script shall be performed.

The Joint Committee of both Houses of Parliament which Asquith set up under the chairmanship of Samuel in 1909 at the instance of a deputation of playwrights led by Barrie, Galsworthy, and Yeats, proposed that the Lord Chamberlain should forbid the performance of plays only on certain grounds specified in their Report. It is understood that the Lord Chamberlain does not license plays which conflict with those proposals. These grounds were: (1) indecency; (2) offensive portrayal of personalities; (3) there were to be no invidious representations of persons living or recently dead – it is believed that the Lord Chamberlain normally prohibits entirely plays about persons living or recently dead, and also the dramatization of recent real-life incidents, even if the protagonists are dead, unless the nearest relatives have been approached and their wishes considered; (4) plays were not to violate sentiments of religious reverence. The Lord Chamberlain forbids the physical appearance of the Deity on the stage, although he permits the indication of a Divine Person by a bright light, or by a voice from off-stage. One of his reasons for this is that he regards himself as legally unable to make his licence subject to conditions – he believes that once he has decided to pass a script this approval must be unqualified so that he could not confine the representation of, say, Christ to a particularly suitable actor or the production of a religious play to a responsible Manager. This raises a difficult legal point which is of quite general application: when an administrative body is given a licensing power without the addition of 'on such terms as he thinks fit', or similar words, has the licensing body an implied power to attach conditions? It is believed – although the matter is not free from doubt – that the Lord Chamberlain takes too narrow a view of his powers in regarding himself as unable to attach conditions of the kind mentioned. No doubt he also prefers that his licences shall be unconditional but he would have no difficulty in enforcing compliance with conditions – the sanction is either revocation of licence of the theatre or the imposition of fines on those presenting the play in breach of the condition. Three other grounds for refusing a licence brought the total up to seven. Plays were not to contain matters conducive to crime or vice, or matters which would impair friendly relations with a foreign power, or matters calculated to provoke a breach of the peace. The Lord Chamberlain observes one other rule which the Report did not specifically mention: no member of the royal family living after the death of Queen Victoria may be depicted on the stage. Perhaps this is to be explained by his close connexion with the royal family in the discharge of his other duties.

That the Lord Chamberlain does not work to a code should not be taken as a criticism. Wisely, he prefers to rely on general criteria such as method of treatment and sincerity of object rather than choice of subject merely. At the same time he does not wish to saddle himself with immutable restrictions, but rather to modify his policy in the light of changing conditions and opinion. He did for instance change his mind about Ibsen's plays. More recently he changed his attitude to plays about homosexuality on the ground that 'this subject is now so widely debated, written about, and talked of that its complete exclusion from the stage can no longer be regarded as justifiable.' He will now approve sincere and serious plays on homosexuality, and incidental references 'which are necessary to the plot and dialogue and which are not salacious or offensive'.

The Lord Chamberlain employs part-time examiners to assist in the discharge of his functions. They have no legal standing, are not established members of his office, and merely advise him in theatrical matters. He personally selects them, on being satisfied that they are well read and practically versed in the Drama, and that they are men of the world with broad interests in other fields. They are not given written instructions, but learn the tradition and temper of the office through working under the supervision of the senior examiner, and have discussions with the Lord Chamberlain, who assumes responsibility for the final decisions which are made in the light of the reasoned opinions furnished to him by the examiners. In cases of difficulty, the Lord Chamberlain consults an Advisory Board comprising persons highly placed in such professions as the Church, Medicine, the Law, Literature, and the Stage: their identities are not revealed. They were consulted, for instance, about the Lord Chamberlain's decisions on homosexuality.

Written reasons are not given in the first instance for total rejection of a play, but a representative will always discuss the matter at the wish of the author or producer. Wherever the Lord Chamberlain insists on minor deletions he does so in writing. In recent years an average of two or three plays per annum has been refused a licence. Deletions, especially with reference to questionable remarks, obscenities, and blasphemies, are more frequent than complete refusals; but sometimes the producer is unwilling to present the play so altered. Criminal prosecutions now average two or three a year; the figure used to be six to twelve annually when road shows flourished. The power of forbidding a play under Section 14 is now rarely exercised; perhaps only once since the last war. The Lord Chamberlain's staff do not systematically visit theatres in order to check performances of plays, but they do investigate complaints made by the public, police, or local authorities. In 1961, for instance, the Lord Chamberlain ordered the deletion of unauthorized references to the Duchess of Argyll from *Fings Ain't Wot They Used T'Be.* In 1958 there was a conviction, when, to the play *You Won't Always Be on Top*, there was added without authority an impersonation of Sir Winston Churchill declaring open a public lavatory. In 1962 he demanded an assurance that the cast of the American revue *The Premise* would stick to the licensed script, and cease improvisation.

LOCAL AUTHORITIES

Something ought to be said about the powers of local authorities in relation to theatres. Theatres – other than those under the jurisdiction of the Lord Chamberlain, that is, broadly, Central London and New Windsor – are licensed by the councils of counties and county boroughs, except that a few have exercised their power to delegate their licensing powers to the justices in petty sessions. No play may be publicly performed in premises which have not been licensed for the purpose. The licensing authorities are empowered by the Theatres Act to make suitable rules for ensuring order and decency. In practice they make detailed regulations about fire prevention, crowd control, and other matters affecting safety. It is believed that the Act contemplated order and decency among the persons frequenting the theatre, which regulations of the kind just mentioned are calculated to promote. It is doubtful whether the Act intended to give local authorities control over the content of the plays themselves, except in so far as that content affects order and decency in the audience at the time of performance in the theatre. Yet frequently among a set of say fifty regulations dealing with safety and order the local authority will have one which seems to extend to the plays themselves. Here are two typical extracts:

All performances shall be of an unobjectionable character.

Nothing shall be acted, represented, recited, or sung which is licentious or indecent, or likely to produce riot, tumult or breach of the peace.

Unofficial bodies like the Public Morality Council have assumed that local authorities do have this power to maintain good moral standards in plays. But the best legal opinion is that such regulations will be valid only in so far as their meaning is restricted to the effect which the play will have on the order and decency of the audience. It would not be open to the licensing authority to cut out dialogue because they thought it obscene; on the other hand, if they thought that, in view of the local conditions, a certain controversial play might lead to disorder in the theatre, they could, under such a power, ban it altogether. Suppose the theatre reacted to a local authority's attempt to ban by contending that the Lord Chamberlain had approved the script and that they proposed to proceed with the performance. Local authorities have licensing functions in very many areas other than theatres, and are implicitly empowered by the relevant statute to revoke licences upon breach. They draft their theatre licences as if they had that power in this instance. It is believed that the effect of the Theatres Act is that, whereas the Lord Chamberlain can revoke a theatre licence in London, a local authority must complain to the justices, who themselves have power to close a theatre upon proof of a breach of licence: it would be for the justices to decide what the regulation meant, whether it was within the power given by the Act, and whether the play violated it. Obviously some local authorities have taken this view that the Act does not authorize them to revoke the licence, for some have secured the passing of local Acts of Parliament empowering them to revoke a theatre licence upon conviction for breach of regulations. It is very doubtful whether a local authority need give a hearing to a licensee before revoking his licence under such a power: this is therefore in form a very wide power. Fortunately, it does not appear to be the practice of local authorities to require the submission of scripts at local theatres and still less to ban any which the Lord Chamberlain has approved.

Licensing bodies usually assign to particular policemen supervision of theatres. Occasionally, they will obtain copies of the approved script in order to compare it with the performance. These licensing bodies also have jurisdiction over all the amateur bodies which perform plays. In practice, there is no systematic check by the police, and still less by the Lord Chamberlain's Department, that such societies are conforming to authorized scripts.

GENERAL OBSERVATIONS ON THEATRE CENSORSHIP

No appraisal of theatre censorship can be made without some general observations on censorship. It is increasingly accepted that administrative bodies in particular circumstances should prevent the risk of subsequent harmful conduct by licensing those in certain activities and prohibiting all others from taking part. It is agreed for instance that it is better to license car-drivers rather than merely to leave them to the Courts' jurisdiction after they have offended against the traffic laws. Does it follow, then, that censorship is justifiable because instead of letting crimes like obscenity and sedition be committed, with consequent punishment of the perpetrators, it prevents the wrongful act from being performed at all?

Obviously, it is in the public interest to reduce crime of

every kind and there would seem to be a prima facie case for any expedient tending to do this. But, as we shall see when we discuss the relevant crimes later, not many of the matters which the Lord Chamberlain prohibits would be criminal. Some would constitute obscenity, and conceivably sedition, or contempt of Court, or criminal libel, but most, such as dramatizing recent real-life incidents, could not be crimes. Occasionally, censorship might prevent not crime, but some wrong for which an individual could claim damages: a representation on the stage might be libellous, for example. Although this would not be as important as crime prevention, the argument might be advanced that it is desirable to prevent incidents arising which might provoke actions for damages. Yet the Lord Chamberlain forbids plays about individuals even though their facts are accurate: one could say that English law lags behind that of other countries in not awarding damages to those with whose private lives there is a socially inexcusable interference, and that the Lord Chamberlain is trying to make good the deficiency. Even if one made all these concessions, there would remain many matters forbidden by the Lord Chamberlain which are not crimes or wrongs in any common-law country; for instance, inoffensive dramatization of politicians, depiction of say Edward VII, physical appearance of the Deity, and dramatization of English *causes célèbres*. The Lord Chamberlain avoids injuring people's feelings and wounding their susceptibilities and protects institutions such as the monarchy, the Church, the armed forces, and the police, to an extent to which the law could not possibly go. There seems to be no justification for the total prohibition of matters which the community would not be prepared to treat as criminal or as otherwise illegal if they were to be done.

There is a more subtle objection to censorship. Is it not likely that a censor will tend to play safe, to be behind rather than in advance of contemporary public opinion about freedom of speech, that his decisions will tend to operate against the interest in freedom of speech? The

Director of Public Prosecutions has said that if the Lord Chamberlain licensed an obscene play, this would make the Lord Chamberlain guilty of the crime of aiding and abetting, and he could not prosecute the producers without also prosecuting the Lord Chamberlain. The Lord Chamberlain's knowledge of the attitude of the Director of Public Prosecutions, who is in sole charge of prosecutions for obscenity, is obviously going to reinforce this attitude of caution, which, it is suggested, is to be expected of censors. One can hold this view without scoring cheap points by saying that in the past the Lord Chamberlain has banned various plays which are now held to be innocuous – obviously it would be most unfair to him to ignore the climate of opinion at the time of his ban, and not to take account of the readiness with which he changes his mind in the light of advice which he receives and of shifts in public attitudes.

Other objections must be made. How does one justify censorship of plays on the stage, if there is no legal censorship by an outside body in respect of television and radio? Surely one cannot. We have all enjoyed the political cartoon: how does it differ in essence from the play about a politician? What is incalculable is how many worthwhile controversial plays about politics, the Crown, and the Church the British theatre would have had, if dramatists had not known that plays on such themes would be banned. The seven day notice rule prevents improvisation.

If, however, one *is* to have a censor, are our present arrangements satisfactory? We have seen that they are in the hands of the Lord Chamberlain, not in consequence of a carefully thought-out decision of policy, but only through a historical accident. Should the decision rest solely with one man, and should that man be one whose main function is Court ceremonial, however varied his experience may have been in his earlier career? If the discretion of the censor is unlimited, as at present, should not there be some means, either legal or political, of challenging his decisions? The analogy with judges breaks down, both because they are working to rules – they do not have unlimited discretion to say whether particular conduct shall be treated as criminal, for instance – and because there is usually a right of appeal to a higher Court. If unlimited discretion is to remain, accountability to the House of Commons would seem preferable. But these decisions are best not bedevilled by politics. It would therefore be wiser to define the grounds upon which there shall be a discretion to forbid a play, and to judicialize the procedure. In that event, the Court could decide whether the censor did reasonably find in good faith that one of the permitted grounds of refusal was present, but would not be able to interfere with the manner in which he exercised his discretion. Judicialization would also entail the opportunity (not at present given) for those connected with the play to present arguments why the play should be allowed, and the stating of written reasons for rejection by the censor. There would then be no need for political accountability.

It may be asked why censorship has survived so long in its present form in England. Broadway does not have it, nor does Northern Ireland. Most theatrical managers prefer to have it. We have seen that the Director of Public Prosecutions would never prosecute in respect of a play which the Lord Chamberlain has approved, because he would then have to prosecute the Lord Chamberlain for aiding and abetting, which he is not prepared to do. In practice, though not in law, then, the present system ensures that theatrical producers are safe from criminal prosecution so long as they conform to the licensed script. But we have seen already that little of the censoring concerns crime. In so far as, say, libel is involved, the fact that the Lord Chamberlain has approved a play in no way restricts the right of a person defamed by a play to sue the producer in damages – the Lord Chamberlain's licence is irrelevant.

Do proposals for reform which merely improve the procedure of censorship go far enough? The Joint Select Committee of the House of Lords and House of Commons in 1909 recommended that play-licensing should be optional.

Those who wish to secure criminal immunity by seeking the censor's approval should be able to do so, and those who prefer to risk legal consequences should be free to put on a play without prior approval. They recommended, moreover, that a licence should be refused only on grounds specified by Parliament. These proposals are a distinct improvement on the present arrangements. There seems no adequate reason for compulsory censorship, no evidence that much irremediable harm would be done if it were abolished. Theatrical managements do not require this protection. It is only of any importance in regard to obscenity, and their legal advisers would ordinarily be able to decide whether a play came within the scope of that crime. No doubt obscene scripts are sent to and rejected by the Lord Chamberlain, but a few stiff punishments would soon curb the purveyors of the obscene in the theatre, even without any censorship.

The conclusion is then that although the present system of censorship is very much fairer and more enlightened than many of its critics have suggested, its procedures certainly could be improved, if we must continue to have theatre censorship. On balance, there seems no adequate reason for maintaining the present machinery, on either a compulsory or an optional basis.

Cinema

THE CINEMATOGRAPH ACTS

In 1909 Parliament passed 'an Act to make better provision for securing safety at cinematograph and other exhibitions': the cinema was a new form of public entertainment, and, in view of the risk of fire, clearly needed official supervision. Accordingly, the Act provided that an exhibition 'for the purposes of which inflammable films are used' required a licence: county councils and county boroughs were made the licensing authorities, and county councils were expressly authorized to delegate their powers to justices sitting in petty sessions. These licensing bodies might grant licences to such persons as they thought fit to use the premises specified in the licence for the above purpose on such terms and conditions and under such restrictions as, subject to regulations of the Home Secretary, the licensing bodies might determine. Many had supposed that the only conditions authorized would relate to public safety and order; and that any other conditions would be void. When confronted with a power to impose conditions which on a literal interpretation seems unrestricted, the Courts frequently have given that power a restricted meaning in the light of the general purpose of the Act. A former permanent head of the Home Office, which originated the Act, has written that the Home Office never supposed that local authorities were being given a power to censor films.

However, soon after the Act was passed some local authorities responded to local pressure by refusing to allow the exhibition of films of which they disapproved. An exhibitor challenged the legality of this action, and, surprisingly, failed, the Court holding that the licensing power did extend to matters affecting public morals.[1] Faced with the prospect of conflicting decisions on particular films the cinematograph industry pressed the Home Office to centralize film censorship. The Home Office refused to introduce legislation setting up compulsory national censorship: obviously they shirked undertaking a new duty which might expose their chief to continual criticism in Parliament and the Press. Working in close cooperation with the Home Office, the industry itself set up in 1912 a voluntary and unofficial body, the British Board of Film Censors, to certify and classify films for public exhibition. Thereupon, the Home Office, after consultation with licensing authorities, and in the light of representations from welfare organizations about the impropriety of many of the films then being exhibited, began to encourage licensing authorities to make use of the Board's work so that suitable and reasonably uniform standards of censorship might be applied. The Home Office recommended to the licensing authorities certain 'model' conditions which they might attach to cinema licences. They are based almost entirely upon the British Board of Film Censor's censorship and classification of films. Licensing authorities are not bound to adopt recommendations made by the Home Office; the Cinematograph Act leaves decisions to the discretion of the licensing authority. In any event the model conditions are framed so as to leave unimpaired the statutory discretion of licensing authorities to accept, reject, or modify any of the decisions of the Board under the Cinematograph Act, 1909 – indeed, a condition attached to a licence that the Board's rulings must always be followed, has been held void because the final decision must be that of the licensing body, not of the Board.[2] The legal position, in brief, is that the British Board of Film Censors has no official statutory existence; it is a private body set up by the cinematograph industry, which derives its authority from the fact that when the local authorities license cinemas they usually stipulate that the films ordinarily conform to the Board's ruling – a stipulation which a Court of first instance has surprisingly held to be valid and which has gone unchallenged ever since.[3] The only important legal change since 1909 is the passing of the Cinematograph Act, 1952. This for the first time extended the powers of licensing bodies to non-inflammable films. It also put on a firm legal basis the power of licensing bodies to make conditions or restrictions on the admission of children to films designated as unsuitable for children and indeed imposed a duty on them to consider such restrictions. In all other respects the legal position about licensing set out above remains unaltered.

CENSORSHIP IN PRACTICE: THE BRITISH BOARD OF FILM CENSORS AND LOCAL LICENSING AUTHORITIES

What then happens in practice? First, the power to delagate to justices has been widely exercised, so that more then half of the country's seven hundred cinema-licensing bodies are justices. Many other local authorities have delegated the powers to their watch committees, and on even to its health, sewerage, and cemeteries committee. Of 487 licensing bodies which answered a canvass all but 32 had adopted the Home Office's model conditions.

The main provisions of the model conditions are as follows. No film shall be shown, and no poster or other advertisement of a film in or outside the premises shall be displayed, which is likely to be injurious to morality or to encourage or incite to crime, or to lead to disorder, or to be offensive to public feeling, or which contains any offensive representation of living persons. If the licensing body serve a notice on the licensee that they object to the exhibition of any film on any of these grounds, that film shall not be shown. No film which has not been passed by the Board shall be exhibited without the express consent of the licensing body. The next provisions refer to the Board's classification: Category A, for films passed as more suitable for exhibition to adult audiences; Category U for films passed for general exhibition; Category X for films passed for exhibition provided that no child under sixteen is present. No 'A' film is to be exhibited (without the licensing authority's consent) while any child under, or appearing to be under sixteen, is present, unless that child is accompanied by a parent or other person over the age of sixteen *bona fide* in charge of such child. No 'X' film is to be exhibited while any child under sixteen is in the cinema. A licensing authority, even though it has adopted the model conditions, is free to reject the Board's classification either by refusing to permit the exhibition of a film in accordance with that classification, or by allowing its performance in disregard of the Board's refusal or restricted classification. Conditions sometimes imposed by authorities which do not follow the model conditions include: specific permission to be sought before exhibiting 'X' films on Sunday; synopses of all 'X' films to be submitted in advance so that the authority may, if it chooses, view any such film before deciding whether to permit its exhibition.

How does the British Board of Film Censors go about its

work? The President of the Board is selected in this way: the Council of the Kinematograph Producers' Association, of which the Secretary to the British Board of Film Censors is *ex officio* secretary, makes a recommendation to a joint committee which consists of representatives of the British Film Producers' Association, the Federation of British Film Makers, the Association of Specialized Film Producers, the Kinematograph Renters' Society and the Cinematograph Exhibitors' Association. Prior to this meeting there will have been consultation with the Home Office, the Association of Municipal Corporations and the County Councils Association. The joint committee of the industry makes the actual appointment. The President appoints examiners, who, together with the President and the Secretary (who is now appointed by representatives of that committee which appoints the President) constitute the Board. None of the Board's members is connected with the film industry, and its revenues are derived from fees charged for all films submitted for censorship. In the past the Home Office has exercised some influence on the Board. Some appointments, both to the presidency and to the influential secretaryship, have been of persons with Home Office connexions. There are authenticated examples of governmental interference before the Second World War. In 1939 the Home Secretary admitted under questioning in the House of Commons that the Board had consulted him about certain films before deciding whether to recommend them for exhibition. In 1938 the Secretary of State for India arranged with the British Board of Film Censors to prevent production and exhibition of a film about the Indian mutiny at Lucknow. Again, in 1935 a pacifist film of the Peace Pledge Union was refused a certificate on the ground that it might lead to disturbances, whereas in the following year a Territorial Army film was approved and widely exhibited. In recent years the Board has attained strength and independence. Its present Secretary has no Home Office antecedents, and there seems to be no significance in the fact that its President, Lord Morrison of

Lambeth, is a former Home Secretary. The Home Secretary was at pains to protest in the House of Commons his inability to prevent the exhibition of *Rommel*.[4] There is no reason to believe that the Board now consults government departments on any decisions, and still less that it ever submits to governmental pressure. Each film is seen by two or more examiners; films in which important problems occur will also be seen by the Secretary or President, or both, and matters involving important changes of policy will usually be discussed by the President with all the Board's examiners. Sometimes the Government has interfered with the exhibition of films without attempting to exert pressure on the Board. The Board does not control news reels, although local authorities could, but in practice do not, require them to be approved before exhibition. In September 1938, at the time of Chamberlain's visit to Hitler, four out of the five cinema news companies exhibited films favourable to the Government – the fifth, Paramount, included interviews with persons opposed to appeasement: the Foreign Secretary successfully stopped exhibition of this news reel by persuading the American Ambassador to intervene with Paramount. In 1959 the Foreign Office advised the British participants in a Moscow Film Festival not to exhibit *Carlton-Brown of the Foreign Office* on the ground that it might be misunderstood.

The practice of the local licensing bodies varies widely. Films are sometimes exhibited despite the Board's refusal: Cambridge and Maesteg, for instance, allowed the playing of Brando's *The Wild One*. Manchester's police force has an Entertainments Department, with functions such as are performed in some other towns by the fire service. Its members read the cinema trade newspapers in order to decide which trade shows of films in the city to attend, and they will at least attend all 'X' and 'A' films. They prepare for the chief constable a report on any film which they think ought not perhaps to be shown in the city. This report is forwarded to the Watch Committee who will have a private viewing of the film and then decide whether to allow it to be shown. For example, Manchester refused to allow *The Savage Eye* to be exhibited, although it won an award at the Edinburgh Festival. If an application is made to exhibit a film which the Board rejected, the Committee will view that also. By arrangement, Manchester police circulate their reports on films to many north-western towns. Whatever Manchester has approved without reservation these other towns will also approve ordinarily without further check: in the remaining instances they will usually view and decide for themselves. London and the Midlands have more formal consultative arrangements. Birmingham has delegated the task to the licensing justices, who have appointed women inspectors for the discharge of both cinema- and theatre-licensing functions. These inspectors attend shows, and, if they make unfavourable reports, two nominated justices attached to whichever of the city's five police districts is affected visit the cinema within twenty-four hours. These justices also attend trade shows if the local cinematographers' association so request them because they are doubtful about booking a particular film. Occasionally they change the Board's classification. Birmingham has an arrangement with Walsall, Redditch, Willenhall, Dudley, Stourbridge, Smethwick, Wolverhampton, West Bromwich, and Warwick to invite representatives from all of them whenever it views a film in consequence of having received a complaint. Although each authority reserves liberty of action, in practice uniformity is achieved, so that exhibited films do not acquire notoriety through being banned in neighbouring towns – there will be no 'Banned in Birmingham' posters. The administrative county of Warwickshire is not a party to this arrangement: thus, in 1961, it banned *Saturday Night and Sunday Morning*, which Birmingham and the other boroughs allowed to be exhibited in accordance with the Board's 'X' certificate. London County Council joins forces with the county councils of Surrey, Middlesex, Berkshire, and Essex and the boroughs of Croydon, East Ham, and West Ham in viewing films which have been the subject of complaint or have not been passed by the Board, but these bodies do not necessarily make uniform decisions. Some local authorities always accept the Board's rulings; others never vary them without asking the Board to give reasons for their decision.

The British Board of Film Censors does not follow the American practice of publishing a detailed code of rules for the production of films, e.g., 'open-mouth kissing' is not to be shown, 'pansy', 'S.O.B.', 'son-of-a', and other listed expressions are forbidden. Its task is also easier because in Britain there are no unofficial powerful pressure groups systematically viewing and censoring films, whereas in the United States dozens of organizations such as the General Federation of Women's Clubs, the National Legion of Decency (a Roman Catholic organization) and the Daughters of the American Revolution publish regular reports to their members and the trade. Contrary to popular belief, violence and horror, not sex, is the Board's primary concern. The Board rejects films for other reasons, too. It denied a certificate to the film *Operation Teutonic Sword* because it believed that it contained matter defamatory of a living person, General Speidel of the German armed forces. Its judgement was vindicated in the sense that, when certain local authorities allowed the film to be shown despite the Board's refusal, the General successfully sued the distributors for libel. At the same time one wonders whether the Board should not leave it to the ordinary Courts to protect a man's reputation. The situation is the more disquieting in that the Board was also influenced in its decision to reject by the fear that the Board might itself be liable for defamation if it authorized the exhibition of a defamatory film. It would surely be undesirable if the Board were to deny a certificate to every film which it thought might be defamatory of some living person; the Courts can be relied on to afford remedies for libel victims. The Board encourages the growing practice of submitting the scripts of films to it in advance of production. Where the Board cannot approve a film in the form submitted, cuts are usually suggested, and if these are substantial, if they involve reductions in scenes rather than definite eliminations, or if there are other good reasons, resubmission of the appropriate reels is required. Sometimes cuts are made at the request of a film company in order to avoid the restriction of a film to the 'X' or 'A' categories, since there are often financial advantages in 'U' or 'A' as compared with 'X' films.

GENERAL OBSERVATIONS ON FILM CENSORSHIP

How is one to appraise this system of cinema censorship? It seems to be generally agreed that the Board tackles the task in an intelligent manner, and that, particularly with the development of the 'X' certificate since 1951, few sincere and serious films are denied public exhibition. For example, this category has permitted such films as *Room at the Top, La Ronde, Death of a Salesman,* and *Baby Doll* to be seen in unabridged versions by the adult British public. On the other hand, because it has sometimes been thought commercially unprofitable to exhibit solely on an 'X' classification, some serious films have never been made at all, or else like the school film *Spare the Rod* (1961) have been produced in a watered-down version. Obviously, if the statutory system of local licensing is to continue, the Board fulfils an essential function in making unnecessary the submission of all films to all licensing authorities. But why have local censorship at all? It is responsible for much local expenditure, and argument that local bodies know the peculiar quirks and susceptibilities of their own folk seems thin in a small homogeneous country. It seems a waste of public funds that conferences of local authorities and the Board have to be convened so that the local authorities and the Board can understand the reasoning underlying each other's decisions. There is another objection to the present system of local licensing. It is the practice to make the licence revocable for breach of condition: consequently local authorities have a much wider power to close down cinemas than theatres. Moreover, local authorities (with the laudable exception of the London County Council, do not usually give a licensee the right to appear personally and to be legally represented before them when a licensing decision is taken. Licensing justices usually do afford this facility – in Liverpool, for example, the justices listened to counsel's arguments before refusing the usual twelve months' renewal to a cinema which had persistently published offensive posters – and licensees are seriously prejudiced when the licensing is carried out by local authorities. Fortunately their lot is to some extent improved by the Act of 1952, which gives those aggrieved by the revocation of a licence the right of appeal to Quarter Sessions.

If local censorship were abolished the choice would then be between putting the Board on a statutory basis and giving its decisions legal effect, or leaving the industry free to continue to operate a Board which would be shorn of the indirect legal sanctions which at present attach to its rulings. If the Board were legally recognized, there would be a strong case for widening its membership and ensuring its judicial independence. In order to keep the decisions out of the political arena, it would also be desirable to enact the grounds on which rejection and classification are to be based. Its decisions should be unchallengeable in Parliament and only subject to judicial review if the powers were exceeded. Perhaps such a body should listen to any arguments in support of a film made by its sponsors and be required to give reasons for its refusal to comply with the sponsors' requests. Some of the grounds on which films have in recent times apparently been censored should be excluded. Take the treatment given in 1954 to *The End of the Affair*, of which its director, Edward Dmytryk complained in the *New York Herald Tribune*: the censor refused permission to include a news reel shot of the royal family on the balcony of Buckingham Palace on V-E Day on the ground that to associate the royal family with the film could be improper – yet Dmytryk stated that a representative of the royal family itself eventually permitted the shot.[5] There has also been complaint that the British Board is hypersensitive on religious matters: parts of the script of *The Left Hand of God*, which passed the Code of the Motion Picture Association of America and the Legion of Decency, were either altered or deleted at the behest of the British Board. In short, the Board may be subject to criticism (though to a lesser extent) in largely the same areas as the Lord Chamberlain. In its regulation of obscenity, horror, and violence it will have universal support, but not in an interpretation of 'offensiveness' which appears to be unduly deferential to monarchy, the Church, and similar institutions. No doubt censorship of this latter kind is infrequent, but it would be better to make its exercise impossible.

It would not be inconsistent to abolish theatre censorship and yet to retain national censorship of films, either legal or unofficial. Factors like the large attendance of children and the facility for portrayal of horror justify making a distinction between the two media.

Radio and Television

B.B.C. AND I.T.A.: THE LEGAL POSITION

The British Broadcasting Corporation is a body incorporated by royal charter. There are nine governors (including the chairman and the vice-chairman) who are appointed by the Crown on the advice of the Prime Minister: three of the governors are 'national' governors, representing Scotland, Wales, and Northern Ireland. The powers of the B.B.C. to provide sound and television broadcasting services and the controls to which they are subject are to be found in the Licence and Agreement of 1 July 1952.[6] The key figure is the Postmaster-General; he grants the licence, and without it there can be no broadcasting. The B.B.C. is directed not to broadcast its own opinion on current affairs or on matters of public policy, and in 1927–8 was directed not to broadcast matters of political, industrial, or religious controversy.

The Licence and Agreement requires the publication of various programmes; for instance, Clause 15(2) orders the broadcast of 'an impartial account day by day prepared by professional reporters of the proceedings in both Houses of the United Kingdom Parliament.' Clause 15(4) of this Licence provides that 'The Postmaster-General may from time to time by notice in writing require the Corporation to refrain at any specified time or at all times from sending any matter or matter of any class specified in such notice.' And what if the B.B.C. were to disobey a direction from the Postmaster-General? Clause 24 provides for the revocation of the Licence by the Postmaster-General upon non-compliance with a direction of his – and the approval of Parliament is not required either for the cancellation of the licence to broadcast or indeed for the revocation of the royal charter. Clearly these are water-tight legal controls.

The Independent Television Authority is set up directly by the Television Act, 1954, in order to provide television broadcasting services additional to those of the B.B.C.: the I.T.A. is to have a chairman, deputy chairman, and at least five other members, appointed by the Postmaster-General, three of whom represent Scotland, Wales and Northern Ireland respectively. The Act contemplates that programmes shall be provided, not by the I.T.A., but by programme contractors under contract with the I.T.A. Surprisingly enough, the Act lays down no procedures for the award of these highly lucrative contracts.[7] This contrasts with the American prescription of procedures of a judicial kind calculated to ensure that these decisions are arrived at fairly and impartially. In fact the I.T.A. interviewed some applicants but not others – presumably it interviewed those whom it appointed. In the event, two of the first four contracts were allocated to companies backed by right-wing newspapers. The Act contains several rules about the content of programmes which will be examined later. The contracts between the I.T.A. and the programme contractors must include power to require submission of scripts in advance, power for the I.T.A. to forbid the broadcasting of specified matters, and power to ensure that nothing shall be broadcast without the previous approval of the I.T.A. These powers must not be exercised unless the I.T.A. is satisfied that some breach of contract which it apprehends makes it necessary. The contracts must also contain such provisions as the I.T.A. thinks necessary for ensuring that the programme contractors comply with the rules about the content of programmes. If a programme contractor violates its contract in any of these respects, then the I.T.A. can demand the payment of penalties not exceeding £500, £1,000, and £1,500 for the first, second, and subsequent breaches respectively. After three penalties have been imposed, the I.T.A. may, in the event of a subsequent breach, and after first giving the contractor opportunity to make representations, suspend for a period or end completely the broadcasting of that contractor's programmes. Suppose that the I.T.A. fails to enforce its contract against a defaulting programme contractor. The Act merely provides that 'it shall be the duty of the Authority to satisfy themselves that, so far as possible, the programmes broadcast by the Authority comply with' the requirements of the Act. These words were deliberately drafted in this loose discretionary form so as to impose no enforceable legal duty on the I.T.A.; they have no legal effect, they are merely words of exhortation which the I.T.A. can disregard without any legal consequences. The Act does not impose duties directly on the programme contractors; it relies on the I.T.A.'s securing their compliance with the Act by enforcing its contractual rights against them. The public has no means of knowing to what extent the I.T.A. interferes with the programmes of the companies. The I.T.A. refuses to give details about this on the ground that it 'would serve no purpose' and would be 'undesirable'. Why this is so is not explained.

By notice in writing the Postmaster-General may at any time require the I.T.A. to refrain from broadcasting any matter or classes of matter specified in the notice. Unlike the similar power with respect to the B.B.C., non-compliance

does not threaten the power to broadcast (although the
I.T.A., like the B.B.C., has a licence from the Postmaster-
General, this licence differs from that of the B.B.C. in that it
is silent on programme content and therefore makes no
express provision for revocation on non-compliance with
directives): the Act merely adds that it shall be the duty of
the I.T.A. to comply. At most, the Postmaster-General could
obtain in Court an order of mandamus requiring the
I.T.A. to comply: in the unlikely event of matters going so far,
perhaps the members of the I.T.A. could then be committed
for contempt of Court if they still did not comply with the
Postmaster-General's notice after he had obtained the
order of mandamus against them.

The Postmaster-General has the power to prescribe the
actual hours during which broadcasting shall take place.
Both the B.B.C. and the I.T.A. are required to broadcast any
Government announcement at the time specified by the
Postmaster-General: this refers not to statements about
Government policy, but to official announcements; for
example, the calling up of certain classes of reserves in the
armed forces. In practice police messages and the like are
broadcast without a direction. The B.B.C. complains that the
power is not confined to Ministers: it has complained that
civil servants have occasionally tried to insist that certain
views be inserted in news bulletins; sometimes the B.B.C.
has had to refuse.

We have been discussing the legal obligations of the
B.B.C. and the I.T.A. contained in the Licence and statute
respectively: the matters to be discussed next do not rest
on the law.

BROADCASTING AND POLITICS

By virtue of an agreement between the Conservative
Party, the Labour Party, and the B.B.C. in 1947 (usually
referred to as the 'aide-mémoire'), the full terms of which
are set out in the Beveridge Report on Broadcasting
(1951),[8]

In view of their responsibilities for the care of the nation the Government should be able to use the wireless from time to time for Ministerial broadcasts which, for example, are purely factual, or explanatory of legislation or administrative policies approved by Parliament; or in the nature of appeals to the nation to co-operate in national policies, such as fuel economy or recruiting, which require the active participation of the public.

The intention here is clear: a typical example would be the Postmaster-General asking the public to post early for Christmas, or the Minister of Transport explaining new speed limits under a new Road Traffic Act. The agreement continues:

It will be incumbent on Ministers making such broadcasts to be as impartial as possible, and in the ordinary way there will be no question of a reply by the Opposition. Where, however, the Opposition think that a Government broadcast is controversial it will be open to them to take the matter up through the usual channels with a view to a reply. (i) As a reply if one is to be made should normally be within a very short period after the original broadcast, say three days, the B.B.C. will be free to exercise its own judgement if no agreement is arrived at within that period.

The 'usual channels' are in fact the Government whips. An incident during the Suez affair illustrates the working of this rule. Sir Anthony Eden, the Prime Minister, broadcast on B.B.C. sound radio and television. The Government Chief Whip refused the Labour Chief Whip's request for a broadcast in reply, on the ground that the Prime Minister's broadcast was a non-controversial Ministerial one within the terms of the agreement set out above. The Labour Chief Whip appealed to the B.B.C. who exercised their power under the agreement to allow a reply on radio and television by Mr Gaitskell, the leader of the Opposition.

By the 1954 Act, the I.T.A. had to satisfy itself that 'no matter designed to serve the interests of any political party is included in the programmes.'[9] These words of the Act necessarily overrode, for the I.T.A., whatever was in the aide-mémoire. Although, as we shall see, parts of the aide-mémoire are treated as applying to the I.T.A. as much as to the B.B.C. the I.T.A. was in a different position from the B.B.C. in regard to these Ministerial broadcasts. Before a Minister made what he regarded as an uncontroversial factual broadcast it would plainly be the duty of the I.T.A. to examine the script in order to ensure that it was not designed to serve the interests of the Government party, and to refuse the broadcast altogether if it found that it was a party statement: there could be no question of the I.T.V. deciding after the broadcast, on appeal by the Opposition, to allow a politically controversial reply. The I.T.A. had to decide in advance whether the broadcast was an impartial Ministerial one; if it rejected the broadcast, its decision was final; if it permitted it, the Opposition was not entitled to an answering broadcast. However the 1963 Act repealed this duty of I.T.A. to prevent party statements. The I.T.A. still has to decide in advance whether the broadcast is impartial; if it is not, it must arrange beforehand for another broadcast in order to comply with its duty under the 1963 Act of satisfying itself of the impartiality of any series as a whole.[10] On the other hand, the B.B.C. has no choice but to allow a Minister to broadcast what the Postmaster-General says is uncontroversial, but it has an unfettered power to allow a reply.

The aide-mémoire also provides:

A limited number of controversial party political broadcasts shall be allocated to the various parties in accordance with their polls at the last General Election. The allocation shall be calculated on a yearly basis and the total number of such broadcasts shall be a matter for discussion between the parties and the B.B.C.

The B.B.C. is prohibited from sending any other controversial party political broadcasts. The Act of 1954 (proviso lii to section 3 (1)) expressly permitted the I.T.A. to relay all the B.B.C.'s party political broadcasts.[11] The 1963 Act has repealed this proviso so that the I.T.A. is not legally bound to take these broadcasts, and in practice the parties have to fall in with the I.T.A.'s own suggested times, which of course will exclude the peak advertising revenue-earning hours. In 1961 one of the programme contractors announced that it would not relay party political broadcasts unless the parties indemnified it against all damages and costs awarded against it in libel actions arising out of such broadcasts – no doubt the attempt by Mrs Barbara Castle to obtain damages for libel from Mr Christopher Chataway occasioned this attitude. The contractor was correct in saying that it would be answerable for any such libels, because, as we have seen, it is by agreement and not compulsion that these broadcasts are made. On the other hand, if the libel were contained in a Government announcement, i.e. a broadcast which the Government can compel the B.B.C. and I.T.A. to make, the B.B.C. and I.T.A. would probably not be liable.

The Beveridge Report criticized adversely the refusal of the Government in the nineteen-thirties to allow Mr Churchill to broadcast comments on its India policy. In consequence, the aide-mémoire provides that the B.B.C. reserve the right, after consultation with the party leaders, to invite to the microphone a member of either House of outstanding national eminence who may have become detached from any party.

The most controversial aspect of relations between Government and broadcasting authority in recent years has been discussion of matters being debated in Parliament. During the war, when of course there was no effective Opposition, a Minister prevailed on the B.B.C. to let him make a broadcast, on a subject unconnected with the war effort, the night before it was to be debated in the House of Commons. Repenting of this weakness in face of governmental pressure, the B.B.C. then itself made a rule for its own protection that it would not allow broadcasts by anybody in anticipation of parliamentary debates. This was incorporated in the aide-mémoire without discussion, and almost by accident. Again the B.B.C. had second thoughts and became irked by its own rule. The Beveridge Report recommended its repeal, but Sir Winston Churchill's

Government rejected this proposal by the Beveridge Committee. Then the B.B.C. showed commendable courage. When the parties turned down its proposal that the governors should decide how much discussion of political issues would be broadcast, on an undertaking that no members of parliament would be allowed to broadcast within 14 days before parliamentary debates, it refused to renew this provision of the aide-mémoire and thereby forced the Government to take upon themselves the odium of imposing it. Without consulting Parliament, the Postmaster-General in 1955 issued directions in the same terms as those contained in the aide-mémoire, to both the B.B.C. and I.T.A. (which, as we have seen, are legally binding): that they should not,

on any issue, arrange discussions or *ex parte* statements which are to be broadcast during a period of a fortnight before the issue is debated in either House or while it is being so debated, and that when legislation is introduced in Parliament on any subject, they shall not, on such subject, arrange broadcasts by any member of Parliament which are to be made during the period between the introduction of the legislation and the time when it either receives the Royal Assent or is previously withdrawn or dropped.

The responsible Press, commendably putting on one side its own interests, was unanimous in its condemnation of this Governmental policy. In 1956 a Select Committee was set up to consider the matter. It found that any restrictions should be reduced to the smallest extent that is practicable (and would have gone further had not its terms of reference precluded it) and that the only justification which could be claimed for any policy of restriction was the necessity of upholding the primacy of Parliament in debating the affairs of the nation. The Government refused to implement the Report, but instead agreed to suspend the fourteen-day rule for an experimental period of six months. The price exacted was an undertaking by the B.B.C. and I.T.A. that they would continue to act in a way which would not 'derogate from the primacy of Parliament' as the forum for debating the affairs of the nation.[12]

Subsequently, the fourteen-day rule was suspended indefinitely, and remains suspended today. Both bodies are free to arrange discussions and talks on any political matters – they are themselves to be the judges of what derogates from the primacy of Parliament. For the time being then, the I.T.A, may, without the incumbrance of the direction, include programmes relating to matters of political controversy or current public policy; the only statutory duty is to take care that due impartiality is preserved considering, when there is a series of programmes, that series as a whole.[13] Programmes like I.T.A.'s *Free Speech*, and B.B.C.'s *Tonight* can pursue their course of political discussion, either by members of Parliament or others. Whether the whips will allow M.P.s to broadcast freely is another matter – Lord Boothby has told how, when a member of Parliament, he received orders from the Tory whips restricting his T.V. appearances in particular programmes to a specific number.[14] Whereas, however, the B.B.C. could invite, say, the Earl of Avon or Lord Franks to speak on a controversial issue, the I.T.A. could not, unless it was satisfied both that to do so was consistent with its statutory duty to preserve 'due impartiality'. Government control of British Forces Network programmes remains: Lord and Lady Tedder could not broadcast on the 'Malcolm Clubs' for the armed forces – their scripts were controversial and critical of Air Council decisions.

The next question is broadcasting in connexion with parliamentary elections. The answer might seem clear enough in view of what has been said already: both bodies free to transmit all the party broadcasts, and to hold such impartial and balanced discussions of political issues arising in the campaign as they think fit. Unfortunately, however, this question is further bedevilled by Section 63 of the Representation of the People Act, 1949, which makes infringement of the following a crime and a corrupt practice:

No expenses shall, with a view to promoting or procuring the election of a candidate at an election, be incurred by any person other than the candidate, his election agent and persons authorized in writing by the election agent on account (a) of holding public meetings or organizing any public display; or (b) of issuing advertisements, circulars, or publications; or (c) of otherwise presenting to the electors the candidate or his views or the extent or nature of his backing, or disparaging another candidate: Provided that paragraph (c) of this sub-section shall not restrict the publication of any matter relating to the election in a newspaper or other periodical.

Whatever the restrictions are, then, they apply to B.B.C. and I.T.A. but not to newspapers. Equally clearly, the restrictions are statutory, and operate regardless of what arrangements to the contrary might appear to be sanctioned in the aide-mémoire or other agreements between the parties and the broadcasting bodies. The significance of any infringement being declared by the Act to be a corrupt practice is that, regardless of any arrangements 'through the usual channels', the election might be declared void by an Election Court.

In 1958 Granada, a programme contractor, gave extensive coverage to the Rochdale by-election, including speeches by all the candidates, with the support of I.T.A. and in the face of opposition from the political parties. In three subsequent successive by-elections, Conservative candidates refused invitations from the B.B.C. to take part in programmes with the other candidates. The B.B.C. therefore cancelled the programmes on the ground that it would infringe Section 63 unless all candidates participated. In the General Election of 1959 the B.B.C. and I.T.A. were willing to put on, first, programmes relating to a particular constituency in which all the candidates appeared, secondly, regional programmes in which selected candidates appeared, not as candidates, but as party spokesmen not talking about constituency issues and thirdly, party political broadcasts by the leaders. Both bodies believe that the law permits this but no more, and the B.B.C. is pressing for the extension of the statutory exception for newspapers to broadcasting bodies.[15]

Are these legal interpretations correct? The Section is a difficult one to interpret, but no doubt broadcasting is a method of 'organizing (a) . . . public display . . . or otherwise presenting to the electors the candidate or his views'. Equally clearly 'expenses . . .' are 'incurred' within the section by such broadcasting. The key words in the section are 'with a view to promoting or procuring the election of a candidate at an election', and above all the words 'with a view to'. Do they mean that the offender must be acting 'for that purpose', or that an objective view of his conduct would be that he did so intend, or merely that a result of his conduct, regardless of his intention, is that the election of a certain candidate is procured? The third interpretation would have absurd consequences: if one candidate gave so inept a performance that his rival won, there would then be a contravention of the section. Moreover, 'with a view to' literally connotes a state of mind, either assumed or actual, on the part of someone. You may say that nobody would be guilty of something so serious as an election offence unless he had a guilty mind in the sense of actually seeking to prefer one candidate. In practice that would be difficult to prove. That is why the Courts will normally presume that a man intends the natural consequences of his acts. The previous Representation of the People Act used the words 'for the purpose of', on which it was held by the Court of Criminal Appeal that a man could not disclaim an intention to promote a candidate if he must have known that that would be the result of his act.[16] Moreover, in other statutes, the words 'with a view to' have been held to bear that same meaning – if the object aimed at was the prohibited result, then the act was deemed to be done 'with a view to' that result. On this approach – which is therefore the most likely interpretation – the offence will be committed if the broadcasting body either actually intended to, or did something which was substantially certain to, promote or procure the election of a particular candidate.

If this last interpretation is the correct one, have the B.B.C. and I.T.A. properly applied the Section? If some but not

all of the candidates in a particular constituency broadcast
this will probably advance their cause at the expense of the
non-broadcasters, and the B.B.C. and I.T.A. would be right
to refuse the broadcast. Conversely, to allow all the candidates to speak is not to promote the cause of one, and they are
right in believing that they do not commit a crime by doing
that. But what of the regional and national broadcasts in
which the speakers will speak as party men and not as
candidates? Presumably, the argument of the broadcasting
bodies is that this is not very likely to assist the speaking
candidate. This is surely doubtful: if a candidate is given
five minutes on a regional programme, is it not calculated
to give him an advantage over those candidates who do
not appear at all, even though he does not speak about
constituency matters? After all, how much of an electoral
address is about constituency, as distinct from either
regional or national issues? On the whole, the stand taken
by the B.B.C. seems inconsistent. If the offence is committed
even though the body does not actually intend to favour one
candidate, then having one candidate speak in the absence
of his rivals, whether on the constituency, regional, or
national platform seems likely to have the same kind of
effect in each case. Equally, of course, these remarks apply
to I.T.A.'s duties under the Representation of the People Act,
but it, unlike the B.B.C., has the further duty under the
Television Act to ensure that political debates are balanced.
If, on the other hand, 'with a view to' demands that the
B.B.C. or I.T.A. actually have as their aim the favouring of
one candidate at the expense of another, there would be
no justification for denying a broadcast to x because his
rival Y had rejected an invitation to broadcast.

It may be that the above discussion has not covered every
aspect of governmental interferences with programmes.
The Press and the Opposition accused the Government of
attempting backstairs interference at the time of Suez. On
another occasion South Africa's Minister for External
Affairs complained that a Panorama feature on apartheid
had been broadcast in the face of an express request of the

United Kingdom Government that it be postponed. Apparently Panorama did not broadcast the interview with Bidault at the time it was filmed because the Government requested its postponement so as not to jeopardize Common Market negotiations, although it did broadcast it seven weeks later after the Common Market talks had broken down.

So far we have been examining relations between the broadcasting companies and the Government of the day. Parliament itself also exercises supervision, although the Government is not responsible to Parliament for the day to day running of the B.B.C. and I.T.A. and has denied, for instance, any obligation regularly to monitor programmes. At question time in the House of Commons the Postmaster-General is often asked about the B.B.C. and I.T.A. Questions about the alleged failure of the I.T.A. to enforce compliance by the programme contractors with the requirements of the Television Act are frequent, and are usually countered by denials of responsibility for such day-to-day activities of the I.T.A. Again, in 1959, the Minister refused to ban a Week's Good Cause appeal for the Family Planning Association which the B.B.C. had refused to cancel despite outside pressure. The daily motion for the adjournment of the House of Commons is sometimes used to air grievances: an allegation of excessive Welsh nationalism in Welsh B.B.C. broadcasts led to the setting up of a Select Committee which cleared the B.B.C. of the charges levelled against it. Similar accusations of bias in treatment of the Suez crisis were made, to be refuted by the B.B.C. Governors after a full inquiry. Occasionally a motion of censure on the B.B.C. is put down, as when the B.B.C. was alleged to have made statements contradicting facts found by a Parliamentary Select Committee about methods of slaughtering horses. Sometimes, the B.B.C. submits to threats of parliamentary action. When a member of Parliament threatened to raise on the adjournment a projected broadcast by an ex-Queen's Scout who had been expelled from the movement for being a Communist political officer, the Director-

General cancelled the recorded broadcast within two hours.

OUTSIDE PRESSURES ON BROADCASTING AUTHORITIES

Other forms of informal pressure influence the B.B.C. A documentary about sending a worker to Coventry was cancelled, consequent upon Trade Union Congress comment; when on Easter Sunday the B.B.C. put on a play (*Family Portrait*, previously licensed by the Lord Chamberlain) which presented a Christian doctrine acceptable to some denominations but not to Roman Catholicism, the Director-General apologized to Cardinal Griffin for his 'grave error': no doubt this approach would rule out many of the miracle plays, at least at periods like Easter and Christmas. Public bodies, too, restrict the freedom of the B.B.C. British Railways withdrew a promise of facilities for a television Special Inquiry into railways in which there would be raised such matters as dirty lavatories and unpunctuality; Salford City Council resolved never to allow broadcasts about the city without its express permission because of a television programme on the city's health services.

INTERNAL CONTROLS

Editorial control within the B.B.C. is largely in the hands of programme producers. Occasionally written directives on specific matters are issued – there is a detailed one on violence from the Controller of Television Programmes.[17] Light entertainment producers are given lists of forbidden subjects, such as royalty and the Church. In general, producers are expected to know the B.B.C.'s attitudes; when in doubt they refer to their superior or sometimes to their equals. For example, religious allusions in a non-religious programme would be referred to the Head of Religious Broadcasting.[18] Like other censors whom we have considered, the B.B.C. in its self-censorship is at great pains to avoid upsetting susceptibilities. It will ban a record by Petula

Clark entitled *The Sky* because it finds offensive a veiled reference to God. It will remove Malcolm Muggeridge and Lord Altrincham from its programmes because they have written magazine articles which criticize the monarchy. It will ban records of Noel Coward's musical *Sail Away*, which American audiences have listened to unrestricted for years. It is difficult to resist the conclusion that the tendency within the B.B.C., especially before commercial television, was to lean over backwards so as not to give offence to any 'important' section of the community. The B.B.C. denies that it has any code and maintains that its key personnel merely instinctively understand what is expected of them by the governors and Director-General. But it is believed that lists of forbidden subjects have been compiled from time to time for producers.

By the Television Acts it is the duty of the I.T.A. to satisfy itself that, so far as possible, nothing is included in the programmes which offends against good taste or decency, or is likely to encourage or incite to crime or to lead to disorder or to be offensive to public feeling. Particularly controversial is the question whether scenes of violence on commercial television amount to a breach by I.T.A. of its duty under the Act. The argument of Sir Edwin Herbert, a director of Associated Rediffusion, is that 'these representations of the violent and sordid are a means of working out of the system the quite clear public liking for violence and the sordid side of life'. He added: 'I believe this mood will pass, but while it persists it is inevitable that to a greater or lesser degree it should be recognized by those who have to cater for the public taste.' I.T.A. insist, moreover, that programmes likely to contain violence are previewed. It mentions also that the problem of violence on television is studied actively by its children's advisory committee, with whose advice about the principles for children's programmes it must until July 1964[19] comply, subject, in the words of the Act, 'to such exceptions or modifications, if any, as may appear to the Authority to be necessary or proper' having regard to its other duties. After July 1964 the I.T.A. has to draw up a code giving guidance as to the rules to be observed in regard to the showing of violence, particularly when large numbers of young persons may be expected to watch, and has to secure that the provisions of the code are observed.[20]

No religious service or propaganda may be broadcast without I.T.A.'s approval. Sermons by the Archdeacon of London have been withdrawn by I.T.A. because of their political slant. The I.T.A. must comply until July 1964 to the same extent as for its children's committee with the recommendations on religious propaganda and services of a religious advisory committee 'representative of the main streams of religious thought in the United Kingdom'. The B.B.C. has similar committees for religious and children's broadcasting but their functions are only advisory – the Roman Catholic church in its memorandum to the Pilkington Committee on broadcasting recommended that the B.B.C. be subject to the same obligations touching its religious committee as I.T.A.

One matter peculiar to I.T.A. is the control of advertisements. It is the duty of I.T.A. to secure that the requirements of the Act on advertisements are complied with. These include: they must be clearly separate from the rest of the programme, they must not be inserted by religious or political bodies, or directed towards religious or political ends or relate to industrial disputes. *Daily Worker* advertisements were refused because the *Daily Worker* was found by the I.T.A. to be a body having wholly or mainly political objects; films by the Institute of Directors were refused because they had a political end, advertisements for family planning are refused because they are directed to religious ends. Notice that the decision of the I.T.A. on advertisements is not subject to appeal to any court or tribunal. Detailed comment on Television advertising will be made in Chapter 4.

The Act imposes another restriction on I.T.A. No programme may offer 'a prize or gift which is available only to persons receiving that programme, or in relation to which any advantage is given to such persons.'[21] Some may rejoice that this prevents our following the American habit of playing Bingo on television. A few naïve souls were under the delusion that it prevented the giving of prizes to quiz contestants; but it is those 'receiving' the programme, not the participants, who must not be offered prizes.

A COMPARISON WITH CINEMA AND THEATRE CENSORSHIP

How does broadcasting compare with film and theatre censorship? Films may be exhibited on television even though the British Board of Film Censors has refused a licence: one example was *The Warsaw Ghetto*. Frequently 'X' films are televised without notification of their classification. All this is undeniably legal. It seems pointless to require television to heed British Board of Film Censors classifications unless there is similar treatment of other plays and features. There is pressure from the film industry for uniform treatment in cinema and television. At least, it should be possible to keep 'X' films off peak family viewing periods and to require that the programme announcements and *T.V. Times* and *Radio Times* state their British Board of Film Censors classification. In theory, the restrictions on televised plays are less severe than on theatre productions. In practice, matters may sometimes be different; the handling of Graham Greene's *The Complaisant Lover* is revealing. Associated Television had presumably submitted the script to I.T.A. in advance. I.T.A. required seven cuts in the script which the Lord Chamberlain had approved for the theatre. When Graham Greene complained in *The Times*, the I.T.A. replied that it objected to the following:

The expression 'arse over tip'; dialogue about sex and the cigar butt; dialogue about the girls in Curzon Street; a reference by Clive (the lover) to the cigar incident; the sentence 'You need your bloody sign'; Clive's unnecessary use of the word 'bloody'; the dentist's speech concerning his wife's habit of touching his face and saying 'Thank you'; the wife's speech 'What a bastard you are', and a sentence referring to 'the love with two backs'.

94

I.T.A. relied on its duty to ensure that nothing is broadcast which offends good taste or decency or is likely to be offensive to public feeling, and did not feel that the standards of the theatre were 'necessarily correct for the very different medium of television'. The B.B.C. and I.T.A. are legally free to put on types of play which the Lord Chamberlain will always reject, for example, plays about twentieth-century members of the royal family (needless to say, this freedom is not exercised), or about other persons recently dead.

Revue satire of the kind common in the theatre was seldom broadcast until recently. Broadcasting considers itself unable to present plays, sketches, or songs on political themes or personalities: the difference here between broadcasting and theatre is striking. The broadcasting bodies have been unnecessarily cautious in their interpretation of their obligation to maintain 'due impartiality': political satire need not be, in the words of the Television Act's prohibition, 'designed to serve the interests of any political party', and the Act's other relevant requirement that those providing the programmes show due impartiality as regards matters of political controversy certainly does not require every programme, whatever its nature, to be politically impartial. The B.B.C. has made a welcome break from its past in its new television satirical programme, *That Was The Week That Was*. Now that the Act of 1963 has deleted the former I.T.A. ban on any 'offensive representation of or reference to a living person', the way seems clear for I.T.A. to do the same.[22]

CHAPTER 4

FREEDOM OF EXPRESSION (2): THE PRINTED WORD AND ADVERTISING

The Printed Word

HISTORY OF THE FORMER CENSORSHIP

FROM the sixteenth century the Crown assumed the prerogative power to grant printing privileges and thereafter treated this power as its monopoly. The Crown was concerned at the threat to the established order of Church and State presented by unrestrained printing. Philip and Mary therefore granted a charter to the Stationers' Company in 1556 which confined printing to members of the Company and its licensees. In return the Company undertook to search out and suppress all undesirable and illegal books. The censorship was political and religious, not moral. The system continued throughout the Tudor and Stuart eras. The Licensing Act of 1662 illustrates how it worked. All printed works had to be registered with, and licensed by, the Stationers' Company. A licence was required to import, and to sell. Printing presses had to be registered, too. Wide powers to search for and seize suspected printed matter in shops and houses (except those of peers) were given.

In 1695, when the current licensing statute expired, the House of Commons refused to renew it, although the House of Lords voted for its renewal. Thus, the licensing system lapsed, never to be re-introduced. The end came, not through any decision of principle, but merely through complaints at abuses in operation and the difficulty of devising a workable machinery of control. Since that time there has been no legal censorship of books – Milton's

Areopagitica (1644) was written in a successful attempt to ward off a parliamentary threat to reinstate the licensing of printing – although until 1855 newspapers were subject to a tax designed to make them too expensive for the masses. Freedom of the Press from licensing restriction was soon seen as a vital common law right, as this quotation from the leading eighteenth-century jurist shows:[1]

The liberty of the press is indeed essential to the nature of a free state; but this consists in laying no previous restraints upon publications, and not in freedom from censure for criminal matter when published. Every free man has an undoubted right to lay what sentiments he pleases before the public; to forbid this, is to destroy the freedom of the press; but if he publishes what is improper, mischievous or illegal, he must take the consequences of his own temerity.

During the Second World War, Defence Regulation 2D empowered the Government to suppress a newspaper without previous warning if it was systematically publishing matter calculated to foment opposition to the prosecution of the war. Thus, the *Daily Worker* was suppressed in 1941, and the *Daily Mirror* was officially threatened with suppression in 1942 because it published a cartoon allegedly calculated to cause unrest in the armed forces and merchant navy: the cartoon depicted a shipwrecked seaman, and implied that the petrol which he and his shipmates were trying to bring across the Atlantic was being used for non-essential purposes. At the end of the war censorship was at once removed.

OTHER PRESENT-DAY RESTRAINTS

There is, then, no official censorship of printed works. There is, however, one form of unofficial censorship of books, the Index of the Roman Catholic Church. The rules are contained in the papal code of canon law. Certain classes of books are banned without inclusion in the Index, such as translations of the Scriptures by non-Catholics, and books attacking religion or morals, or upholding the validity of divorce. The 12 categories of forbidden books are considered more important than the Index of specific books. The Pope can also ban particular books throughout the world, and each bishop may do so in his own diocese. Books on the Index include all the works of Balzac, Stendhal, and Zola, Richardson's *Pamela* and Gibbon's *Decline and Fall*, and total some four to five thousand in all. The Index is revised periodically by a small congregation of cardinals and priests although one wonders how efficiently this revision is done. Dusty polemical tracts by obscure seventeenth-century and eighteenth-century writers abound, but there is no mention of Marx, Lenin, or Freud, for instance. The punishment for printing or reading books written by apostates, heretics, or schismatics in defence of their views is instant excommunication. Cardinals and bishops are not bound by these prohibitions. Clergy and laymen may for grave reasons obtain permission from the local bishop or the Pope to read a condemned book. No doubt, for instance, a Roman Catholic undergraduate might apply for permission to read a condemned book like Machiavelli's *Prince*, if it were set for his degree examination. One wonders whether Roman Catholics 'work to rule', and whether the choice of a few of the prohibited books has been motivated by political considerations. No Catholic may publish a work of a religious character without the prior approval of one of the diocesan censors appointed by the bishops. Priests and members of religious orders need permission before publishing a book or article on any subject whatever. A book by one of them which has received the bishop's imprimatur may still find itself in the Index.

Selection of books – even though it falls short of censorship – must also have a restrictive effect. In this connexion, the decisions taken by the library committee of the local authorities, and by the persons responsible for choosing school books, are of interest. In the absence of detailed surveys, it is difficult to assess their effect. Two points are relevant: there seems little publicly expressed dissatisfaction; secondly, although a hundred years ago there were active and powerful societies for the prevention of vice, library selection committees now seem as free from external pressures as our theatre and cinema censors. True, there is the Public Morality Council, with high-ranking membership of the main religious denominations, but it does not appear to attempt that kind of detailed interference with the work of elected representatives on local government bodies. Commercial distributors, too, can exercise a restrictive influence: for example, W. H. Smith & Son, which has a monopoly at various points of distribution, such as railway stations, refused to sell a pamphlet by Randolph Churchill which criticized the Press.

In 1949 the Royal Commission on the Press reported its findings.[2] The Press has no statutory duty to be impartial politically in the way that, say, the I.T.A. has, and we have seen that Parliament even exempted it from the provisions of Section 63 of the Representation of the People Act, 1949. The Commission found evidence of the Press's 'willingness to be satisfied with what at best corresponds only roughly to the truth and of readiness to make statements on inadequate evidence.'[3] 'Through excessive partisanship, or through distortion in the interests of news value' all the popular papers and certain of the quality papers fell short of the requirements of truth and fairmindedness. The Report abounds with examples, and no doubt the reader will add his own. For example, the *Daily Express* reported a speech by Marshall, United States Secretary of State. The Commission found its report 'not merely inadequate; it was a travesty', the exact opposite of the true impression of the speech was given – 'it was a case . . . amounting virtually to suppression, which appeared to be associated . . . with the political views of the proprietor,'[4] Lord Beaverbrook, with whose policy the speech was made to conform by being distorted. Another typical example was an article in the *Observer*, while the Commission was sitting, which made categorical statements about the Commission's proposals: many of these statements were 'not only untrue but devoid of any resemblance to the truth'.[5] The Report condemned this practice of dressing up uninformed guesses as facts. Of course the Report also found evidence of triviality and sensationalism in the popular Press.

The Commission found evidence that advertisers occasionally seek to influence the policy of a newspaper, but none of concerted pressure to induce a newspaper to adopt a particular policy. It thought that only newspapers which were financially less strong avoided policies detrimental to advertisers' interests. A Scottish newspaper, for example, refused to insert any advertisements for auction sales of property on which there appeared the name of solicitors who had successfully sued them on behalf of clients for libel. Instances of similar conduct have occasionally come to light since the Commission reported. When, some years after the Commission had reported, the Classics Club complained to the General Council of the Press that the leading music magazines refused to advertise its records because they were price-cutting the large record companies, the Press Council replied that it is a recognized principle in journalism that an editor has the sole and absolute right to reject any advertisement which is submitted to him, and nobody can question his decision.

The Press Council also defended the refusal by *The Times* to publish advertisements of Dr Marie Stopes's book, *Married Love*. On the other hand, it condemned, in 1962, the Society of West End Theatre Managers for an attempt to influence editorial policy when most of its members withdrew advertisements of their productions from the *Observer*, which refused to discontinue a weekly 'Quick Theatre Guide' which contained potted criticism of the shows.

The Commission uncovered one instance of governmental pressure. The *Glasgow Herald* opposed appeasement at the time of Munich: the editor and proprietor were invited to see a senior member of the Cabinet who pointed out to them their shortcomings and indicated the Government's dislike of their editorial policy: the pressure was resisted successfully and the *Glasgow Herald* adhered to its editorial view. One recalls also that the Press was persuaded not to mention the relationship between Edward VIII and Mrs Simpson, and the application by Prince Philip for British nationality. When the Government is attacked in the Press on false grounds it can of course utilize Parliamentary time to defend itself. For instance, some of the inaccurate statements in Koestler's articles on capital punishment in the *Observer* in 1956 reflected on the Home Office: a parliamentary question and answer were used as a vehicle for the Government's denial of the assertions contained in the articles.

The Commission thought that the system by which the Press took news from Government departments through Public Relations Officers needed careful watching, because of the obvious dangers of totalitarianism if the Press relied on them instead of making independent inquiry. There is a Services, Press, and Broadcasting Committee of five officials and eleven representatives of Press and broadcasting which unofficially agrees on the draft of D notices, i.e. information about defence matters. In this way agreement is reached on the amount of information to be published about specific matters. The workings of this committee are examined more closely in Chapter 8.

THE PRESS COUNCIL

Perhaps the most important recommendation of the Commission was that there should be set up a General Council of the Press. This Council was in no sense to be a Government organ, but a voluntary body set up by the Press. A lay chairman entirely unconnected with the Press and a twenty per cent lay membership were recommended. The Commission recommended that a body set up along these lines should endeavour to safeguard the freedom of the Press and to encourage the growth of a sense of public responsibility and public service among journalists.

In 1953 the organizations of the Press did set up a General Council of the Press with functions broadly similar to those recommended. But it consists entirely of persons engaged in full-time journalism. The Royal Commission on the Press, 1961–2, recommended that if the Press did not establish, within a specified time, an authoritative General Council with a lay element as recommended by the 1949 Commission, the Government should introduce legislation for the establishment of such a body.[6]

The work of the Council can be assessed in the light of its annual reports which are available to the public. Broadly speaking, it has concerned itself with matters affecting the freedom of the Press to obtain information and with complaints from the public both about the methods used and standards of reporting. For instance, the *Daily Sketch* smuggled a girl reporter into the grounds of the Duchess of Kent's (now Princess Marina) home in the boot of a car in the hope of her attending the Duke's twenty-first birthday party. She had to be escorted off the premises by the police when her statement that she was a personal friend of the Duke who had mislaid her invitation was challenged. The Council severely condemned the editor's conduct. Frequently the Council has criticized newspapers for intrusion into private lives or for failing to correct inaccurate statements in subsequent editions when their attention was drawn to them. It had also criticized what it regarded as the unwholesome exploitation of sex in articles by Diana Dors in the *News of the World*.

On the whole, however, the Council shows that tendency to defend the Press to be expected of a body so one-sided in composition. For example, the *People* and the *Sunday Express* distorted Malcolm Muggeridge's article on the Queen in the *Saturday Evening Post*. Muggeridge's protest was rejected by the Council although of course it had to admit the distortions: it did not ask the newspapers to publish corrections, apparently on the ground that anybody who disparaged the royal family must reasonably expect British newspapers to take extracts out of context and base their comments solely on these extracts. Little attention has been given to such problems as the buying up by newspapers of exclusive news rights in individuals. The criticism is made that the Press Council has no teeth: editors cock a snook at it, continue to intrude into people's private lives, and fail to correct statements whose falsity the Press Council has exposed. All this is true, but it is difficult to see how the Council could be given greater powers. To give a private body powers of fining or suspension seems impracticable. No doubt newspapers are guilty of unwarranted and offensive invasions of private lives; no doubt they should correct errors. But is it not the function of the ordinary law of the land to deal with such matters just as the law of defamation is a weapon against the Press? We shall consider later whether the law confers adequate protection on the citizen against the Press in these matters. It may be that the slogan 'Freedom of the Press' which properly connotes freedom to publish without prior restraint, has been deliberately and cynically used by the Press to give them unjustified powers of obtaining information. Of course what is a trespass by an ordinary citizen should be and is an actionable wrong by a journalist too – the Press is not above the law. The question for later consideration is whether the Press as a pressure group has moulded the law into a form which inadequately protects the citizen against activities in which the Press particularly engages.

Even in its present capacity as a voluntary and recommending body, it does seem that the procedure of the Press Council leaves much to be desired. Complainants are not allowed to appear unless the Council invites them, and it is not its normal practice to do so. Neither Press nor Public are invited to its meetings.

Particularly indicative is the Lady Chatterley affair. The *Guardian* and the *Spectator*, when reporting and commenting on the trial of Penguin Books Ltd, printed the word 'fuck' which had, of course, been used during the trial. Following its usual practice when examining what it decides to be matters of public interest about which no member of the public has complained to it, the Council considered this behaviour of the *Guardian* and the *Spectator* without even informing them that it was doing so. The Council decided to rebuke them: the *Spectator* first learned of this when the Council's hand-out appeared in the newspapers. This hand-out gave the impression that the decision was unanimous – in fact a member then revealed that there were dissenting views and the decision was that of a minority of the membership. The chairman of the Press Council held that it was justified in condemning the *Spectator* unheard because the *Spectator* had criticized the Council, and the Council's action, therefore, was 'surely part of the cut and thrust of public debate'; the Council claimed the same right as the Press to criticize without preliminary warning. The member was publicly criticized by the chairman for blowing the gaff and resigned. The chairman's contention was that the Council, like the Cabinet, must observe the doctrine of collective responsibility.

Obviously, the Council does not regard itself as a judicial body. But should not even a voluntary body follow the basic procedures of fair play – giving a fair hearing to both sides to a controversy and stating whether or not the decision is unanimous? The analogies of public debate and the Cabinet are both inapposite here. In 1963 there has been belated and grudging acknowledgement of public criticism of the Council in the introduction of a lay chairman (Lord Devlin) and a further lay element not exceeding 20 per cent of its voting membership.

In some areas the law imposes a prohibition on publication: some aspects of this are dealt with in the section on Contempt. Mention might be made here of the Judicial Proceedings (Regulation of Reports) Act, 1926. This makes it a crime to publish in relation to any judicial proceedings any indecent matter or indecent medical, surgical, or physiological details which would be calculated to injure public morals. In particular, the Act makes it an offence to publish in relation to proceedings for divorce or nullity any particulars other than the following: the names, addresses, and occupations of the parties, the charges, legal argument, and the judge's summing up and verdict. The

Press must not publish the 'juicy' details of the evidence. One notices the relish with which the Press publishes full reports of proceedings in Court which escape the ban: Courts-Martial for naval misbehaviour with W.R.E.N.S., claims for breach of promise to marry, or actions for seduction.

Advertising

LEGAL CONTROLS

Advertising presents a sharp conflict of competing interests. The advertiser of the product wishes above all to sell his product and to beat his competitors. The agent whom the advertiser employs has to prove his ability to sell the product. The owner of the medium through which the product is advertised, whether newspaper or periodical, poster or television, requires the advertising revenue in order to stay in business. Massed against this powerful trio are the general public. The trio rest their case on the virtues of freedom of expression, and freedom of business competition. The opposing interests are more complex: that the consumer should have full, frank, and accurate statements of the quality of the product advertised; that public safety, public amenities, and public morals should not be imperilled; and that business competitors should not be subject to unfair trade practices.

Is the individual member of the public adequately protected against false advertising? Sometimes he used to have an action for breach of contract. For example, in 1891, the Carbolic Smoke Ball Company, the makers of a 'Carbolic Smoke Ball', advertised in the *Pall Mall Gazette* a reward of £100 to any person who contracted influenza or a cold after having used the balls as directed and stated that they had deposited £1,000 in a named bank to show their sincerity. Mrs Carlill read the advertisement, bought the balls, and contracted influenza. The Court awarded her £100 damages for breach of contract.7 But advertisers do not fall into this trap nowadays. The company was liable because its lodging £1,000 in the bank suggested that the advertisement was no mere puff. Today's advertisers take care that their advertisements are mere puffs which do not subject them to contractual liabilities. 'X's slimming pills, guaranteed to reduce your weight' will give no remedy to the unfortunate purchaser who remains as fat as ever. The law ordinarily allows him to recover compensatory damages against anybody who has fraudulently made a false statement to him on which he has acted to his loss. In practice, however, no one who has been taken in by a false advertisement has very much chance of recovering damages. The Courts require the clearest proof of fraud; they limit their protection to statements of fact, as distinct from opinion. Those who merely indulge in 'sales talk' are safe. The Courts are guilty of muddled thinking about fraud: they think that to charge somebody with fraud is so serious that such a finding should only be made in a very clear case. But the issue is not whether the advertiser should be sent to prison, when such an attitude would be justified, but whether a member of the public who is out of pocket through relying on a seller's false statements should recover his loss from him. In the United States, the law of fraud is much more comprehensive than in England, although even there it is recognized that it does not in itself afford adequate protection to the consumer against the wiles of the advertiser. Suppose that the advertiser has not been fraudulent, but merely negligent. Normally of course, victims of negligence can recover compensation. English law has in the past been most reluctant to hold that there was any liability for causing financial loss to others by making negligent *statements*. It is true that the House of Lords has recently recognized that in some circumstances there might be a liability. Nonetheless, in all probability it remains the law that advertisers will not ordinarily be liable for their false statements, however carelessly made. Only in the rare case where the victim could show that the advertiser had such special skill or knowledge that he would know that the victim was relying on his statement so that the advertiser would assume responsibility for its accuracy, would the victim have a remedy against the advertiser.[8]

Nor is the law of contract of any use to the consumer. If the person from whom he buys the product tells lies about it, those misrepresentations will in some cases form part of the contract, so that when they are not made good an action lies for breach of contract. English law, however, has a firm rule that those who sue for breach of contract must be parties to the contract. Advertisements of products are made by the manufacturer, but the purchase is normally made from the retailer. The customer's contract is with the retailer, not with the manufacturer, so that he can never sue the manufacturer for breach of contract on the basis of false advertising. Some American judges, on the other hand, are extending the benefit of a manufacturer's warranty to the eventual consumer, although he has no contract with the manufacturer-advertiser.

Nor does the ordinary law adequately protect the business competitor. Suppose that an advertiser makes false statements about his product so that sales of his rivals fall off. English law only gives damages in the rare case where the rival can prove that his customers were misled by the advertisement into believing that they were buying the rival's product. This relief is not adequate: we are concerned with the case where the advertisement makes no reference to the rival's product, but tells lies about the product sold, so that its sales increase at the expense of its rivals. English law has no remedy, whereas in the United States the injured rival tradesman could recover damages against the lying advertiser.

Parliament has passed a considerable number of Acts which are designed to protect the citizen against particular advertising abuses, by making them crimes. Betting circulars cannot be sent to those under twenty-one years of age; money-lenders are restricted in advertising; hire-purchase advertisements must indicate the size of deposit and the number and amount of instalments; unrestricted advertisements for the sale of company shares are forbidden; indecent or obscene hoardings are prohibited. Most important are the restrictions on advertising medicines, food, and drugs. Commercial advertisements which prescribe cures for cancer, venereal disease, tuberculosis, diabetes, epilepsy, Bright's disease, cataract, glaucoma, and paralysis are forbidden. It is a criminal offence to publish an advertisement which either falsely describes any food or drug or is calculated to mislead with regard to its nature, substance, or quality. There is a most surprising gap in the criminal law in the case of the Merchandise Marks Acts. These Acts are concerned to restrain false descriptions of goods, and yet they have never been phrased so as to cover advertisements.

Parliament has sometimes intervened to prevent advertising from becoming a nuisance, or a danger. Thus, the Civil Aviation (Licensing) Act, 1960, makes it a crime for an aircraft to advertise while in the air over the United Kingdom or territorial waters in such a way that the advertisement is visible from the ground. The Noise Abatement Act of the same year prohibits the use of loudspeakers on the street for advertising purposes, except that between noon and 7 p.m. sounds other than words may be made in an inoffensive way from a vehicle to inform the public that perishable goods for human consumption are on sale from that vehicle: thus the chimes of the ice cream van are inoffensive. Local bye-laws often contain other restrictions.

A well-known restriction is that on poster and other outdoor advertising contained in the Town and Country Planning legislation. The planning authorities, that is, the Minister of Housing and Local Government, and the local government authorities, are empowered to regulate all outdoor advertising displays except those on vehicles such as buses or minicabs, or within buildings and enclosures such as football grounds and therefore not visible from outside. They are to have regard to both amenity and public safety in exercising their powers. 'Amenity' is recognized to have a varying content, so that certain areas of natural beauty such as the Peak and Lake Districts (in all about one fifth of the country) are defined as special areas where large scale commercial advertising is prohibited. It would obviously be impossible to require every advertisement in the rest of the country to be considered by a planning authority. Advertisements are, therefore, divided into two groups, those which must have individual approval, and those where consent is deemed to have been given. Even in a 'deemed consent' case a specific advertisement may be challenged. Whether an advertisement is of the kind that ordinarily requires individual approval or of the challenged 'deemed consent' kind, the decision on it is normally taken by the local planning authority, acting in the interests of amenity and safety. From that decision an appeal lies to the Minister, some member of whose Department will in fact decide – there are usually about 1,500 to 2,000 appeals a year. In any event all advertisement sites must be clean, tidy, and safe, and a 'deemed consent' one must be no hindrance to traffic. Most important of the 'deemed consent' category are advertisements on business premises. These may be displayed with deemed consent, if they conform to certain requirements as to size of lettering, height from the ground, and the like, and refer to the business or trade conducted on the premises, the goods sold or services provided, or the qualifications of the person carrying on the business. It is generally agreed that planning authorities have struck a fair balance between advertiser and public, and that the standards of outdoor advertising have improved in consequence.

REGULATION WITHIN THE INDUSTRY

This survey of legal controls on advertising has shown that they are patchy and inadequate. The advertising industry itself practises a degree of self-regulation which is unsuspected by the general public.

The firms engaged in poster advertising have trade

associations known as the British Poster Advertising Association and the London Poster Advertising Association. These two associations have a Joint Censorship Committee on which are also represented the Solus Outdoor Advertising Association, the British Transport Commission, and the Theatres' National Council. Outdoor advertisers are encouraged to submit doubtful posters for prior approval. The Censorship Committee also considers complaints about existing posters. It has no coercive legal powers but is so representative that we may assume that posters banned by it will not in practice be exhibited in Britain. It works to a code, embodying a number of prohibitions. Posters must not depict murder, violence, obscenity, or nudity, and they must not be calculated to foment social unrest or to wound the susceptibilities of newspapers or to offend religious groups. Personal attacks on members of the government are forbidden, and so are advertisements of treatment for serious diseases. False advertisements and those which disparage the products of others ('knocking' advertisements) are prohibited. Two acts of censorship by this Committee illustrate its approach. The *Guardian* newspaper wished in 1960 to reproduce as a poster a cartoon by David Low, entitled 'Alas! A New Generation', but the Censorship Committee banned it. Pressed by the *Guardian*, the Committee, contrary to its usual practice, gave its reasons: that the poster infringed foreign susceptibilities by insinuating that all Germans were Nazis. The *Guardian*'s objective had been to warn those Britons who thought that 'It couldn't happen here'. Under protest, the *Guardian* agreed to an amended title, 'A New Generation?'. After complaints from brewers the Committee advised the banning of a poster in Birmingham in 1954 which bore the words 'One for the road may be one for the grave'. This infringed the Committee's rule about 'knocking' advertisements. Questions were asked in the House when the point was made that the poster merely implemented the Highway Code and the Christmas policy of the Minister of Transport. The Minister declared his inability and unwillingness to do anything about the Committee's ban or about any other of their interpretations of their code. Similarly the Association has asked outdoor advertising contractors not to display Ministry of Health anti-smoking posters, and has thereby prevented local authorities from putting them on commercially-owned sites.

The Newspaper Proprietors' Association and the Newspaper Society, trade associations of London and provincial newspapers respectively, also have a joint committee and a common code of advertising rules. These rules include the usual ones: for example, 'knocking' is forbidden. Little reporting of its bans appears in the Press. It is regrettable that advertisements from finance companies appear from time to time, even in the 'quality' newspapers, which contain promises that are not sustained by the booklets for which the advertisements invite the reader to apply. Even though newspapers take inadequate steps to check the accuracy of invitations for money, they are sometimes responsive to abuses in their advertising columns which are brought to their notice. Housewives have recently been plagued by 'switch-selling': some product is advertised at a bargain price, but the salesman who appears at the door of the person answering the advertisement attempts to foist upon her some other dearer product. As usual these days, it was the B.B.C. that brought home on television the extent and nature of this commercial practice. To their credit, once others had convinced them of the abuse, the Associations responded by requiring undertakings of advertisers which were framed widely enough to prevent their practising the abuse through newspaper advertisements, although the Molony Committee on Consumer Protection (1962) has evidence that these undertakings were sometimes evaded.[9]

The British public's long-standing gullibility where patent medicines are concerned has caused special attention to be given to the control of advertisements recommending them. The statutory prohibitions already mentioned are obviously insufficient in scope. The trade associations previously described are all represented on a Committee which operates the British Code of Standards relating to the Advertising of Medicines and Treatments. The Code forbids claims to cure ailments or symptoms of ill-health, and offers of medicine or advice for those serious conditions or diseases which should receive the attention of a medical practitioner. Prizes and 'money back' offers are forbidden. Advertisements must not mislead, or induce fear. Expressions like 'Female Pills', 'Never Known To Fail', or those which imply the stimulation of sexual virility are forbidden. The Code contains long lists of conditions for which advertisements are prohibited: for example, ulcers, and 'chronic or persistent rheumatism' (though other forms of rheumatism may be the subject of an advertisement). Hence the stress in advertisements on 'relieve' and the concentration on 'permitted' diseases – coughs, cold, influenza, etc. Eighty per cent of the drug manufacturers also have an association which has similar objects. They agree to submit their advertisements in advance to test their compliance with the Code of Standards on Advertising Practice of the Proprietary Associations of Great Britain, and disputes are referred to an advisory panel of two doctors, two members of the Executive Committee of the association, and an independent chairman. Despite all this machinery, the medical profession remains not wholly satisfied. In the *Lancet* in September 1961 an obstetrician complained that medical theories and practice were being recommended, misinterpreted, or ignored for the sake of selling more goods. Products no better than other substances obtainable at a fraction of the cost were bolstered up by false or pseudo-scientific theories. This advertising was specially directed at the least educated section of the community and at the older age groups. Plainly, practices of this sort are not, and cannot be, controlled by the codes described.

The regulations in connexion with food labelling and advertising have also been found inadequate. The Ministry of Health has tried to fill the gap in an unofficial way by producing, after consultation with the Medical Research Council, a Code on the Advertising, Labelling, and Composition of Food. As is to be expected of such a non-legal arrangement, the citizen is unacquainted with this Code, and in practice does not avail himself of the protection which it purports to confer on him. Typical rules of the Code are that an advertisement should not refer to a vitamin unless the product advertised contains one sixth of a person's daily requirement of that vitamin and should not describe the product as 'rich' in vitamins unless it contains one half of the daily requirement of the vitamins.

TELEVISION

The Law[10]

Television advertising, where there is a blending of legal and self-regulating controls, demands separate examination.

The Television Act, 1954, regulates television advertising to some extent. By Section 4 it is the I.T.A.'s duty to ensure that the provisions contained in the Second Schedule are complied with. That Schedule contains certain rules about advertisements, which the Postmaster-General may amend by regulation with the approval of each House of Parliament. The I.T.A. is also under a duty to consult him about the classes and descriptions of advertisements which must not be broadcast, and to carry out any of his directions thereon. The I T.A. must appoint an advertising advisory council (A.A.C.) with powers which include that of preparing a code of standards of advertising conduct.

In summary, this is all the law has to say on television advertising. Of what value is this legal protection? The duty of the I.T.A. to observe the rules of the Schedule about advertisements is mandatory, not discretionary. Therefore, while, as we have seen earlier, the law cannot interfere with the merely discretionary functions regarding programme content contained in the Act, the law could operate if the I.T.A. failed in its duties with respect to advertising. Many lawyers believe that the private citizen is powerless to secure performance of these duties. It may well be that he could not obtain from the High Court an order of mandamus (with its sanction of punishment for contempt upon disobedience) commanding the I.T.A. to carry out its duty. Yet the Court could probably grant an injunction to the citizen restraining the I.T.A. from violating it. Many lawyers deny this. It is true that the citizen could not bring these proceedings of his own initiative unless he could show that the I.T.A.'s breach damaged him particularly – he could himself sue, for example, if the I.T.A. refused his own advertisements but accepted those of a competitor. It is submitted, further, that in any event a citizen can sue for an injunction if he obtains the Attorney-General's consent. Suppose that an interested citizen believes that religious advertisements are being broadcast in violation of the rules, the Attorney-General may himself sue, or, if he consents, the citizen may bring a relator action, for an injunction. (It is a weakness of the Act that the citizen is helpless if the Attorney-General refuses his consent. The citizen is not entitled to know the reasons for refusal – they may be party political – and cannot appeal to any body against that refusal.) The rule forbidding any implication of commercial sponsoring in a programme is contained in a separate sub-section and no duty to enforce it is imposed on the I.T.A. – it is very doubtful whether there is any legally enforceable obligation to observe it. The I.T.A. approves of advertisers booking space at a time when the advertiser knows that a particular programme is being televised: this practice is not prohibited by the Act.

The citizen's position is even weaker if he complains that the I.T.A. has disregarded the recommendations of the Advertising Advisory Council. The Act merely requires the I.T.A. to comply 'subject to such exceptions or modification, if any, as may appear to the Authority to be necessary or proper, having regard to the duties incumbent on the Authority otherwise than under the sub-section'. The section has been deliberately phrased so as to give the I.T.A. the last word – the test is not what is necessary but what appears to the I.T.A. to be necessary. This provision is useless to the citizen. In another respect the protection afforded by the Advisory Council's recommendations is illusory. The Post-master-General can override any of the Council's recommendations about methods of advertising or forbidden advertisements.

Operation of Advertising Controls

The A.A.C. is appointed by the I.T.A. and consists of 'a committee representative of organizations, authorities, and persons concerned with standards of conduct in the advertising of goods and services (including in particular the advertising of goods or services for medical or surgical purposes)'. Of the twelve members five are medical, dental, and pharmaceutical experts, five are engaged in the advertising industry, one is the secretary of the Retail Trading Standards Association, and one is a professor of economics. All the members except the chairman are nominated by representative professional bodies. The complaint is often made that the committee is overloaded with advertising men (who must be expected to be biased) and that there are no experienced disinterested citizens such as teachers and representatives of consumers' organizations. The Act is difficult to interpret. It could be argued that teachers and other citizens are not 'concerned with standards of conduct in advertising', that the Act requires some specialist connexion. The I.T.A.'s interpretation is curiously ambivalent: it obviously finds it necessary to overload with advertising men, yet it has a professor of economics. He is there because the I.T.A. asks its unofficial advisory committees in Scotland and Ulster to nominate one member each – Scotland nominates an advertising man, Ulster has nominated Professor Denison. Either his appointment is invalid or the I.T.A. has made the committee unrepresentative on the whole.

The A.A.C. duly drafted a code of Principles for Advertising which the I.T.A. and Postmaster-General accepted without amendment. They are published. They forbid misleading advertisements, and they embody *in toto* that British

Code of Standards for the Advertising of Medicines and Treatments which has already been summarized. There are special restrictions on advertisements for mail orders, home-work schemes, investments, hire purchase, and instructional courses. Many advertisements are forbidden: for instance, those from moneylenders, matrimonial agencies, fortune tellers, undertakers, and tipsters; and those concerned with betting (including pools); contraceptives, and cures for smoking and alcoholism. It is not clear whether the A.A.C. is legally concerned with methods as distinct from content of advertising but, in practice, it treats them as within its powers – for instance, it has advised the I.T.A. about the use of substitute materials in advertising ice-cream and jellies and of other devices 'to achieve verisimilitude'. Although the A.A.C. revises its Principles from time to time it also makes other rules which are not reproduced in the Principles – the reasons for this differentiation are obscure. For instance, in 1959–60 it laid down conditions calculated to restrain 'switch-selling' of domestic appliances, when the goods offered would not be the ones advertised. The A.A.C. also occasionally considers particular instances of misleading advertisements which the I.T.A. brings to its notice. It was on its advice that a toothpaste advertisement claiming protection against decay was withdrawn in 1958, after complaints by the British Dental Association's representative on the Committee.

The A.A.C. is not concerned at all with the day-to-day control of advertising – it usually meets about four times a year. The day-to-day acceptance of advertising is in the hands of the programme contractors, who have formed the Independent Television Companies Association (I.T.C.A.). All advertising scripts are referred to the copy sub-committee of the I.T.C.A.'s advertisement committee. There is close liaison between that committee and the I.T.A., mainly through the advertising control officer of the I.T.A. The I.T.C.A.'s advertising committee regards it as its main function to work to the Principles for Television Advertising. Nonetheless it works out detailed rules of its own, only some of which are available to the public. For instance the I.T.A. Code of Principles restricts advertisements in children's programmes – advertisements must not suggest that children lack loyalty or are inferior if they do not buy a certain product. Yet after consultation with the I.T.A. and A.A.C. the I.T.C.A. has made detailed rules about children's advertising which are not found in the Code of Principles, e.g. such an advertisement must not start with the word 'FREE'. Legally, these rules of the I.T.C.A. have no effect – there is no duty on the I.T.A. to see that they are observed. The Code of Principles provides that 'no advertisement shall contain any statement intended to promote sales by unfair competition with or reference to competitive products or services'. This rule is ambiguous. Does the word 'unfair' govern 'reference' as well as 'competition', in which event an advertisement would not violate the code when it correctly stated that the product was superior to 'Y'? It is submitted that on balance this is the correct interpretation of the Code. Yet the I.T.C.A. committee rules that there is no question of accepting an advertisement when it identifies the competing product, however accurate the statement. What can a manufacturer do who claims that he is prejudiced – as he may well be to a serious extent – by this wrong interpretation of the Code? He is helpless. The Act only requires the I.T.A. to see that advertisements comply – it gives no remedy to an advertiser who complains that the programme contractor imposes more stringent conditions unless – and this is unlikely – he can invoke the statutory prohibition against discrimination. Conversely, if the proper interpretation of the Code is that all comparisons are prohibited, a manufacturer whose product was compared with the advertised one would have a cause of action against the I.T.A.

We have been considering in detail the codes of general principles. Let us turn to the specific rules of the Act itself – those in the Second Schedule. These rules are the concern of the I.T.A., not the A.A.C. Paragraph 1 states that the advertisements must be clearly distinguishable as such and recognizably separate from the rest of the programme – the 1963 Act prohibits subliminal advertising.[11] Paragraph 2 requires that the amount of time given to advertising in the programme shall not be so great as to detract from the value of the programme as a medium of entertainment, instruction, and information. From these statutory provisions the I.T.A. makes its own interpretative rules, which are sometimes summarized in its annual reports.[12] At present (1963) the amount of spot advertising in any clock hour must not exceed seven minutes. These interpretative rules have no legal effect; a citizen could not complain to the Courts that there were eight minutes of advertising in one hour. He would have to prove a violation of Paragraph 2 itself, which of course is worded so vaguely as to be practically free from judicial review. Conversely, if he did sue the I.T.A. it would be no defence that it had conformed to its interpretative rules if the Court found that this rule was based on a misinterpretation of the Schedule of the Act.

Paragraph 3 enacts that 'advertisements shall not be inserted otherwise than at the beginning or the end of the programme or in natural breaks therein'. It is submitted that the I.T.A. continually violates this by allowing advertisements *both* in breaks and at the beginning and end of programmes, whereas the Act says that they may only be inserted at the beginning or end, *or* in natural breaks. The Attorney-General should sue the I.T.A. to restrain this illegality, or alternatively allow a citizen to do so.

The schedule requires the I.T.A. to obtain the agreement of the Postmaster-General on rules about the interval between periods for advertisements and between advertisements and certain programmes which must not be interrupted by advertisements; if no agreement is reached, the Postmaster-General can decide the issue. These agreements need not be published but the annual reports of the I.T.A. have set out agreements about religious broadcasts, royal ceremonies, and events such as the Football Association Cup Final at which a member of the royal family is seen to be present (unofficial Rule 1 (c) provides that 'in cases of doubt about the application of this rule to particular occasions, the I.T.A. shall consult the Press Secretary, Buckingham Palace'). This class of statutorily agreed rule must be distinguished from, say, the rule that tobacco advertisements shall not appear during and immediately before or after children's programmes. This latter rule is also not published but is not subject to the Postmaster-General's agreement and in contrast with the royal family rule does not require an interval of so many prescribed minutes between programme and advertisement.

Paragraph 6 precludes advertisements on behalf of any body whose objects are mainly political or religious, and any which is directed towards any religious or political end or has any relation to any industrial dispute. The I.T.A. has rightly construed this as affecting local as well as central government, and as affecting advertisements by non-political bodies directed towards political ends. Both the Institute of Directors and the *Daily Worker* have come under this ban.

No doubt the I.T.A. and programme contractors are at great pains to conform to the Act. Nonetheless, one has an uneasy feeling that the elaborate machinery is geared to protect business in general and also such obvious establishment bodies as the royal family, political parties, and religious institutions. Is the viewer equally protected? If he feels that those provisions of the Act which are for his protection – restrictions on advertising time for example – are violated, what can he do? There is no machinery for his complaint to be heard personally. There is no independent body charged with the task of monitoring programmes on his behalf: this is not a function of the advertising-industry-dominated A.A.C. Some advocate independent machinery for deciding whether particular advertisements are too jarring, too strident, too boringly repetitive. The annual reports of the I.T.A. are coy about condemning manufacturers and advertising agents – their delinquencies are played down and offenders are never named. One looks in vain in the reports, for instance, for the incident when a lady from London, W14, complained to the Postmaster-General about claims in advertisements by Hovis and B.P. Energol Visco-Static Oil – eventually it had to be admitted that the advertisements made claims which could not be substantiated and they were withdrawn. It is not suggested that the Act is being widely flouted – apart from the controversial 'natural breaks' provision – but one would prefer to see more concrete evidence that the interests of the citizen, both as viewer and potential buyer, are rated by the advertising men as highly as those of industry. The citizen wants the true facts about products: as interpreted by the programme contractor the rules deny him comparative factual data and leave him largely with meaningless superlatives. It is consistent with this lack of balance that the public is given insufficient access to the rules which are applied to advertising – however many different purchases the citizen makes at Her Majesty's Stationery Office he cannot come away with a full list of the rules of television advertising. These rules are his concern, as well as that of advertisers and programme companies.

The B.B.C. is precluded by its licence from broadcasting commercial advertisements. The Director-General has issued an internal directive which in some twenty detailed rules prescribes how the B.B.C. is to avoid giving publicity to any person or organization, except where this is necessary for providing a full service under its Charter.[13] The difficulties which the B.B.C. experiences in practice through trying to be consistent are obvious to viewers and listeners.

BRITISH TRANSPORT COMMISSION

The advertising policies of the former British Transport Commission have come in for press criticism: whether this is because they were inferior or because the nationalized industries are a popular target of the Press is hard to say. The criticisms are mainly on two counts: one, that they allow too many obscene, or at least suggestive advertisements, especially advertisements for brassières and cinemas (although their code forbids advertisements which 'depict or refer to indecency, obscenity, nudity, or strip-tease'). The second is that they have a clause in their code which has no counterpart in the others except that of I.T.V.: politically controversial posters are forbidden. One would have thought that the need for such a clause was obvious in the case of a nationalized industry, but there is room for argument that it has been interpreted too widely. Quaker advertisements for disarmament have been banned; a poster advertising a meeting of civil servants to protest against the Treasury's attitude to a pay claim was also banned. The *Sunday Citizen* was prohibited both by the Commission and the British Poster Advertising Association from advertising a series of articles on Germany which might have offended Germans. Their code may even be interpreted so as to reject any advertisements seeking any reform of the law by Parliament, for it states: 'Any advertisement, whether displayed by a political party or not, which is likely to be construed as politically controversial is not acceptable'.

THE FUTURE

Hitherto the Minister of Housing and Local Government has given businesses a very free hand with advertisements outside their premises and has not sought to subject them to detailed legal requirements: a frequent consequence has been a clutter of advertisements outside tobacconists, newsagents, and mixed businesses, which, because they are too many, too crowded, and are badly arranged, spoil local amenities. With the Minister's blessing, the industry formulated in 1960 a Code of Standards for Advertising on Business Premises, which has produced some improvement. The Government has dropped hints that it will invoke its powers of town planning control (which it undoubtedly already has under the Town and Country Planning Act, 1947) if the industry does not, by its voluntary code, control this rash of mass-produced advertising facia boards which has broken out on shop fronts all over the country. Some other organizations endeavour to maintain standards in various advertising media. The Retail Trading Standards Association, a retailers' trade association, is active, and sets up tribunals to hear complaints. The Advertising Association, a trade association, has an investigation department which aims at preventing and suppressing abuses.

There can be no doubt, then, that the advertising industry has been taking vigorous steps in an attempt to put its own house in order. In the past, pressures on it have been few, but the recent development of consumer organizations has made the struggle less one-sided, and produced more response from the industry. *Which?*, *Shopper's Guide*, television, the Advertising Inquiry Committee and other activities of Francis Noel-Baker, M.P., the setting up by the Government of the Molony Committee on Consumer Protection, have all contributed to this changed atmosphere. The advertising industry, realizing that the forces concerned to subject it to proper control are marshalled, in 1961 set out to produce a new code of advertising practice and a constitution for its own advertising standards authority. This body, the self-styled Advertising Standards Authority, was set up in 1962 in order to promote and enforce standards of advertising. Significantly, five of the eleven members are directly and professionally concerned with advertising and no representatives of consumer organizations were appointed or invited to be represented. Perhaps it might 'view with concern' advertisements which masquerade as editorial or news matter, or even in the future reconsider whether to deny the consumer information about the merits of competing products is in the public interest. But it is not very likely that it will enforce its rulings. If one could rely on all of the following the Authority would be important: that no member would accept the custom of an advertiser or agency who violated the code; that all hearings were in public; that full lists of violators were published; that members of the public could bring complaints and be represented; that pre-publication scrutiny was being attempted at least on a sampling basis; that a large staff of full-time investigators was being employed.

Everything points to none of these elements being found in the new arrangements, so that the Authority will be able to afford no substantial protection to the public.

In short, the scales have hitherto been weighted very heavily in favour of the advertiser against the consumer. The advertising industry was content with the *status quo* until recent developments began to imperil its advantages. The industry sees the risk of more legal control: this it will endeavour to avoid by this self-disciplinary body, like the Press Council. It is significant that in 1961 such diverse bodies as the Conservative Political Centre, the Labour Party, the Retail Standards Association, and the Advertising Inquiry Committee all published documents recording their dissatisfaction with the present legal controls of advertising.

The defects are obvious. The common law affords inadequate protection in actions for damages by aggrieved citizens: the fault here is with the judges who have failed to use the opportunities open to them to maintain a fair balance between citizen and advertiser. Secondly, the legislation which imposes criminal sanctions is too diffuse and haphazard. A typical gap is revealed by the statement in the House of Commons of the Parliamentary Secretary to the Board of Trade that, reprehensible as the practice is, the law is powerless to prevent national newspapers advertising for sale reconditioned washing machines even though those who respond to advertisements of this type are visited by salesmen who offer them no such models but only new ones at four times the advertised price. Thirdly, and partly in consequence of the second weakness, enforcement of the criminal law is weak – systematic investigation of breaches is non-existent. Fourthly, far too much is left to self-regulation by the trade which as yet has made no attempt to control some areas of advertising, such as advertising on vehicles of the products or services of the vehicle owners. Of course, enlightened sections of the trade realize that objectionable advertising harms not only consumer and competitor, but all business interests involved in advertising. There is no reason to expect the advertising industry to succeed in keeping its own house in order when the Press Council has so conspicuously failed. The belated arrangements recently made are, as has been seen, likely to be ineffective. The problem is more serious than that of the Press in the sense that infringements directly affect the pockets of poorer sections of the community.

There is no hope of the Courts effecting any improvement. The first need is for new legislation providing better remedies in actions for damages when false advertisements are issued. A new criminal code of advertising standards is called for, to some extent consolidating the existing miscellaneous rag bag of Acts, but also giving the force of law to many of the common form provisions in the existing unofficial code within the industry.

Many of these proposals will be ineffective unless new enforcement machinery is introduced. The Federal Trade Commission of the United States points the way. This governmental body has the investigation staff to unearth for itself illegal advertising practices: it examines half a million every year. These illegalities include false advertising which constitutes an unfair method of competition, and deceptive or misleading practices which are contrary to the public interest. As of course it punishes misrepresentations of composition and character of products wherever advertised, claims to cure, and false disparagement of products. Its standard weapon of control is the cease-and-desist order. When, after a hearing, it declares a practice illegal, it issues an order to the offender requiring him to abandon the illegal practice, and large fines are imposed for failure to comply with this cease-and-desist order. A case of 1960 is typical:[14] an advertisement stated that the product was capable of preventing 'the common type of baldness'. After taking expert evidence, the commission found that ninety-five per cent of cases of baldness were caused by endocrine, hereditary, and age factors, in which the product was useless. Even though the product might benefit the remaining five per cent of cases, the failure positively to disclose this limitation in the efficiency of the product was a ground for a cease-and-desist order: a Federal Court confirmed this decision by the commission.

A body with powers similar to those of the commission seems to be the minimum requirement in Britain. Admittedly, such a body might not prevent the harm from being done before its order became operative. To impose legal censorship of advertising would be too sweeping a move; if the fines were large enough they would effectively discourage deliberate violations. It was in line with the general level of the Molony Report of the Committee on Consumer Protection that its only reason for rejecting a body like the Federal Trades Commission was that 'we do not find the model ... a congenial one'.[15] The present practice of the advertising industry is to encourage puffery as much as possible. As the advertisers well know, so long as they use subjective words of no defined meaning, 'scrumptious', 'excellent', 'delicious', 'tasty', and the like, they are immune. This must be accepted; there is a limit to how much the citizen can be protected against himself. She is a very gullible Mrs 1963 who takes any notice of debased language of that kind. There is the less need to worry about puffery so long as prominent factual statements of the composition of many kinds of product are insisted on by the new statutory code. One would like to see an end of the present 'no-knocking' rule of the trade – a factual comparison of one product with another is surely what the consumer wants, despite the view of the Molony Report that 'no-knocking' is preferable to rationalizing and justifying competing claims. Yet it would be difficult to enforce a rule that no advertisement shall be refused on the ground that it makes a comparison with another product.

The single biggest advantage of having such a commission would be the systematic inspection of advertising matter. Even though there would be no censorship in advance of display, the knowledge that staff was employed full time throughout the country in scrutinizing advertisements would be a most potent factor in restraining illegalities on the part of advertisers.

CHAPTER 5

FREEDOM OF EXPRESSION (3): OBSCENITY AND DEFAMATION

FREEDOM OF EXPRESSION

So far we have been examining those restraints on freedom of expression which operate before publication. We must now consider the ways in which the law intervenes with regard to publications already made. First there is the law of obscenity.

Obscenity

THE LEGAL POSITION UNTIL 1959

Our starting point is the prosecution of Sir Charles Sidley in 1663 for his behaviour after a drinking orgy. In the words of the report:[1]

He was fined 2,000 marks, committed without bail for a week and bound to his good behaviour for a year, on his confession of information against him for showing himself naked in a balcony and 'throwing down bottles (pist in) *vi et armis* among the people in Covent Garden, *contra pacem* and to the scandal of the government'.

To hold this conduct criminal was an innovation. There was however more than mere obscenity here – there was an element of public indecency towards a captive audience and the case certainly did not purport to declare a separate crime of obscenity. Nonetheless this case was made the basis for convicting in 1727 one Curl for publishing a porno-graphic book. Curl's case firmly established the crime of publishing obscene libels.[2] From time to time afterwards prosecutions for pornography followed regularly, but growth of the trade led to the passing of the Obscene Publications Act, 1857, which empowered magistrates to order the destruction of obscene books and which made this procedure the more effective by authorizing the grant of warrants to the police to search suspected premises. Its sponsor, Lord Campbell, assured the House of Lords that he had no desire to interfere with works of art such as those of Ovid or the Restoration dramatists, Wycherley and Congreve:

'The measure was intended to apply exclusively to works written for the single purpose of corrupting the morals of youth and of a nature calculated to shock the common feelings of decency in a well-regulated mind.'[3]

In 1868 there was decided *Hicklin's* case,[4] the leading case on obscenity, which arose out of an order by Wolverhampton magistrates for the destruction of 'The Confessional Unmasked', a Protestant tract which contained obscene extracts from allegedly Roman Catholic publications and which purported to expose the iniquity of the confessional. The Queen's Bench Division upheld the magistrates' order, Chief Justice Cockburn stating that 'the test of obscenity is this: whether the tendency of the matter charged as obscenity is to deprave and corrupt those whose minds are open to such immoral influences and into whose hands a publication of this sort may fall'.

In 1923 the United Kingdom signed an international convention for the suppression of the circulation of and traffic in obscene publications, and shortly afterwards, upon Sir William Joynson-Hicks's becoming Home Secretary, there was an increase in prosecutions for obscenity. There was a new development now: a burst of prosecution of serious works of literature. The *cause célèbre* was the Government's application in 1928 for a destruction order in respect of *The Well of Loneliness* by the widely-praised Radcliffe Hall. Norman Birkett, counsel for the defence, had assembled forty expert witnesses, including Desmond MacCarthy, E. M. Forster, and Julian Huxley, but the Bow Street magistrate refused to admit their evidence about the book, on the ground that he alone was to judge whether it was obscene, and ordered its destruction. In the ensuing twenty-five years there was a gradual cessation of prosecutions in respect of literature, but in 1954 came a sudden revival. Hutchinson, Heinemann, Secker and Warburg, Werner Laurie, and Arthur Barker were all prosecuted for publishing allegedly obscene novels, and, most notorious conviction of all, *The Decameron* was ordered to be destroyed by Swindon magistrates (although this destruction order was reversed by quarter-sessions on appeal). In the prosecution of Secker and Warburg for *The Philanderer*, Mr Justice Stable summed up to the jury in a manner which received great praise in the Press:5

'Turning for a moment to the book that you have to consider, it is, as you know, in the form of a novel. Remember the charge is a charge that the tendency of the book is to corrupt and deprave. The charge is not that the tendency of the book is either to shock or to disgust. That is not a criminal offence. The charge is that the tendency of the book is to corrupt and deprave. Then you say: "Well, corrupt and deprave whom?" to which the answer is: those whose minds are open to such immoral influences and into whose hands a publication of this sort may fall. What, exactly, does that mean? Are we to take our literary standards as being the level of something that is suitable for the decently brought up young female aged fourteen? Or do we go even further back than that and are we to be reduced to the sort of books that one reads as a child in the nursery? The answer to that is: Of course not. A mass of literature, great literature, from many angles is wholly unsuitable for reading by the adolescent, but that does not mean that a publisher is guilty of a criminal offence for making those works available to the general public. I venture to suggest that you give a thought to what is the function of the novel. I am not talking about historical novels when people write a story of some past age. I am talking about the contemporary novelist. By "the contemporary novelist" I mean the novelist who writes about his contemporaries, who holds up a mirror to the society of his own day. The function of the novel is not merely to entertain contemporaries; it stands as a record or a picture of the society when it was written. Those of us who enjoy the great Victorian novelists get such understanding as we have of that great age from chroniclers such as Thackeray, Dickens, Trollope, Surtees, and many others of that age.

'In the world in which we live today it is equally important that we should have an understanding of how life is lived and how the human mind is working in those parts of the world which are not separated from us in point of time but are separated from us in point of space; and that we should have this understanding (particularly at a time like today when ideas and creeds and processes of thought seem, to some extent, to be in the melting pot and people are bewildered and puzzled to know in what direction humanity is heading and in what column we propose to march). If we are to understand how life is lived in the United States of America, France, Germany, or elsewhere, the contemporary novels of those nations may afford us some guide, and to those of us who have not the time, opportunity, money or, possibly, the inclination to travel, it may even be the only guide. This is an American novel written by a citizen of the United States of America, published originally in New York, purporting to depict the lives of people living today in New York, and to portray the speech, the turn of phrase, and the current attitude towards this particular aspect of life in New York. If we are going to read novels about how things go in New York, it would not be of much assistance, would it, if, contrary to the fact, we were led to suppose that in New York no unmarried woman or teenager has disabused her mind of the idea that babies are brought by storks or are sometimes found in cabbage patches or under gooseberry bushes?

'This is a very crude work, as you may think. You will consider whether or not it does seek to present a fair picture of aspects of contemporary American thought in relation to this problem. You will, no doubt, further consider whether or not it is desirable that on this side of the Atlantic we should close our eyes to a fact because we do not find it altogether palatable. ...'

The jury, who had been told previously to take the book home and read it as a book, not picking out bits here and there, found the accused Not Guilty.

The prominence and praise rightly accorded to this passage are calculated to deceive. After all, it was only one judge's summing up. Contrast it with the trial of Hutchinsons in respect of *September in Quinze* at the Old Bailey three months later. The judge, Sir Gerald Dodson, told the jury, who convicted:

'A book which would not influence the mind of an Archbishop might influence the minds of a callow youth or girl just budding into womanhood. ... It is a very comforting thought that juries from time to time take a very solid stand against this sort of thing and realize how important it is for the youth of this country to be protected and that the fountain of our national blood should not be polluted at its source.'[6]

Indeed, such judgements were more characteristic of the judiciary as a whole than was that of Mr Justice Stable.

This outburst of activity prompted the Society of Authors to set up a Committee presided over by Sir Alan Herbert. This Committee produced a bill for reform of the law which was introduced in the House of Commons in March 1955 by Mr Roy Jenkins, M.P., under the Ten Minute Rule, although it got no further.

Contemporaneously with the doings of the Herbert Committee, the Government introduced a bill to deal with horror comics. Despite its lukewarm reception in the national Press on the ground that it was a piecemeal solution of a larger question, it was enacted as The Children and Young Persons (Harmful Publications) Act, 1955. The Act applies to any book or magazine of a kind which is likely to fall into the hands of children or young persons and consists of stories told in pictures, being stories portraying the commission of crimes or violent, cruel, repulsive, or horrible acts or incidents in such a way that the work as a whole would tend to corrupt a child or young person into whose hands it might fall. It is an offence to print, sell, publish, let on hire, or possess for those purposes any such work.

Obscene publications furnish an outstanding example of how difficult it sometimes is to frame laws to attain objectives on which there is general agreement. Most people would agree that the law should punish and prevent pornography, but that it should not interfere with serious literary works. What, then, was wrong with the law of obscenity in, say, 1955?

The overriding problem is, What do we mean by 'obscene'? The standard answer was that of *Hicklin's* case, a 'tendency to deprave and corrupt', which unfortunately Chief Justice Cockburn did not define with any precision. Is its meaning obvious? He gave us a clue to what he meant by his view that the book in question 'would suggest to the minds of' the reader 'thoughts of a most impure and libidinous character'. But when is a thought 'impure'? Only when it relates to sexual passion? To normal sexual intercourse? In the marriage bed, or outside? To perversions? Do books on sex in marriage corrupt or deprave? What degree of causal relationship must there be between the book and the sexual thought? Do we know when and how and to what extent the reading of a particular book will arouse sexual passions, either in itself or with the aid of other stimuli, and, if only with the aid of the latter, is this sufficiently causal? In any event should the law concern itself with men's thoughts? It is no answer that lustful thoughts are sins according to religious doctrine. Or is the law really looking to the depraving and corrupting *consequences* of stimulating sexual thoughts, i.e. forms of sexual conduct condemned by contemporary society? Is this what the Courts mean when they speak of corrupting 'the morals'? The difficulty here of course is that nobody, judges included, can measure the effect of a book on the sexual behaviour of the reader. Or are 'deprave and corrupt' not limited to sex? Do they extend to that bane of the cinema, the emphasis on horror and violence?

A related question is whether the Courts are to fulfil a social function. Why used Ibsen's *Ghosts* and Shaw's *Mrs Warren's Profession* to be regarded as obscene? Surely on the social ground that they attacked existing conventions. Is a book obscene because it is calculated to bring about a change in the accepted moral standards of society? From this it is not a big step to condemn the offensive, the vulgar, the shocking as obscene.

So far the charge against the law of obscenity is that it failed to face up frankly to the difficulties of defining obscenity. We now pass to more specific grounds of complaint.

The law did not require the Courts to consider the work as a whole. Prosecuting counsel were encouraged by many judges to select the 'highlights' from the book, to quote them with emphasis out of context and thereby convince the jury of the obscene character of the work. One can imagine what counsel could do with James Joyce's *Ulysses*, for example.

We have seen that English law soon turned its back on the promise given by the sponsors of the Obscene Publications Act, 1857, that an allegedly obscene work would be judged, for the purposes of that Act, by its effect on the ordinary person. *Hicklin's* case talked of the effects on the minds of the young: in Mr Justice Stable's words, the test of the fourteen-year-old schoolgirl. Should not the standard be that of the normal person, unless the abnormal or the young are shown to be the probable readers? It is true that judges occasionally mentioned the relevance of the circumstances of the publication. In *Hicklin's* case itself Chief Justice Cockburn said:

'A medical treatise, with illustrations necessary for the information of those for whose education or information the work is intended, may, in a certain sense, be obscene, and yet not the subject for indictment; but it can never be that these prints may be exhibited for anyone, boys or girls, to see as they pass.'

There is no clear judicial guidance of when and for what purposes 'circumstances of publication' were relevant. One would have desired at least a finding that the probable readership should be judged by considering such circumstances of publication as the nature of the advertising material, the publisher's reputation, the channels of distribution, the price and quality of the books sold, but nothing explicit emerged.

We pass naturally from this last point to the relevance of the literary, scientific, and educational values of the work. There was no authoritative decision on whether these were defences to a charge of obscenity. Certainly the judges refused to hear evidence from expert witnesses on them, so that in practice the defence could not be established.

The position of the author was a difficult one. Under the Act his books could be destroyed without his being made a party to the proceedings. His works could be castigated as obscene without his knowledge. But let us suppose that the accused bookseller or other publisher communicated with him. The Courts would not hear him as a witness. Were they right? Is the author's purpose in writing the book material either to the literary value of the work or even to the question of whether it is 'obscene'? This is not the same question as one with which it is often confused: should a man be guilty of obscenity even if he had no intention 'to deprave or corrupt'? Remember that quite often the accused is not the author, but the bookseller or the publisher. Should a judge say: 'You have published the work; it is obscene, therefore you are guilty, regardless of whether you intended to corrupt or deprave'?

ATTEMPTS AT REFORM

With these comments on the law of obscenity in mind, we now turn to the efforts made to reform it.

In 1955 and 1956 Mr Hugh Fraser, M.P., and Lord Lambton, M.P., made two further attempts to launch the Bill previously introduced by Mr Roy Jenkins. In March 1957 the Bill was referred to a Select Committee on the second reading. This Committee took a great deal of evidence but was unable to complete its inquiry by the end of the parliamentary session. Another Select Committee carried on in the next session and reported to the House of Commons in March 1958.

This Report was a first-class document reflecting the thorough examination made of the problem. The Committee were impressed with the existence of a sizeable and lucrative trade in pornography, both in books and postcards. In 1954 167,000 books and in 1957 22,000 postcards had to be destroyed. The number of books and postcards destroyed greatly exceeds the number of articles the subject of prosecution because, as the Director of Public Prosecutions explained to this Committee, a system of 'disclaimers' is operated whereby the possessors of obscene books are given the opportunity to agree, without proceedings being instituted, to their destruction. The Committee made proposals for facilitating its suppression. Their proposals sought also to clarify the law of obscene publications. Briefly, they approved Mr Justice Stable's approach to the definition of obscenity, proposed that the effect of the work as a whole be considered, that a defence of literary or artistic merit be afforded, and that the author have a right to be heard. In November 1958 Mr Roy Jenkins introduced a Bill designed to implement these recommendations. The Committee's report was debated in December 1958, when the Government expressed its agreement with many of the recommendations, but dissented from some, especially the defence of artistic merit and admission of expert evidence thereon. The Bill proceeded on its way but had a stormy passage in the face of considerable Government opposition and amendments. Ultimately, after some Government concessions and compromises (some possibly stimulated by Sir Alan Herbert's characteristic decision to oppose the Government's candidate at a by-election on the stand of the Government's unwillingness to promote legislation) there emerged in July 1959 the Obscene Publications Act, which must now be examined.

THE OBSCENE PUBLICATIONS ACT, 1959

The Act incorporates many of the Select Committee's proposals for strengthening police powers to suppress pornography. Previously the police could not obtain a search warrant without evidence of previous sales: the mere fact that the books were stored by some disreputable wholesaler in a Soho attic was not enough. Now a warrant can be had on evidence that they are being kept 'for publication for gain'. Equally desirable is the new power to search stalls and vehicles, and to seize business documents which might uncover the wholesaler and producer concealed in the background. Although the Act repeals the Obscene Publications Act, 1857, it retains the power of Justices of the Peace to order the destruction of the obscene works.

Section 1 of the Act provides that an article is obscene if its effect is, 'if taken as a whole, such as to tend to deprave and corrupt persons who are likely, having regard to all relevant circumstances, to read, see or hear the matter contained or embodied in it.' This section contains many good features. The book must be considered as a whole. What matters is the effect on those who are the probable readers in the circumstances. Section 2 confers a desirable defence on those charged with the crime of publishing obscene matter: they are not guilty if they prove that they 'had not examined the article ... and had no reasonable cause to suspect' that it was obscene.

Section 4 provides that no offence is committed 'if it is proved that publication of the article in question is justified as being for the public good on the ground that it is in the interests of science, literature, art, or learning, or other objects of general concern.' Moreover, the opinion of experts as to the 'literary, artistic, scientific, or other merits' is admissible evidence. The Act also meets the objection that an author's reputation and royalty-earning power may be taken away from him without his knowing. Even though he is not summoned, he is now entitled to show cause why his books should not be forfeited. Moreover he can appeal against a forfeiture order made by justices although he did not appear at the trial before the justices: this enables an author who first learned of the proceedings when the forfeiture order was made still to challenge the order.

We can further evaluate the Act by considering the important prosecution of Penguin Books Ltd for publishing *Lady Chatterley's Lover* by D. H. Lawrence.[7] At the trial Mr Gerald Gardiner, Q.C., Penguin Books' counsel, argued that since the purpose of the Act was to suppress pornography, but not to censor literature, it was of paramount importance to consider the intention of the author. The difficulty with his argument, however, is that D. H. Lawrence was not the accused. Be that as it may, Mr Justice Byrne ruled 'that it is not open to the Defence to call evidence to prove that there was no intention to deprave or corrupt', and his ruling presumably meant that no evidence of Penguin Books' intentions, as well as those of D. H. Lawrence, was admissible on this issue. Whether the decision is correct is another matter. The judge's reasoning was that before the Act there was no need to prove intention, and the Act had not altered things. Yet, as we have seen, it was far from clear whether, before the Act, in the absence of intention there would necessarily be criminal liability – indeed, two months after his ruling, a higher Court, the Court of Criminal Appeal, decided that before the Act 'it would no doubt have been necessary to prove an intention to corrupt.'[8] When the Select Committee recommended a new Act containing those words which in fact found their way into Section 1, they said, in response to the Society of Authors' view that proof of guilty knowledge should be required, that these words enabled the accused to rebut the presumption of intent to corrupt. In short the new form of words was used precisely because it was believed to have the opposite effect to that which Mr Justice Byrne has given to it. Well, it may be asked, why did not counsel point this out to him? The answer lies in a peculiarity of English law – that Courts are not allowed, when trying to interpret Acts, to look at what Parliament and its committees said about them – the reasons given are that it would create confusion, that different meanings might be given in various parliamentary reports, that the Courts must rely on the language of the Act, and that the citizen is entitled to rely on the words of the Act, without having to read parliamentary debates as well. None of this satisfactorily answers the suggestion that we should look at the parliamentary material only if the meaning of the Act is not on its face clear. Although *R. v. Penguin Books Ltd* is a decision only at first instance and one therefore which other trial judges would be free to disregard, one's guess is that they are likely to follow his ruling on this point. Perhaps the point is not very important: after all, there is the separate defence of public good. One other point about intention: a publisher is not guilty if he had no reasonable cause to know the work to be obscene; and he is not guilty unless the jury find that the work did tend to deprave or corrupt. Mr Justice Byrne also held that in connexion with the defence of literary or other merit 'one has to have regard to what the author was trying to do, what his message may have been, and what his general scope was.'[9]

Prosecuting counsel in his opening address tried to follow the pre-Act practice of reading the 'juiciest' parts to the jury. Mr Justice Byrne rightly stopped him; the Act requires the jury to view the book as a whole, although Lord Radcliffe has stated that this rule will not protect society from being contaminated by what it reads, since it does not read books as a whole.[10] The trial was adjourned so that the jury could read the book in the jury room: the judge refused to let them take it home to read.

The case also threw light on the defence of public good. The judge explained to the jury that, if they found the book not to be obscene, then the accused were not guilty. If the book were obscene, then the jury had to decide whether publication was for the public good. Because the jury merely recorded a verdict of Not Guilty it is impossible to know whether they found the book not obscene, or for the public good, or both. Indeed it may be that some thought it obscene but in the public good, and others both not obscene and in the public good. The judge told the jury:[11]

'As I understand that Section, it was not the intention of Parliament to provide immunity to an author or publisher who published an obscene book *simply* because that work had literary or other merits. In my own view, and I am telling you this as a matter of law, the important words in that Section are the words that the publication "is justified as being for the public good"; and that being so I give you this direction as a matter of law. ... it was not the intention of Parliament by that Section to say, "Well, if somebody who is a skilful author is prepared to write filth, and write it very well, he will escape conviction." What has to be established, that is to say the probability of the matter has to be established, is that the merits of the book are so high that they outbalance the obscenity so that its publication is for the public good.'

This direction is undoubtedly correct in so far as it stresses that the publishers of a book which has literary merit do not always have a defence: the Act provides that they are not guilty if the publication is justified as being for the public good, in deciding which the opinion of experts on its literary and other merits is admissible. The one criticism to be made of this part of the summing-up is that the judge may seem to have treated 'literary merit' and the 'interests of literature' as interchangeable terms. The Act says that the test of public good is (among other things) 'the interests of literature'; 'literary merit' is admissible but is not made the criterion of public good.

Two other rulings by the judge seem sound. The first is the interpretation of the 'literary, artistic, scientific, or other merits' of which the Act permits expert evidence: he held that 'other merits' covered evidence by the Bishop of Woolwich on the *ethical* merits, because this is a merit tending to establish that the publication was for the public good. Secondly, he would not let the expert witnesses say whether the book was published for the public good; they were experts on literary or other merits, but not on public good, which it was for the jury alone to evaluate. He further ruled that the onus was on the defence to prove public good; the Act is not explicit about this, but the ruling was to be expected. The effect of all these rulings is to make the expert evidence – both sides can offer it, although, for reasons unknown, the prosecution did not in the *Penguin* case – very important. It will be difficult to prevent the astute witness from interpolating, with his legitimate opinions on the author's intention and the book's merits, his own views on the author's intention in the context of obscenity and indeed on the rendering of public good.

We said earlier that the old test of 'deprave and corrupt' was vague. The Act merely repeats the words and provides no definition. Mr Justice Byrne had to tell the jury what they meant:[12]

'to deprave means to make morally bad, to pervert, to debase, or corrupt morally. The words 'to corrupt' mean to render morally unsound or rotten, to destroy the moral purity or chastity of, to pervert or ruin a good quality, to debase, to defile. . . . just as loyalty is one of the things which is essential to the well-being of a nation, so some sense of morality is something that is essential to the well-being of a nation, and to the healthy life of the community . . . and accordingly, anyone who by his writing *tends* to corrupt that fundamental sense of morality is guilty of an obscene libel. . . .'

This is the only help he gave them apart from explaining that it was not enough to shock or disgust. One wonders what the jury made of it. Does this direction suggest that there was no need for special legislation about horror comics?

Two subsequent cases have revealed what are presumably drafting errors or omissions in the Act. In the first,[13] the accused displayed packets of obscene photographs in his shop window, with a ticket attached marking them at 10s. The police prosecuted under Section 1 of the Act which provides that any person who 'distributes, circulates, sells, lets on hire, gives or lends it, or who offers it for sale or for letting on hire' commits the crime when the work is obscene. We have seen that the Select Committee had been anxious to catch the man who could not be proved to have sold. Certainly the Act is wide enough to permit the forfeiture of these obscene photographs, but here there was a charge for the crime, not merely a search and seizure. Now it is a rule of contract that there is a binding contract only when there is an offer and an acceptance, and that for a shop to ticket an article is not for it to make a binding offer to sell it at that price – the law has in mind that more than one acceptor might come along. The Court chose to interpret 'offer for sale' in the Act in the light of this rule and to hold, therefore, that the shop manager was not guilty – his was not a binding offer to sell at 10s., therefore there was no offer for sale within the Act. This decision seems to conflict with the obvious purpose of the Act, and it seems to have been unnecessary to interpret 'offer for sale' in this restricted way. At first impression this decision might seem to render nugatory the penal provisions of the Act in a large number of cases since its effect appears to be that the police can only get a conviction on proof of a sale or specific offer. There is, however, one gleam of hope even before Parliament finds time to pass an amending Act. If the accused is indicted, and not merely tried summarily before magistrates as this man was, for a crime, it is open to the Court to convict him of an attempted crime. Perhaps if he had been charged with selling, not offering for sale, he could have been convicted of attempting to sell by ticketing the goods in the shop window.

In the *Ladies Directory* case,[14] the accused, Shaw, published a periodical, the *Ladies Directory*, in order to assist prostitutes to ply their trade, when, as a result of the Street Offences Act, they were no longer able to solicit in the streets. It was a booklet of some twenty-eight pages, most of which were taken up with the names and addresses of women who were prostitutes, together with a number of photographs of nude female figures; the matter published left no doubt that the advertisers could be got in touch with at the telephone numbers given and were offering their services for sexual intercourse, and, in some cases, for the practice of sexual perversions.

One of the offences charged was of publishing an obscene article in breach of the Obscene Publications Act, 1959. Shaw was convicted on this and appealed to the Court of Criminal Appeal, on the ground that the judge failed to direct the jury that Shaw's honesty of intention was relevant. The Court rejected this plea, saying:[15]

'If these proceedings had been brought before the passing of the Obscene Publications Act, 1959, in the form of a prosecution at common law for publishing an obscene libel, it would no doubt have been necessary to establish an intention to corrupt. But the

Act of 1959 contains no such requirement and the test of obscenity laid down in section 1(1) of the Act is whether the effect of the article is such as to tend to deprave and corrupt persons who are likely to read it. In other words obscenity depends on the article and not upon the author.'

Shaw also contended that, since the persons likely to read the *Ladies Directory* were persons who had come to Soho and Paddington to look for prostitutes, they would be already depraved and corrupt, so that the magazine would not deprave and corrupt them. The Court would have none of this argument: they said that 'the fallacy in this argument is that it assumes that a man cannot be corrupted more than once and there is no warrant for this.'

Another offence with which Shaw was charged is perhaps more important in connexion with freedom of expression. This was conspiracy with the prostitutes to corrupt public morals on the ground that the advertisements would induce readers to fornicate and indulge in perversions. The Court of Criminal Appeal affirmed his conviction on this charge, but gave him leave to appeal on this charge to the House of Lords since a point of law of general public importance was involved – they refused leave on the obscenity charge, presumably on the ground that it was clear that intention was irrelevant.

The House of Lords held that it was a crime to conspire to corrupt public morals, and that it was rightly left to the jury to decide whether these advertisements did corrupt public morals. The gravity of this decision can be measured by some of the views of Lord Reid, who dissented in the House of Lords. He pointed out that there are wide differences of opinion on how far the law ought to punish immoral acts done in private, that Parliament, not the Courts, should decide this, that men will not know in advance whether their conduct is going to result in their imprisonment, which will depend on how juries choose to interpret expressions like 'to corrupt public morals'. The House of Lords did not decide that any act which corrupted was a crime; they said that a conspiracy to corrupt was – all rested on the conspiracy between Shaw and the advertising prostitutes.

The case has serious implications for other cases like the *Lady Chatterley* one. The Act prevented prosecutions under the old common-law rules of obscene publication by providing that 'a person publishing an article shall not be proceeded against for an offence at common law consisting of the publication of any matter contained or embodied in the article where it is of the essence of the offence that the matter is obscene'. Shaw pleaded that he could not therefore be charged with conspiracy since the conspiracy relied on was the obscene publication. The House of Lords rejected this plea: the offence of conspiracy 'did not "consist of the publication" of the magazines, it consisted of an agreement to corrupt public morals by means of the magazines which might never have been published'. This seems a highly technical point. There will always be sufficient agreement for conspiracy whenever author and publisher sign a contract: all the protection given to the accused by the Act can be side-stepped if the police choose to prosecute for conspiracy to corrupt public morals. And Viscount Simonds said that it was desirable that this charge of conspiracy should be brought where a doubt existed whether a conviction of obscenity under the Act could be obtained. A perusal of the report of the Select Committee and of Hansard shows that nobody ever thought of this – not surprisingly since it was not realized before this decision that there was a general crime of conspiracy to corrupt public morals. But when Parliament talked of 'the essence of the offence that the matter is obscene' did they not intend to cover conspiracies of this sort, or at least would they not have framed the wording widely enough so as to catch it had they addressed their minds to it? Be that as it may, nothing short of a new Act can override the decision in the *Ladies Directory* case. The protection given by the Act is in practice now seen to be much more restricted, the decision in *R.* v. *Penguin Books Ltd* notwithstanding, than had previously been thought. One law lord had previously complained that the Act 'succeeds in providing for the protection of people who write books, which is not quite the same thing as "to provide for the protection of literature"':[16] the Court of which he is a member has made that success, if any, very short-lived.

PROCEEDINGS FOR OBSCENE PUBLICATION

The vast majority of prosecutions for obscene publications are undertaken at the instance of the police, although there is nothing to prevent a private individual from prosecuting. From the societies for the suppression of vice in the eighteenth and nineteenth centuries to the Public Morality Council or the Catholic Teachers' Federation of today there is never a shortage of bodies willing to assist the police in uncovering obscenity, although one's impression is that the British pressure groups in these matters are not very influential. One case decided since the 1959 Act might appear to have hampered police prosecutions by ruling that, where policemen of the Obscene Publications Department at Scotland Yard bought the obscene photographs and admitted in cross-examination that such photographs aroused no feelings in them whatsoever, commission of an offence was not proved. But the Court of Criminal Appeal added that, in the absence of evidence that the sale of the articles seized would be restricted to persons not susceptible to their influence, the sellers were rightly convicted on a charge of conspiracy to publish obscene articles.[17]

If the police (as distinct from a private individual) contemplate prosecution, they are required by the Prosecution of Offences Regulations, 1946, to report to the Director of Public Prosecutions. The Director is empowered to advise the police whether to prosecute and, if he thinks the case sufficiently important, to take over the prosecution himself. The department of the Director classifies all works reported to it into (a) material in respect of which destruction orders have previously been made, (b) material in respect of which destruction orders have been refused, (c) fresh material which it considers should be put before the Court, (d) fresh material which it thinks not to be obscene. In doubtful cases, the Director seeks advice from the Treasury Counsel before prosecuting: no doubt this happened in the case of *Lady Chatterley's Lover*. At one time the Home Office used to circulate to police forces lists of books condemned by the Courts, but it no longer does this. The Select Committee recommended that the functions of the Director should not stop at advising on prosecutions, but that obscene publications should be added to that list of crimes which cannot be prosecuted without his consent. The Committee was anxious to promote uniformity, and thought that, since the Director had all the tabulated information on which to advise, it would be little extra administrative labour for him to decide whether to allow prosecution. It pointed out that consent is needed for prosecution under the analogous Children and Young Persons (Harmful Publications) Act, 1955. The Government resisted this recommendation on the ground that the definition of obscenity is necessarily so imprecise that it would be improper for the Executive to usurp the Court's task of deciding what is obscene by screening all prosecutions. When the Bill was in Parliament the clause requiring consent of the Director for prosecutions had to be dropped under Governmental pressure.

The Home Office is the Government department concerned, as part of its responsibility for enforcing the criminal law, with the supervision of matters relating to obscene publications. The police forward reports of all convictions and detention orders to the Home Office, which maintains records and statistics. Similarly, the Home Office is notified of seizures by H.M. Customs and the Post Office. The Home Office acts as a liaison between the Post Office, H.M. Customs, and the Director of Public Prosecutions for the purpose of advising on action to be taken. It is also the authority, designated by the United Kingdom under the

international convention for the suppression of pornography, for informing other states of obscene matters being
distributed. In practice it even reports books which it
believes to be obscene, although no prosecution has been
launched in the United Kingdom. The best known is
Lolita, an American novel which had never been the subject
of prosecution in England when the Home Office wrote to
France about this 'highly obscene' book so as to secure the
suppression of an English language version being printed
in France. Of course, since that time, *Lolita* has been
published in England. When Durham County Education
Committee complained about the pin-up girls on chewing
gum imported from the United States, the Board of Trade
stated that it fell outside the control of import licences to
censor wrappers, and the Home Office ruled that they were
not obscene in the accepted sense.

There have, from time to time, been waves of prosecutions
for obscenity. Who, if anyone, has initiated them? The
question is hard to answer. Attempts to pin the blame on
the Home Secretary have not succeeded beyond doubt.
There may be several factors: stepping up of the porno-
graphic trade, enthusiastic officials in the departments
concerned, hints thrown out by the Lord Chief Justice in
cases concerning other obscene publications.

CUSTOMS AND POST OFFICE

The Customs Consolidation Act, 1876, prohibits the
importation of indecent or obscene works. Customs officers
are empowered to seize them. They are armed with a black
list compiled by the Commissioners of Customs and Excise,
a list which includes books which have not been the subject
of prosecutions. If a person asks to see this list in order to
know which books he may buy abroad and import, he will
be refused.[18] He must take his chance of seizure on his
return home. A well-publicized example was the seizure of
Genet's works in French which Birmingham Corporation
had bought for their reference library – although it was

pointed out in a debate on the motion for the adjournment
of the House of Commons that the British Museum and
Reading University stocked the books, the Financial Secretary to the Treasury defended the seizure. A person whose
books are seized has a month in which to notify the Commissioners that he objects – the Customs officers do not
tell him this – after which the books are automatically
forfeited. If he objects within the month, the matter goes
to Court. The Customs authorities refuse to return the book
so that he can read it and thereby prepare his defence.
Those dissatisfied with the seizure of books by the British
Customs authorities might reflect that Irish Customs seized
the *Observer* because it contained an article on Family
Planning, that Australian Customs seized Donleavy's
The Ginger Man, and that South African Customs seized
the children's classic, *Black Beauty*. The Customs officials
can also prosecute for the offence of importing obscene
articles, though the number of seizures greatly exceeds the
number of prosecutions. The Customs witness before the
Select Committee stoutly and successfully resisted, on the
grounds of administrative convenience and expense, a
proposal that no destructions be made without Court order.
It is important to notice that the Act of 1959 does not apply
to these customs offences; therefore all the old defects of
the law remain here: literary merit is no defence, expert
evidence is probably inadmissible, selected 'juicy' parts of
the book may be read, and so on.

The Post Office Act, 1953, makes it an offence to send a
postal packet which encloses obscene matter, and authorizes
officials to detain and destroy such materials. Once again
the protections of the 1959 Act do not extend to offences
under this Act. In 1959 the Post Office was seizing *Lady
Chatterley's Lover*, yet in 1960, before the trial, the Customs
officers were allowing it to go through.

LOCAL AUTHORITIES

Some local authorities, Bradford, for example, have local

Acts of Parliament, making certain conduct relating to obscene publications offences within their area. It is not generally realized how widespread local acts are; there is no readily available compilation of these offences, and the citizen has inadequate opportunity of knowing what the law is. It is perhaps for this reason that the Home Secretary pursues a certain course on a related matter. Some local authorities have by-laws referring to obscene publications, but for a long time now when local authorities submit, as they must, by-laws for his approval, he has refused approval if they deal with obscenity. Local authorities exercise power in other unofficial ways: it is the practice for many seaside towns to have unofficial approved lists of comic picture postcards, which it is agreed shall not be the subject of prosecutions. Blackpool, for instance, has an unofficial censorship committee. It is of interest that the Postcard Association, which represents most of the manufacturers and wholesalers in the trade, is pressing the Home Office to set up an independent national censorship board: the Association complains that what one local authority approves will be prohibited elsewhere.

Defamation

This branch of the law gives money damages to those whose reputations have been harmed by disparaging and defamatory statements. The law is complex, both in substance and in procedure, and only its outlines will be given here. It is a story of competing interests. The Englishman (and the Irishman) attaches a great importance to reputation. Put him on a jury in a libel case and he will often award more damages than a judge will give to the permanently incapacitated victim of a road accident. For instance, when a film of Rasputin might have implied that a Russian princess, an *émigrée* in Britain when the film was made, had been seduced by him, the damages awarded in 1934 were £25,000 – say £80,000 at today's value of the pound.[19] Opposed to this tendency is the powerful pressure group of the Press, concerned, of course, to restrict the scope of libel and damages awarded as much as possible – witness the proprietor of the *Daily Mirror* saying in 1962 that the liberty of the Press is drastically curtailed against the public interest because excessive damages are awarded by juries to the libel victims. First, the Press has always been so willing to pay very high fees to counsel in libel actions that the subject has never failed to attract highly-skilled lawyers; in consequence there has been woven into the subject a degree of technical and procedural subtlety not to be found in any other comparable branch of law. Involved in this is the effort to keep as much away from the jury as possible in the hope that matters which the judge must then decide will receive a decision more sympathetic to the Press. The judge has the last word on all the complex *legal* questions: only if the plaintiff has succeeded in all of them is the jury allowed to consider whether on the *facts* the plaintiff's case is proved. For instance, it is often said proudly that in England the jury decides whether a statement is defamatory. But if the judge rules that the statement is not capable of being defamatory the jury never has the chance to decide the point. And even if the trial judge does let the jury decide, the Court of Appeal can still overrule the jury's verdict that the statement was libellous by holding that the trial judge should never have left the issue to the jury because the statement could not be defamatory. Reinforcing these attempts to shape the judicial process are even more successful attempts to persuade Parliament to cut down the liabilities of the Press in libel. The most recent landmark, the Defamation Act of 1952, gave the Press many important exemptions from liability which it had previously never enjoyed. When the Legal Aid and Advice Act, 1949, introduced a widespread scheme for affording financial aid in bringing law suits defamation was one of the few types of litigation left completely outside the scheme.

THE MEANING OF 'DEFAMATORY'

A statement is defamatory whenever it would tend to lower the plaintiff in the estimation of right-thinking members of society generally. It is not enough that the plaintiff is made to look ridiculous or a laughing-stock; the statement must be an attack on his character or reputation. *That Was The Week That Was* can indulge in its satire without saddling the B.B.C. with heavy libel damages. Even if a right-thinking person would not shun him it is enough if most would do so – for this reason it is libellous to call a man 'insane'. It may be that if a substantial and respectable proportion of society would think less well of a person, provided that this reaction is not plainly anti-social or irrational, then a statement is defamatory. On this view, it would be actionable to say that a man is a non-unionist or works during strikes. On the other hand, the Court of Appeal would be right in having held that it was not actionable to allege that a member of a golf club had sneaked to the police about an illegal fruit-machine in the clubhouse.[20] What was libellous yesterday may be harmless today – it would have been defamatory to call a man a German in 1940 but not in 1963. In order to be libellous the attack must be on the character of the plaintiff. One of the excuses of the Press for not criticizing the products of manufacturers has been that it would expose it to libel actions. Of the many reasons why this is a false view, the first is that to find fault with goods is not to attack the character of the maker. To say that X's cooker is slower to heat, harder to clean, has less usable oven space, than Y's cooker, is not to defame X, the maker of the cooker. (Nor is it normally that other wrong, injurious falsehood, because only those who act from malice are liable for that.)

A statement may be innocuous on its face, and yet have a secondary and defamatory meaning: this lawyers call an innuendo. To put a top-flight singer's name third, instead of first, on an advertising bill for a concert was actionable;[21] a caption under a newspaper photograph to the effect that it was Mr C and his fiancée was defamatory of the plaintiff, the wife of Mr C;[22] to include a cartoon of an amateur golfer in an advertisement for chocolate implied that he was prostituting his amateur status.[23]

PUBLICATION

The libel must be published to somebody other than the plaintiff: a man's reputation cannot suffer unless third parties hear something to his discredit. The plaintiff must also show that the statement is about him. For this reason the civil law is powerless to interfere with group libels: for instance, attacks on Jews or Roman Catholics as a class: when no particular members of the group are pointed at, no individuals can sue.

LIBEL AND SLANDER DISTINGUISHED

The difference between libel and slander is unimportant. Anything communicated in a permanent and visible form is libel, anything temporary and audible is slander. Thus books and letters may convey libel, whereas spoken words (except on radio and television) will usually be slander. To place the effigy of the plaintiff near effigies of convicted murderers in Tussaud's waxworks exhibition was a libel.[24] Libel may be also a crime where the publication is likely to endanger the public peace; slander is not a crime. The distinction is relevant for one other reason; sometimes, in order to win in slander, the plaintiff must prove that he has suffered some material loss in consequence of the defamatory statement. There is not even this difference between libel and slander in the following cases: where the slander imputes a crime; where it imputes that a person has venereal or some other contagious disease; where the words are calculated to disparage the plaintiff in any office, profession, trade, or business; and where the words impute unchastity or adultery to any woman or girl.

DEFENCES

When somebody consents to a publication of defamatory matter he cannot sue. The Racing Calendar published the report of an inquiry by the Jockey Club into the running of a horse trained by the plaintiff; although this report stated that the horse had been doped, and that the plaintiff was warned off, he was held to have no action on the ground that by taking out a Jockey Club trainer's licence he had impliedly consented to publication in the Racing Calendar of any reports by the Jockey Club on his conduct as trainer.[26]

There is no liability whenever the statement made is substantially true. The expert who has made an accurate scientific assessment of the manufacturer's products can report his findings confident in the knowledge that he has nothing to fear from the law of libel. Until 1952 every material statement had to be justified. By the Act of that year 'a defence of justification shall not fail by reason only that the truth of every charge is not proved if the words not proved to be true do not materially injure the plaintiff's reputation having regard to the truth of the remaining charges'. The completeness of the defence of justification must be emphasized. Even if the defendant be inspired by malice, or even if, when he made the statements, he did not believe them to be true, if in fact they are true, his defence is good. This makes the consequences of the failure of the English law to protect privacy so serious. Newspapers are free in this country to rake up a man's forgotten past, and ruin him deliberately in the process, without risk of incurring tortious liability.

Even if the statement is false, there may still be no liability. Some statements are said to be absolutely privileged. Thus an M.P. can in the House of Commons say whatever he likes about anybody; he may use the occasion deliberately to blacken a business rival in order to divert profitable contracts to his own company, knowing that everything he says is completely false, and positively desiring to ruin his rival: he is completely exempt from libel, and so are the Press and television when they accurately report his speech. Hence the frequency with which M.P.s spurn the challenge to repeat outside the House the disparaging remarks which they have made in it. Communications passing between senior civil servants are also absolutely privileged, but not, say, letters exchanged between directors of Imperial Chemical Industries Ltd. Statements made in Court, whether by judge, lawyer, litigant, or witness, enjoy the same privilege: fair, accurate, and contemporaneous reports in newspapers and broadcasts of judicial proceedings can also never be the subject of libel actions.

Whenever it is in the public interest, or in the interest of the person making the statement and the person to whom it is communicated, that the statement be made, the maker of the statement, even though it be false and defamatory, has the defence of qualified privilege so long as he makes it without malice. There is malice if the maker does not believe in the truth of his statement, or if he is actuated by some improper motive, such as spite or ill-will. A newspaper may report that an athletics body has deprived an amateur of his status on the ground that he has been paid to run; it will not be liable even though the athlete can prove that he received no payment, provided that it has accurately reported the body's decision. Fair and accurate newspaper and broadcasting reports of proceedings of local authorities, public bodies, and company meetings are also qualifiedly privileged. The manager of a company may inform his directors of his suspicion that the cashier is falsifying the accounts – however untrue, this is no libel if done without malice; for it would be an instance of a common interest between the maker and the recipient of the statement.

It is also a defence to make a fair comment on a matter of public interest. The defence covers the public conduct of persons holding public office or of those engaged in local government or management of religious institutions. Plays, broadcasts, the work of an architect, are other examples. Publishers may be annoyed at the scathing reviews of their books, but are remediless when the comment is one that an honest man, however biased and prejudiced his views, might have made. This is one more reason why the Press could freely criticize products offered for sale to the public. One House of Lords decision on fair comment arose when Lord Kemsley sued Michael Foot as editor of *Tribune*.[26] *Tribune* attacked a newspaper (with which Kemsley, the newspaper proprietor, was not connected) by publishing an article headed 'Lower than Kemsley'. The House of Lords held that Foot would have a defence of fair comment if an honest man would have complained that the Kemsley Press was low: after this ruling Kemsley dropped the proceedings. Whenever qualified privilege or fair comment is pleaded, no written questions about the defendant's sources of information or grounds of belief are allowed. When the *Daily Telegraph* published an allegedly defamatory letter about a radio show it did not lose the defence of qualified comment when it emerged that the letter was written anonymously from a false address and therefore the newspaper could not prove that the writer was not actuated by malice.[27]

Sometimes a libel may be published innocently. Thus, a newsagent will not be held answerable for the libel in the magazine which he sells, for he is a mere distributor who could not ordinarily be expected to know of the libel. Before the Act of 1952, newspapers were held answerable in the following cases: The *Sunday Chronicle* published a fictional article about 'Artemus Jones'; the writer of the article did not know of the plaintiff, of that name, who was a former contributor to the newspaper, but the managing editor, on reading the article in proof, had thought at first that the plaintiff was intended.[28] In another, the *Daily Express* published an account of the trial for bigamy of 'Harold Newstead, thirty-year-old Camberwell man': the reporter had included the address and occupation of the Harold Newstead of whom this was a correct report, but the sub-editor deleted it; this want of particularity caused readers to think that the plaintiff, another Harold Newstead of Camberwell, of about the same age, was meant; it was held to be no defence that the words were true of, and intended to refer to, another, and the jury was held to be justified in finding that the words referred to the plaintiff.[29] The Act of 1952 has for the first time given newspapers a defence when they unintentionally defame a person.

In practice, therefore, those who take reasonable care about what they say have little to fear from the law of defamation. When newspapers (or those with whom they insure for libel) are caught by the law of libel, it is usually either because their reporters and proof-readers have been careless in not detecting the offending material, or because in the interests of circulation they have taken a calculated risk.

The general verdict on the law of defamation is: the obstacles in the way of the plaintiff's success are severe and probably larger than they ought to be; on the other hand, once the jury are allowed by the judge to try the issues they redress the balance by awarding damages on a generous scale.

There is nothing to support the Press view that the law of libel prevents newspapers from commenting on many matters about which the public should know. The Press cannot, for instance, hold the law responsible for its inept and cowardly showing in the Profumo affair; a newspaper which publishes the truth cannot be held liable to the victim, whether he be a Minister or a nonentity.

CHAPTER 6

FREEDOM OF EXPRESSION (4):
CONTEMPT OF COURT AND
CONTEMPT OF PARLIAMENT

Contempt of Court

IN this section we are concerned with the restrictions imposed upon those who wish to comment on judges and trials. There are two issues: whether the law embodied in these restrictions is sound, and whether, however good in itself, it is liable to work unfairly if judges are allowed to judge in their own causes. The power of restriction arose in this way: it used to be the law that in some cases a man who hindered another from having a fair trial (whether criminal or civil) could be indicted for a crime (called a contempt of Court) tried by a jury in the usual way. In the early seventeenth century the Star Chamber assumed jurisdiction to punish these contempts. Soon after the Star Chamber was abolished in 1641 the ordinary judges themselves began trying these contempts summarily. When this was challenged in 1765 the Court held that the practice was lawful;[1] since that date this summary method has continued unchallenged, whereas trial by jury for such contempts is now obsolete. The judges now act as if the law has always conferred on them this summary power. There can now be no doubt that they used not to have such a power, that they usurped it on the dissolution of the Star Chamber, and that the authorities relied on in the decisive case of 1765 did not warrant that decision. The power (which cannot be exercised by County Court judges or other judges in inferior Courts, such as magistrates) is now too entrenched to be altered except by Act of Parliament. (One might ask: why does it matter that a crime is tried summarily by a judge instead of on indictment in the usual way? First of all, the accused is denied a jury; there is nothing to stop the judge who is himself the victim of the alleged contempt from trying the charge. In some Courts the accused has no right to a personal hearing on the charge; he is only allowed to swear an affidavit. The judge can impose a fine of unlimited amount, he can impose a term of imprisonment of any duration he chooses, or indeed send the accused to prison and leave him there indefinitely, and until October 1960 the law gave the accused no appeal.)

CONDUCT WHICH INTERFERES WITH THE FAIRNESS OF A TRIAL

Any conduct that tends to bring the authority and administration of the law into disrespect or to interfere with litigation is a contempt of Court. We are concerned here only with those contempts which concern freedom of expression. The Press and broadcasting are obviously the most important media, but theatrical productions, cinema newsreels, sermons, and speeches have all fallen foul of the law of contempt.

It is obviously of the first importance that every accused should have a fair trial. Important though freedom of speech and freedom of the Press be, a 'freedom' which deprived prisoners of a fair trial could not be countenanced. In the United States, the Press is free to assist in detection of crime, to interview witnesses and suspects and report their observations, to comment on trials as they proceed, and to give opinions on the guilt of suspects. Englishmen should be proud of the fact that none of these things can happen in England: the law of contempt stands in the way.

This is not to say that the British Press has not tried to interfere. For instance, in the early nineteen-twenties national newspapers used to assign teams of their staff to investigate crimes. In 1924 the *Evening Standard* published misleading information about discoveries in a murder case. The newspaper also obtained from a witness information and a promise not to speak to anybody but themselves about the case, but, doubting whether she would resist the wiles of other newspapers, they arranged that she should stay out of the way with the wife of a sub-editor.[2] The proprietors were fined £1,000 for contempt, disabused of the notion that they were fulfilling a public duty, and sternly informed that any future offences of that kind would be dealt with by imprisonment. This put a stop to that type of activity on the part of the British Press.

The overriding aim of the law of criminal contempts is to ensure that the jury enters upon its task free from bias. For example, after a criminal trial where the jury disagreed, and the accused published an article before the re-trial in which he attacked the reliability of one of the leading witnesses in the case, members of the jury at the re-trial might well have been prejudiced by recalling what they had read in his article, and accordingly the accused was punished for contempt.[3] The English method of criminal prosecution creates a particular risk of prejudice. A person who is charged by the police with a crime is not tried at once. The matter is first referred to examining magistrates who hear the evidence of the prosecution in order to decide whether there is a prima facie case for committing him for trial. As we shall see, this investigation is normally carried out in open Court. At the eventual trial journalists are free to report the proceedings contemporaneously. But it does not follow that these proceedings consist of the same evidence as that heard by the magistrates. The following cases illustrate what sometimes ensues.

In 1954 an *Evening Standard* reporter was attending a murder trial at Chelmsford Assizes. He telephoned an account to head office which was an inaccurate statement of the evidence given. The inaccuracy lay in the fact that evidence prejudicial to the accused (which had wrongly been allowed to be given by the examining magistrates) was prohibited by the judge at the assizes.[4] Presumably, the reporter thought that he had heard at the trial what in fact he had only previously heard before the magistrates. The untrue account which appeared in the *Evening Standard* (on sale in Chelmsford that evening) could have prejudiced the jury, who might very well have read the newspaper at home before returning to Court the following day to continue their duties. The proprietors were fined £1,000 for contempt.

Another incident arose out of the trial of Dr Bodkin Adams. During his trial for murder *Newsweek* published matter highly prejudicial to the doctor which was not given in evidence at his trial. This publication was held to be contempt.[5]

Some Sunday newpapers have sought to increase their circulations by writing articles which purport to expose criminals who have not yet been brought to justice. In1956 the *People* published an article, prepared by its crime reporter Duncan Webb, demanding that one Micallef be arrested and prosecuted for his brothel-keeping activities. The only object of the article was found to be to boost sales.[6] Micallef had been arrested the previous month for a crime of this type and had been committed for trial by a Court operating within a mile or so of the *People*'s head office. No evidence of previous convictions is ordinarily allowed at a trial; while Micallef was awaiting his trial, however, not only had the *People* published a list, but the list apparently included many offences for which he had not been convicted; the prejudicial effect on any members of the jury who read the article is obvious. The editor, the proprietors, and Webb were all fined for contempt. It seems just that the Court should have found the offence committed even though the accused's trial had not begun. The editor of the *Daily Mirror* was sent to prison in 1949 for publishing an article, when the murder trial of Haigh was pending, which might have suggested to readers that Haigh was involved in some other horrifying murders.[7]

It was thought at one time that newspapers were free to comment so long as no arrest had been made. In a Scottish case in 1959 the *Scottish Daily Mail* published prejudicial material before the accused was charged but when he was being questioned as a suspect:[8] this was held to be contempt, and a warning was given that if newspapers persisted in the independent interviewing of witnesses in a way that impeded the police, it might be necessary to imprison those responsible. In Scotland, however, there is no public investigation before magistrates, and it did not follow that the decision applied in England. Subsequently, the *Daily Express* and *Daily Mail* were fined in Northern Ireland for publishing information about a person whom the *Daily Express* described as the 'No. 1 suspect'9 – he was later charged. Moreover, the Administration of Justice Act, 1960, recognized that if proceedings were imminent, even though not pending, the crime could be committed. This extension to the period before anybody is charged may appear to place a newspaper in some difficulty. It would be wrong to muzzle a newspaper altogether before arrests are made: newspapers may be capable of uncovering criminal activities. But in practice it is believed that it will not be difficult to define an 'imminent' proceeding and so the rule will not work unfairly against the Press. This example illustrates a recurring problem in drafting statutes. It is comparatively easy to determine the common-sense solution to a problem, but often very difficult to translate it into a form of wording which will convey the sense intended with precision. It is not to be wondered at that parliamentary draftsmen are hard to train, and that many lawyers are found wanting when they turn their hands to this highly specialized and skilled art. It is common for the Press to indulge in such euphemisms as 'the police wish to interview X whom they believe will assist them in their inquiries', or 'X is detained by the police for questioning'. Everyone knows what these statements mean – they seem a clumsy and almost certainly ineffective way of avoiding possible proceedings for libel. X is a suspect, and it is there that the Courts will draw the line for the purposes of contempt – the Press must not publish anything prejudicial to him. Above all, they must be careful not to publish matter of which the law forbids evidence to be given at the trial.

Photographs are a particular hazard for the Press. A flagrant case of contempt was that of the *Daily Record* in Scotland in 1959.[10] A well-known Scottish professional footballer was arrested: ignoring warnings from the police, the newspaper persisted in its inquiries and published a photograph of the accused. Obviously, whenever any issue of identification arises this is highly prejudicial. The newspaper was fined £7,500. It would of course be equally prejudicial to publish a photograph of a suspect before he is charged; this was one of the grounds on which the *Scottish Daily Mail* was convicted in the case cited earlier. Yet it might be countered that sometimes the Press and television organizations publish photographs at the request of the police. This in itself will not ensure immunity from conviction for contempt, but it does suggest that there are circumstances in which the publication of a photograph of a suspect is not contempt. When the Administration of Justice Bill was before Parliament, the Opposition raised the question of defining contempt in the Bill, and in particular the relevance of the public interest which a publication might serve. The Government resisted these proposals on the ground that it was always clear whether a publication was prejudicial to the administration of justice and that the question of countervailing public interest could never arise. But is this so? Suppose the police ask a newspaper to publish the photograph of an escaped convict whom they believe to be committing, since his escape, a series of dangerous crimes. When the convict is ultimately captured and tried for these further crimes might he not be prejudiced by the photograph in the same way as any other accused standing trial? It is submitted that the law ought to be that the newspaper was not guilty of contempt because the public interest in helping to capture a dangerous escaped convict outweighed the risk of prejudicial publication. One cannot, however, say with confidence that the defence of public interest is ever available, and it is to be regretted that the opportunity to clarify the point was missed when the Bill was in Parliament. Newspapers ought not to be put in the dilemma of either failing to protect citizens against dangerous men or exposing themselves to summary prosecution, and it is no answer that the Court would probably only record a formal conviction without penalty, or that prosecutions for such acts are unlikely.

The discussion so far has avoided the question of whether the accused need have a guilty mind. In several of the cases already examined the Court went out of its way to declare that a person was guilty, however innocent his conduct might have been. In the Micallef case against Odhams Press the accused pleaded that they did not know that Micallef had been charged. Lord Goddard held that the issue of intent was irrelevant. In fact his ruling was totally unnecessary; for the Court found that the *People* had failed to take reasonable care to ascertain the facts, and it could therefore have held the accused guilty, not of innocent contempt, but of carelessness. In the *Newsweek* case the distributors, W. H. Smith & Son Ltd, were found guilty, it being held that their defence that they were unaware of the criminal content of the magazine was irrelevant, and, as Lord Goddard observed, the gossipy nature of *Newsweek* and the well-known lack of restraint in American magazines when reporting crime might well have put the distributors on to inquiry into the contents.

Why did the Courts take this line? Not, it is submitted, because they were determined to be ruthless towards the Press. The evidence is all the other way. They have inflicted punishments reasonable in the circumstances and they have shown no tendency to punish the innocent or to interfere when the risk of prejudice was slight. Typical is the recent decision that a newspaper report published between conviction and appeal which, if published before trial, would have been prejudicial because of its likely impact on a jury, was not a contempt because experienced judges of the Court of Criminal Appeal who would alone decide the appeal could be relied on to be completely uninfluenced by such a Press report.[11] Similarly, the Speaker of the House of Commons ruled that the House could discuss the Wedgwood

Benn case (an M.P. eldest son of a Peer who had died) although an election petition had been presented to the Election Court, on the ground that the issues were purely legal, to be decided by judges who would not therefore be prejudiced by a Commons debate.[12]

In one's search for an explanation of judicial attitudes to contempt, one may seek an analogy outside the law of contempt altogether. Consider the outlook of top-ranking civil servants who cling to power at all costs and resist attempts to introduce into their decisions fair procedures with the force of law: a typical example is the attitude of the Ministry of Housing and Local Government to orders for compulsory purchase of land, as revealed in the evidence given before the Franks Committee on Administrative Tribunals and Inquiries. Both judges with respect to contempt and senior civil servants in the discharge of their duties to citizens intend to act fairly but wish to keep the power in their own hands – justice is the judge's concern and he wishes to have unrestricted power to decide when newspapers and others are guilty of contempt. Although the judges have exercised their wide powers with restraint, public opinion would not tolerate the wide powers which they arrogated to themselves in decisions like that of *Newsweek*. The reaction was rapid: the introduction of the Administration of Justice Bill. Senior judges were, however, closely consulted in the drafting of it.

Section 11 of this Act provided that a distributor was not guilty of contempt 'if at the time of distribution (having taken all reasonable care) he did not know that it contained any such matter as aforesaid and had no reason to suspect that it was likely to do so.' The *Newsweek* case had strongly suggested that importers and big distributors of foreign periodicals were likely always to be punished for contempts contained in any of them. The Courts were apparently resolved that such contempts should not go unpunished. The distributors were the only targets, for these foreign publishers had no editorial units in Britain – the man in charge of *Newsweek* in London was found not guilty because he had no control over the content of the magazine – and, contempt of Court not being an extraditable crime, there was no machinery for bringing the publishers from abroad to stand trial. Foreign publishers refused to indemnify Smith's against any fines imposed on them. If these decisions had stood there might well have been a great reduction in the number of foreign periodicals on sale to the British public. This provision therefore relieved firms like W. H. Smith & Son, Ltd, of much anxiety, although its scope must not be exaggerated. The distributor has the burden of satisfying the Court that he could not, by taking reasonable care, have discovered the offending material. It is submitted that, if facts like those of the *Newsweek* case recurred, the Courts could justifiably still convict.

The Act also provides that any person accused of contempt is not guilty if he proves that he did not know and had no reason to suspect that proceedings were pending or imminent. Although the Act reverses the law laid down in cases like Micallef's, its limits must be noted. On facts such as those, presumably the judge's decision would still be 'guilty' because a newspaper specializing in the reporting of sordid crime ought to know that a person has been committed for trial by a Court in the immediate vicinity of its head office. It is easy to imagine the new provision putting newspapers in a dilemma. Nothing is more likely to restrain the Press than uncertainty about the legality of its proposed actions. There is no central register of summonses issued or committals for trial ordered throughout the country. What inquiries should a newspaper make before writing an article about a person? This question of fact remains solely for the judges. It may be assumed at least that once the police have issued their 'wanted to assist them in their investigations' notices, the Press and broadcasting companies publish at their peril.

It has been widely assumed that since the Act publishers will not be guilty of contempt so long as they are innocent. This is erroneous. The rule laid down by the judges that liability arises regardless of the publisher's state of mind remains untouched save on knowledge that proceedings were pending. It will be remembered that the contempt in the *Evening Standard* case lay in a misreporting of the trial at Chelmsford Assizes. Suppose that a Court reporter cabled to head office his report of a trial, and, owing to the fault of the Post Office, there was an error in transmission, so that the report as published, which was a correct rendering of the report as received at the newspaper office, prejudiced a fair hearing. This would still be a punishable offence, and the Post Office would have no liability to the newspaper. For the new defence of 'innocence' specifically refers only to the fact that proceedings were pending or imminent. This Chelmsford case raises another point. The *Evening Standard* pleaded that even if its reporter was careless in sending an inaccurate report, it had done nothing criminal; it had merely published in good faith what had been telephoned to it. The Court held that 'the principle of vicarious liability is well established in these cases and must be adhered to', which means that, once a servant of the newspaper proprietors acting in the course of his employment is guilty of contempt, the proprietors are themselves guilty. Under the Act, the principle of vicarious liability survives, it seems, in that if the editor knows that the proceedings are pending and none of the directors knows, the proprietors will be guilty, and likewise, even if the editor does not know but the managing director, although in his Bermudan retreat at the time of publication, does know, the proprietors will still be guilty. On the other hand, if the reporter knows and the editor is innocent, the reporter but not the editor will be guilty, for the reporter is not the editor's servant. Yet when this point of knowledge is not in issue an editor can be convicted, even though at the time of publication he was away from the office.

Before we leave this branch of contempt some side-effects must be noted. First, a man may be denied a trial by a jury free from prejudice even though newspapers and others have not infringed this law of contempt. Take the case of Albert Jones who was first charged in 1960, not with the murder of

Brenda Nash, whose death after sexual interference was prominently reported, but with the rape of another girl. Shortly after his widely publicized conviction for this rape, he was charged with the murder of Brenda Nash. It is plain that the risk of the jury's being prejudiced against Jones because of his preceding trial was much greater than was the risk in many of the convictions for contempt previously discussed. Yet the conduct of the police, the Press, and the broadcasting agencies did not infringe the law of contempt. Or take the later A6 'homicide case' in 1961–2. The police let it be known that a certain man was sought in order to help with their inquiries into a death in which foul play was suspected. When this man came forward he was charged with a quite separate offence of wounding another person on another occasion and detained in custody. Then the police realized and stated that their suspicions of him in the context of the A6 death were unjustified. The sequel was that the prosecution stated at his trial for the wounding charge that they were now not offering any evidence, and he was forthwith discharged a free and innocent man. Had the police charged him with the A6 crime there would have been a risk of prejudice arising out of the publicity surrounding the other proceedings, and yet no contempt would have been committed.

The Courts are astute to reinforce the law of contempt in other ways. For instance, a Mr Baker was found murdered. The Press discovered the photographer who had been employed to take photographs at his daughter's wedding and paid him £15 for them so that they could publish photographs of the murdered man. His son-in-law sued the photographer for breach of copyright. The Court of Appeal upheld an award of £400 exemplary damages. Such a high sum was justified because it might deter others from supplying 'to the Press information which they know is going to be used in a manner which will be so hurtful and distressing to the people involved'.[13]

Secondly, the legitimate principle that prejudicial comment on a pending case in an ordinary Court of justice must not be allowed is being increasingly abused under the banner of *sub judice*. A peer who wished to raise in the House of Lords matters arising out of the ministerial inquiry into the application for compulsory powers to work ironstone in Oxfordshire was told by Lord Kilmuir, the Lord Chancellor, in 1960 that his inquiry was out of order, because the matter was *sub judice*; although the inspector had completed his inquiry and his subsequent inspection of the site, the Minister had not announced his decision.[14] There is no legal warrant for that reply. The alleged reason was that the objective of the Government was 'to infuse into the operation of these inquiries a real sense of independent judging, with full responsibility, of the issues which are raised'. The guarded tone of this statement must be noted: the casual reader might think that the Lord Chancellor had advanced conclusive argument that these proceedings were judicial like those of a Court, and therefore must be subject to the *sub judice* protection. But soon afterwards Lord Kilmuir was to defend in Parliament a decision reached by a Minister after an inquiry of this type, where the Minister reversed the recommendation of the inspector on new evidence which the aggrieved landowner was not even allowed to see: a course which would be inconceivable in judicial proceedings. Yet in this latter case Lord Kilmuir's stand was legally supportable: that only shows how wrong it would be to think that the ironstone inquiry was comparable to a trial. A careful reading of Lord Kilmuir's statement shows that he did not say so – he merely spoke of the 'object of infusing a sense of judging'. In short, he wishes to have the best of both worlds, a logically indefensible position: to prevent comment on inquiries because they fall within the *sub judice* rule of trials; to allow evidence to be taken behind the back of parties (which is forbidden at trials) because they are not judicial in the sense in which trials are. And finally, the most absurd example, again from Lord Kilmuir a few weeks earlier, when he told Lord Teviot that he could not discuss the verdict the previous day in the *Lady Chatterley's Lover* prosecution, because the matter was *sub judice* pending a possible appeal. The fact is, of course, that no appeal was possible from the verdict of not guilty.[15] Yet the House of Commons discussed the George Blake treason case in 1961 when the time for his appeal against conviction had not expired, and when it did not know whether he had given notice of appeal. The whole problem of parliamentary discussion in relation to *sub judice* needs re-examination. There is often a conflict between the desire not to prejudice a trial and the need for prompt parliamentary discussion of matters of public interest. In 1962 the Speaker of the House of Commons advised against debating the circumstances of dismissal of a charter aircraft pilot because a libel action was pending, and this despite the public interest in aircraft safety raised by the case. It would be deplorable if a man could avoid discussion of any matter in Parliament by the simple expedient of issuing a writ. It is submitted that the Speaker should himself weigh in the balance the conflicting interests involved before deciding whether to allow parliamentary discussion. The problem is quite distinct from the rule that parliamentary debates are not held on matters the subject of inquiry by royal commission or departmental committee – this is merely a convenient rule of parliamentary business.

WHEN IT IS CONTEMPT TO CRITICIZE A JUDGE

The law of contempt imposes other restraints on freedom of comment in relation to the administration of justice, the justification for which demands careful consideration. In certain circumstances it is contempt to criticize a judge. If a judge's character is blackened he can sue for defamation in the same way as anybody else: there is no need for a special crime of contempt in order to protect his reputation. It is desirable that the performance of judges be subject to examination and comment; even more obviously the accuracy of the law laid down by them in their decisions should be the object of fearless scrutiny. Such freedom to criticize is essential if the high quality of judicial administration is to be maintained. It is a fact that English judges are criticized less openly and severely than those in many other common-law countries. This may be, not because such criticism would necessarily be a crime, but because critics are unsure what the law of contempt is and especially how it will be applied by judges confronted with an alleged crime against one of their brethren. It will be recalled that contempts are summary offences tried by judges without a jury.

In 1900 Mr Justice Darling warned the Press before he heard a particular case that, if they published obscene matter given in evidence, he would make it his business to see that the law of obscenity was enforced against them. After the trial ended, an article was published in a local newspaper which stated:

> No newspaper can exist except upon its merits, a condition from which the Bench, happily for Mr Justice Darling, is exempt. Mr Justice Darling would do well to master the duties of his own profession before undertaking the regulation of another.

The publisher was convicted of contempt because of this 'scurrilous personal abuse' of the judge.[16] In 1928 Dr Marie Stopes lost a libel action which arose out of the refusal of the *Daily Telegraph* to publish her advertisement advocating birth control. The *New Statesman* said of this trial that Mr Justice Avory allowed prejudice against her views to influence his summing up and that 'an individual owning to such views as those of Dr Stopes cannot apparently hope for a fair hearing in a Court presided over by Mr Justice Avory'. The editor was found guilty of contempt.[17] These two cases establish that to abuse a judge or impute unfairness to him is the crime of contempt. Lord Hewart's reason for convicting the editor of the *New Statesman* was that 'the gravamen of the offence was that by lowering his authority it interfered with the performance of his judicial duties'. The Court did not consider whether the attack was justified. It is thought that the law of contempt rightly condemns unjustified allegations of corruption or partiality.

But why should it be a crime if the publisher can show that his comment was fair on the facts disclosed? A Committee of 'Justice' under the chairmanship of Lord Shawcross has recently held that such allegations, however true, should be punished as contempt[18] on the ground that complaints should be made only to the Lord Chancellor and members of Parliament, and that the Bar can be relied on to keep the judges within bounds. But the rules of parliamentary debate ordinarily prevent the casting of reflections on judges, and one has not encountered many recent examples of junior counsel successfully resisting domineering judges in the course of trials.

At the same time, the Committee of 'Justice' strongly recommended that fair criticism of a judge should not be discouraged; it had in mind commenting on his competence in the light of the law laid down by him. And it is the law that such criticisms may legitimately be made. The relevant case is one of many which show how fortunate it is that the Privy Council has had jurisdiction over appeals on contempts from overseas, for to that Court we owe most of the wise restrictions and illuminating decisions appertaining to contempt. (English appellate Courts have made no contribution because, as we have seen, no appeal to them used to lie against convictions for contempt.) When a newspaper editor in Trinidad who published a reasoned article on the human element in fixing the length of sentences was convicted of contempt by the local Court he exercised his right under the colonial law to appeal to the Judicial Committee of the Privy Council.[19] Lord Atkin, holding that the editor was the victim of a substantial miscarriage of justice, said:[20]

'But whether the authority and position of an individual judge, or the due administration of justice, is concerned, no wrong is committed by any member of the public who exercises the ordinary right of criticizing, in good faith, in private or public, the public act done in the seat of justice. The path of criticism is a public way: the wrong-headed are permitted to err therein: provided that members of the public abstain from imputing improper motives to those taking part in the administration of justice, and are genuinely exercising a right of criticism, and not acting in malice or attempting to impair the administration of justice, they are immune. Justice is not a cloistered virtue: she must be allowed to suffer the scrutiny and respectful, even though outspoken, comments of ordinary men.'

This judgment has been recognized as authoritative both in the Courts and by the Lord Chancellor in the debate in the House of Lords on the Administration of Justice Bill, 1960. Such freedom is clearly necessary. The law cannot be improved if experts are not free to criticize it in the light of current decisions. Suppose that an appeal to the House of Lords is pending and yet legislation on the subject-matter of the case is being proposed. It is undesirable that newspapers should feel themselves constrained – as has happened – by fear of contempt proceedings from publishing letters on the subject. Suppose, too, that a newspaper feels that it can only usefully discuss the vexed and difficult problem of sentencing with reference to a case which is newsworthy at the time of the article: for instance it might wish to consider the crime of abortion in the light of a sentence of imprisonment just given.

On the discussion so far it might appear that there is a clear-cut distinction; an attack on the man is punished but criticism of his output in the shape of his judicial utterances is allowed. But look at the next case.[21] The magazine *Truth* said of Lord Justice Slesser, when he was trying a case against the Minister of Labour arising out of an Act of Parliament which he had steered through the House of Commons when Attorney-General in the previous Labour Government, that 'he can hardly be altogether unbiased about legislation of this type'. The editor was convicted and fined for contempt. Yet this was a reasoned observation. The Court brought it within the rule that the judge's partiality was assailed, and so good faith and fair comment were irrelevant. In the context was there not force in the accused's contention that he was merely pointing out what is generally recognized: the dangers of *unconscious* bias in specific situations? The Court's reasoning is obvious: this was an accusation of partiality and must be punished. It is submitted that the result is not just: a fair criticism of judicial competence is allowed, but a reasoned and reasonable speculation about a judge's unconscious bias is a crime. The evil results from the sharp distinction between allegations of corruption and partiality on the one hand, and of incompetence on the other. Ordinarily no harm will be done by treating as contempts wild and abusive allegations of judicial corruption. Such attacks should remain illegal: the defect of the present law is that judges can convict even though the accuracy or fairness of complaints of partiality is conclusively proved. In fairness to Lord Justice Slesser he has since recounted that the editor of *Truth* was deliberately committed for contempt behind his back because the powers that be rightly surmised that he would have stopped the contempt proceedings if possible: he could never find out who 'they' were, who insisted that the public interest demanded the editor's committal.[22]

In June 1962 the proprietor of the *Daily Mirror* and *Sunday Pictorial* stated:[23]

The actual operation of the rules against contempt of Court, however, has meant that of recent years no serious criticism of judicial proceedings above the level of Magistrates' Courts has been thought to be possible. In fact there has been little or no such criticism, though a good deal from time to time would have been in the public interest. As judicial proceedings are not criticized in the House of Commons, this means that there is no criticism of proceedings in the higher Courts.

Maybe this reflects excessive caution on the part of the Press, but there is something seriously amiss with a branch of the law which is administered so unpredictably that a big newspaper organization (employing three full-time and eleven part-time barristers to supervise the contents of its newspapers) has to restrain itself in this way.

There have been suggestions that newspapers can commit criminal contempt even though they do not prejudice a fair trial or impute corruption or partiality to a judge: i.e. if they hinder the activities of the police. In the judgment against the *Scottish Daily Mail* Lord Clyde said that 'once a crime has been suspected and once the criminal authorities are investigating they and they alone have the duty to do the investigating'. The inference is that contempt is committed if the police are hindered while attempting the detection of crime. It would be unfortunate if this extension were accepted. It is not concerned with ensuring a fair trial; it rests on the argument that the administration of justice extends beyond that which takes place in the courtroom to the crime-detecting activities of the police force. The objection is the greater when it is seen that such a contempt would be committed however innocent the newspaper, for it does not fall within those exemptions for innocent publications contained in the 1960 Act which we have previously examined. If the police showed that a consequence of the newspaper's investigation of a crime for which there was no known suspect was that they were impeded, that would be enough. Some of the language of Lord Hewart in the first case against the *Evening Standard* is rather similar. It is to be hoped that the English judges will not – though there is nothing to prevent them, unfortunately – extend the law of criminal contempt in this way. There is a separate crime of obstructing the police in the execution of their duty; if a reporter has committed that crime let him stand trial in the ordinary way. Otherwise, the law of contempt should not interfere when there is no prejudice to any person whose arrest is known to be imminent. After all, newspapers occasionally rise above their usual level of ineffectiveness in this respect by actually uncovering some criminal scandal. This is a public service which, within proper limits, should not be discouraged by instituting criminal proceedings against them.

Until the passing of the Administration of Justice Act in 1960 English law had one unenviable distinction. It was the only legal system in Western Europe which ever denied a civilian sent to prison a right of appeal. The reference is, of course, to the law of criminal contempt. Despite some judicial opposition in the course of its passage through the House of Lords, the Bill now provides a right of appeal to those convicted of contempt. At the same time the Act introduces a right for the prosecution not found in criminal law generally; the applicant for committal for contempt has an equal right to appeal against a finding of not guilty. Why this one type of accused person should be prejudiced in this way is not clear. The Act leaves untouched all the other procedural aspects of contempt: trial remains summary without a jury, and punishments are without limit. The suggestion that no prosecution be made without the consent of either the Attorney-General or the Director of Public Prosecutions has not been implemented by legislation, although in practice the Attorney-General is now the usual originator of such proceedings.

RESTRICTIONS ON REPORTING OF CASES

We have seen that a person charged with an indictable offence first has his charge investigated by magistrates whose task is to decide whether to commit him for trial. Newspapers are free to report everything given in evidence at this hearing and, of course, do report sensational cases at great length. The prosecution of Dr Adams on a charge of murdering a patient raised in an acute form the much debated question of whether this freedom is consistent with that overriding need to ensure a fair trial which has been seen to explain much of the law of criminal contempt. Evidence was given before the magistrates that two other patients of the accused had died in peculiar circumstances while under his care. This evidence was not, and could not have been, given at the trial. Is it not clear that the jury might have been prejudiced by having read newspaper accounts of this evidence?

In 1958 the Departmental Committee on Proceedings before Examining Justices produced a valuable report.[24] It pointed out that neither Scotland nor Ireland had the

English system. There is no public examination of an accused before trial in Scotland. In Northern Ireland, the opening statement by the prosecution before the examining magistrates must not be reported, and the accused can ask the Court to extend this ban to any evidence the admissibility of which he has challenged. The main types of evidence which are usually inadmissible at the trial and might sometimes be given before the magistrates in England are lists of previous convictions and accounts of acts similar to the one charged. The magistrates may properly be told of the accused's criminal record when, having decided to commit him for trial, they are considering whether to grant bail. The rules of evidence which determine when evidence of similar facts may be given are complicated. The magistrates may allow such evidence either through misapplying the law, or because they know that it will be rejected at trial if inadmissible. Northern Ireland always forbids reporting of the prosecution's opening speech because the witnesses may not give evidence which bears out counsel's expectations as outlined in his speech. The Committee was convinced that the present English law worked unfairly for the prisoner, and proposed certain radical changes. Newspapers were to publish no more of the committal proceedings than the name of the prisoner and short details of the charge unless he was discharged by the magistrates. After the eventual trial there was to be freedom to report everything given in evidence before the magistrates, and of course the present freedom to report during trial was to be retained. The Government has failed to implement these sensible recommendations. The opposition to the Report on the part of the Press waving the banner of Freedom was of course tremendous, and presumably the Government has been unwilling to incur that hostility of the Press which the introduction of legislation would no doubt provoke. As recently as February 1962 the Government rejected an amendment to the Criminal Justice Administration Bill which would have implemented the recommendations of the

Tucker Committee. Meanwhile those accused must continue to run the risk of being prejudiced.

It should be added that magistrates have already a discretionary power to hold these preliminary investigations *in camera*. The power has been exercised a little more frequently since the trial judge observed in the Adams case that the power might well have been exercised there, but magistrates are understandably reluctant to incur the odium of newspapermen by excluding them from the Court.

Many judicial proceedings take place in chambers, i.e. in private in the rooms of the judge or some other judicial officer. These are often matters preliminary to trial itself, but not infrequently the final hearing of certain types of case. Judges have often held that newspapers could not report such matters, although the extent to which such reports amounted to contempt was disputed. For example, Mr Justice Paull suggested in the course of the protracted litigation between the Duke and the Duchess of Argyll in the early nineteen-sixties (which aroused so much Press attention) that it was essential for the administration of justice that hearings in chambers should not be reported because they concerned only the parties. The Act of 1960 has clarified the law concerning reporting such proceedings by enacting that such reports shall not, subject to certain exceptions, in themselves constitute contempt, and has thereby rejected the views of Mr Justice Paull. The most important exceptions are proceedings relating to wardship or adoption or maintenance of children, matters relating to mentally disabled persons, matters of national security, or matters relating to a secret process which is in issue in the proceedings.

There are also important restrictions on the reporting of some types of proceedings. Reporters may attend divorce trials but they are prohibited from publishing details of the evidence given. It must be remembered also that a vast number of legal disputes are settled behind closed doors by arbitration – one of the main reasons for the popularity of arbitration is its privacy. Judges, too, often request the Press not to report particular parts of a case – the Podola murder case was an example. The Press will comply although it is not obliged to do so.

Contempt of Parliament

We meet here for the first time this separate branch of English law, the law and custom of Parliament. Although this law does not derive either from statutes or from cases by the Courts, it is equally binding on members of Parliament and on ordinary citizens. It gives many privileges to members of Parliament both collectively and individually. There is an analogy with contempt of Court in that a citizen who is in breach of such a parliamentary privilege commits a contempt. He may also commit a contempt even though his conduct does not involve any breach of privilege; if, for example, he casts aspersions on the dignity of the House of Commons. We shall see that the procedures for dealing with these contempts bear some resemblance to those for contempt of Court. Again, only one particular class of contempts will here be dealt with: those which restrict the citizen's freedom of expression.

Both Houses have always maintained the right to prohibit the publication of debates or other proceedings in Parliament. In the eighteenth century John Wilkes, resentful of this aristocratic impatience with the pressure of public opinion, determined to challenge Parliament. The *London Evening Post* had started to print reports of parliamentary debates; in 1771 the House of Commons sent a messenger of the Serjeant-at-Arms to take the printer to the House. When the printer objected the messenger used force: Wilkes, as a city magistrate, convicted the messenger of assault. The House of Commons duly put Wilkes's fellow magistrates in the Tower for this, but Wilkes successfully defied its efforts to bring him to the House. The upshot was that this attempt to muzzle reporting failed, and Parliament no longer attempts to restrict fair reporting of its proceedings; but when its proceedings are reported in bad faith it has continued to hold the publishers liable to punishment, by virtue of the law of Parliament.

Parliament still, however, effectively curtails the activities of the Press in other ways by virtue of contempt powers, as a selection of recent examples will demonstrate. In 1956 the *Sunday Graphic* voiced its disapproval of the attitude to Egypt of Mr Lewis, M.P.: in an article it exhorted those who shared its disapproval to telephone him to that effect, and gave his private telephone number. In consequence Mr Lewis was inundated with calls which prevented him from having other important telephonic conversations on political matters. The House of Commons found the *Sunday Graphic* guilty of contempt of Parliament on the ground that it instigated others to molest an M.P. while in the execution of his duties. In 1960 Mr Pannell, M.P. for Leeds, asked a question in the House about Fascist propaganda leaflets left in telephone books in the Leeds area, and referred in his question to the possibility of instituting criminal proceedings against those responsible. He then received a letter signed with the name of Colin Jordan, organizer, British National Party, saying:

No doubt when you clamour for our prosecution you will be commended by the Jewish civilians of Leeds and their coloured allies for your zeal. You would do well to take into account the possibility that in the resurgent Britain of tomorrow you and your fellow renegades will face trial for complicity in the coloured invasion and Jewish control of our land.

The House of Commons referred this to its Committee of Privileges which found the letter to be a breach of privilege in that it was an attempt by improper means to deter him from the performance of further parliamentary duties in relation to the leaflets.

The House of Commons takes a serious view of any newspaper comments which reflect on the character of the House. The asserted justification is like that used for some contempts of Court: that the respect due to the House is thereby diminished and consequently the performance of its functions interfered with. The *World Press News* published in 1947 an article written by an M.P. on how newspapers could and did persuade M.P.s by buying them drinks to sell secret information acquired in party meetings. The publisher was reprimanded by the House of Commons for breach of privilege: his allegation of insobriety on the part of M.P.s was castigated as a gross breach of privilege. It further transpired that the M.P. who wrote the article was one of the M.P.s who was selling this information to the Press. The House expelled him.[25]

The introduction of petrol rationing after the Suez expedition of 1956 brought more cases. The *Sunday Express* published an article which suggested that politicians had allowed themselves to be unduly favoured over supplementary petrol. This was held by the House of Commons to be a grave contempt on the part of the editor.[26] The editor's contention that he merely wrote of *politicians*, not M.P.s, was rejected. The House found that the article was, *inter alia*, intended to hold it up to public obloquy as a result of its alleged failure to protest against unfair discrimination of which M.P.s were the beneficiaries. The London *Evening News* published a cartoon which stated that it was very thoughtful of M.P.s to look after their supplementary petrol allocations: this was also held to be a contempt. The editor of the *Romford Recorder* was found guilty for heading an article 'M.P.s Too Kind To Themselves'; he made an ineffectual protest to the Press Council that he was not even allowed to defend himself.[27] In a B.B.C. *Any Questions* programme a Mrs Mary Stocks said that 'the only persons who are reasonably well off under the rationing scheme are M.P.s and potential M.P.s who are nursing constituencies and who apparently have as much petrol as they wish to drive round their constituency.' The Speaker ruled that it was a prima facie case of breach of privilege but the Committee of Privileges in the House held otherwise: this criticism was neither intended to hold the House up to public obloquy nor calculated to diminish the respect due to it and so to lessen its authority.[28]

The severity of the parliamentary law of contempt becomes evident when its procedures are examined. A party may be found guilty without having a hearing, as happened in the case of the editor of the *Romford Recorder*, on the ground that where the breach of privilege is clear a hearing is a waste of time. The House can issue a warrant for the arrest of anybody whom it suspects to have committed a contempt and have him arrested without giving him any reason. They may so arrest him in order to require him to appear before the Committee of Privileges. There he may find himself cross-examined by several Queen's counsel, but he himself is not entitled to be represented by counsel, and still less may he insist on cross-examining witnesses. When the House has found him guilty, it is its normal practice to summon him to the Bar of the House. He is expected, not to say invited, humbly to apologize: his punishment is likely to be the more severe if he does not. The powers of punishment are wide. There is a power to commit to prison. High Court judges, lawyers, sheriffs, and magistrates have all found themselves imprisoned under this power. In 1955 two Australian journalists were imprisoned by the House of Representatives of the Australian Federal Parliament because of newspaper articles. In the opinion of the present Clerk of the House of Commons, Sir Edward Fellowes, the indispensability of this power to commit to prison has been amply demonstrated by experience:[29] this argument is difficult to accept in view of the rarity of the occasions in modern times when the House ever commits to prison. The House of Lords has frequently imposed fines, but the House of Commons has not done so for two centuries. Where the offence is not so grave as to warrant any of these punishments the offender is generally reprimanded or admonished by the Lord Chancellor or the Speaker; if he is not in attendance he may be ordered to be taken into the custody of the Serjeant and brought to the Bar of the House.

Is there any need for this crime of contempt of Parliament at all in so far as it bears on freedom of expression? If an M.P.'s character is attacked he has his remedy in an action for defamation. Serious attacks on institutions of government may be punishable as libel, either seditious[30] or defamatory.[31] The forbidding of reports of proceedings is an anachronism. Unlike contempt of Court, comment of Parliament does not, of course, prejudice litigants. What gap in civil and criminal law is there which needs to be filled by this crime? The case for it seems to stand or fall on a residue of instances where Parliament is hampered in the efficient discharge of its duties: the conviction of the editor of the *Sunday Graphic* for instigating the molestation of an M.P. is an example. The fact that such undesirable interferences with the due discharge of parliamentary functions do not fall foul of the criminal law indicates a small gap in judicial machinery, which ought to be filled.

Although there are gaps in the criminal law, it does not in the least follow that offenders should be tried according to the present procedures. No Englishman should be imprisoned without having had the right to defend himself, to be legally represented, to call and cross-examine witnesses, and to be tried by an impartial body, not by his accusers. The House of Commons ought not to treat trials of citizens as one of its functions: disciplining its members is one thing, punishing outsiders is another. It may well be difficult for the House of Commons to behave like a Court: the solution then is for it to relinquish these powers of punishing citizens, by imprisonment or otherwise, just as it has surrendered its jurisdiction over disputed elections to the judges. The present arrangements have only survived because in recent times Parliament has exercised these powers of punishment with moderation. Let the ordinary Courts decide when the freedom of the Press should be curtailed in the interests of the legislature and let the accused have his trial by jury in those Courts of law.

It may be wondered where the ordinary Courts stand at present in relation to the powers of Parliament. These parliamentary powers, it has been seen, do not stem from statute, so that no doctrine of parliamentary sovereignty inhibits the Courts. Each House asserts its right to be the judge of the extent of its own privileges, while admitting that it could not create new privileges. The Courts treat the law and custom of Parliament as part of the ordinary law of the land. Consequently they reserve to themselves the right to declare the extent of parliamentary privileges and they reject the claim of Parliament to be the sole and exclusive judge of its privileges. At any given moment Parliament may claim that it has a certain privilege and the Courts may deny it: there is no machinery for resolving any such dispute. Conflicts are avoided nowadays because the Courts lean over backwards not to interfere in parliamentary affairs.

In the nineteenth century there was a head-on conflict. When one Stockdale had the temerity to bring, and win an action for libel against Hansard for a defamatory statement contained in a parliamentary report, both he and his solicitor were put in prison.[32] Chief Justice Denman rejected Hansard's defence that there could be no libel because this was a matter of parliamentary privilege, over which the Courts had no jurisdiction. The judge was, however, powerless to protect the prisoners, Stockdale and his solicitor, because the House, as it was perfectly entitled to, omitted to state the reasons for imprisonment on the face of the warrants – the Courts cannot challenge a warrant of Parliament which is not illegal on its face; had the warrant set out the facts, the Court would have been free to reach its independent decision on whether the imprisonment was a lawful exercise of parliamentary privilege.[33] The sheriffs of Middlesex were required by the Court to levy execution for the £600 damages awarded against Hansard, but they sought to appease both Court and Parliament by holding the cash which they duly obtained from Hansard. A Court order compelled them to hand over the cash to Stockdale. For doing so the House of Commons imprisoned them. This lively story shows that Parliament has some effective weapons to use against those who rely on decisions of a Court whose authority it will not accept. But the fact that Parliament might get its way is not equivalent to an authoritative declaration of law in its favour. Nothing has happened since the Hansard affair to resolve the kind of conflict which arose there.

CHAPTER 7

FREEDOM OF RELIGION

RELIGIOUS EXPRESSION

DURING the Middle Ages the Church, not the State, controlled the exercise of religious worship and expression of opinion on religious matters. The State recognized and obeyed the law of the Church, which, before the Reformation, was the papal canon law; the State merely helped the Church to enforce the Church's decrees. The link between Church and State remained very close even after the Reformation. The Tudor principle was that they had common objects: the Church should help the State to maintain its authority, and the State should help the Church to punish nonconformists and infidels. The King was the supreme head of both. The Church exercised its monopoly of control over matters of religious expression through its ecclesiastical Courts. These Courts had power to fine persons for not attending church, or for celebrating mass. They had exclusive jurisdiction over heresy, and as late as 1612, in the case of Legate, a heretic was burned in pursuance of a judgment of an ecclesiastical Court.

Blasphemy and other Legal Restraints

The ordinary Courts first interfered in 1618.[1] They claimed jurisdiction on that occasion by analogy with the offence of sedition: if the accused voiced his opinions on religion in such a way as to threaten a disturbance of the public peace, that was the concern of the ordinary Courts. By the end of the seventeenth century the ordinary Courts were exercising this jurisdiction regularly over blasphemous publications. Starting with Taylor's case in 1676,[2] they justified their jurisdiction by the claim that Christianity was part of the laws of England and therefore any reproach of

Christianity was an offence against the common law of the land. Prosecutions for blasphemy were quite frequent in the eighteenth century, too: the publishers of Thomas Paine's *The Age of Reason* were among the victims: later the publishers of Shelley's *Queen Mab* were convicted.

The last two hundred years or so have witnessed a complete undermining of the dominant position of the Church. It is true that there is still an established Church, with the Sovereign as the head, but these two constitutional features are but meaningless survivals of the old political order. As we shall see, all sects are protected by the law, and the State exercises little coercive authority in religious matters. Parliament gave the lead by passing Acts which gradually removed the disabilities of other religions. A critical factor was the rapid growth of the spirit of toleration among educated classes in the eighteenth and nineteenth centuries. Publications such as Locke's *Letters concerning Toleration* and Defoe's *The Shortest Way with the Dissenters* helped to create this new climate of opinion.

The reward of the Protestant Nonconformists for their contribution to the cause of the Glorious Revolution was the enactment of the Toleration Act of 1689, which removed most of their disabilities and legalized their meetings for worship. In face of the opposition of George III, Burke and his followers were subsequently unable at the same time to sweep away the discriminatory laws against Roman Catholics: for some, Roman Catholicism was not a religious error but a political danger. In 1813 the Unitarians were given the same privileges as had been given to the other Protestant Nonconformists in 1689. In 1829 Parliament, no doubt influenced by the fear of revolution in Ireland, passed the Roman Catholic Emancipation Act, whereby Roman Catholics were relieved of their disabilities, allowed to sit in Parliament and made eligible for most public offices. In 1846 Jews were relieved from the disabilities to which they had remained subject. Many of the disabilities had been imposed by requiring forms of oath which the members of particular sects could not take. When the Test Acts were finally repealed in 1828 the taking of the sacrament ceased to be a prerequisite for office. The campaign of Bradlaugh in the Courts and in the House of Commons in the eighteen-eighties resulted in the removal of disabilities for atheists: the Oaths Act of 1888 permitted an atheist to become a member of Parliament upon affirming his allegiance – an oath of allegiance ceased to be insisted on. The same Act also permits witnesses in Court to affirm, instead of being sworn on oath, when they are atheists or when to take an oath is contrary to their religious beliefs.

Parliament gave one other lead which was destined to facilitate a change towards a correspondingly liberal attitude on the part of the Courts. In 1792 it passed the Libel Act, whereby the whole matter in issue on an indictment for libel was to be left to the jury; and libel included blasphemous libel. In the nineteenth century judges and juries were increasingly reluctant to accept the logical implications for the crime of blasphemy of the 'Christianity is part of the law of England' formula. The judgment of Lord Chief Justice Coleridge in 1883 was the watershed. He rejected the principle that Christianity was part of the law of England and told the jury that 'if the decencies of controversy are observed, even the fundamentals of religion may be attacked without the writer being guilty of blasphemy'.[3] Then in 1917 the House of Lords had to decide whether the objects of a company were criminal because they necessarily denied the truth of Christianity.[4] The House of Lords held that those objects were not rendered criminal merely because they were in conflict with Christian doctrine, and that the crime of blasphemy was not committed by honestly denying the truth of Christianity. The crux is the manner in which the blasphemy is published, not its content. Lord Sumner said:[5]

'Our Courts of law ... do not ... punish irreligious words as offences against God. ... They dealt with such words for their manner, their violence, or ribaldry, or more fully stated, for their tendency to endanger the peace then and there, to deprave public morality generally, to shake the fabric of society, and to be a cause of civil strife. The words, as well as the acts, which tend to endanger society differ from time to time in proportion as society is stable or insecure in fact, or is believed by its reasonable members to be open to assault. ... In the present day reasonable men do not apprehend the dissolution or the downfall of society because religion is publicly assailed by methods not scandalous. ... The fact that opinion grounded on experience has moved one way does not in law preclude the possibility of its moving on fresh experience in the other; nor does it bind succeeding generations, when conditions have again changed. After all, the question whether a given opinion is a danger to society is a question of the times and is a question of fact.'

There has been only one subsequent prosecution for blasphemy of the slightest importance. In 1921 one Gott was charged with selling pamphlets in a London thoroughfare entitled 'God and Gott' and 'Rib Ticklers, or Questions for Parsons'.[6] The Court of Criminal Appeal held that it was not enough that the selling of these tracts might provoke a man of strong religious feelings; the issue was whether they might provoke a breach of the peace by anybody sympathetic to Christian ideals, even though not a practising Christian.

This account of the development of the law of blasphemy furnishes an excellent illustration of the workings of the English judicial system. The theory is that the Courts are bound by previous decisions, and that only Parliament can alter the law. Yet there is no doubt that what would have been blasphemy in the seventeenth and eighteenth centuries does not constitute that crime today, although Parliament has not altered the law of blasphemy. It will be noted how anxious Lord Sumner was to stress that the Courts had not amended the law of blasphemy. We have seen how originally the Courts were able to wrest control of blasphemy from the ecclesiastical Courts by emphasizing their jurisdiction over matters affecting public order. Then the ordinary Courts were soon to subscribe to the doctrine that any challenge to Christianity was blasphemous because Christianity was the law of the land. More recently, that view has become completely out of harmony with public opinion, whereupon the Courts have rejected the contention that mere denial of Christianity is the crime of blasphemy. They purport to conceal this change in the law by turning the wheel full circle and saying that the essence of blasphemy is and always has been the publication of material in such a way as to shake the whole fabric of society and to provoke breaches of the peace. Liberty to attack Christian doctrine does not now endanger the safety of the State so that those who voice anti-Christian opinions do not commit the offence.

What of the future? The judges have left themselves free to take account of changes of public attitude by holding that if to express anti-Christian opinions in a certain way at a given time does in fact in the opinion of a jury shake the fabric of that society or provoke a reasonable element in it to breaches of the peace, this could still be punishable as blasphemy. This no doubt explains why Governments have from time to time refused to abolish the crime of blasphemy.[7] A more practical issue is whether the protection, however limited, which the law of blasphemy at present affords against attacks on the Church of England, extends to other religious denominations, whether Christian or not. In 1838 Baron Alderson held that a scurrilous attack on a Roman Catholic nunnery could not be blasphemy.[8] He said that 'a person may, without being liable to prosecution for it, attack Judaism, or Mahomedanism, or even any sect of the Christian religion (save the established religion of the country)'.[9] But the reason for his decision was that the Church of England was the established religion and so part of the constitution of the country. We have seen that that idea is now exploded. Are we to say that an attack on any Christian doctrine, or indeed on any other religion, can be blasphemous provided that it is calculated to endanger the public peace? One can scarcely believe that protection of Christianity is now confined to the Church of England. Whether one could commit blasphemy by handing out ribald anti-Muslim tracts in the Arab district of an English seaport is a more debatable question.

Restraints Outside the Law

The discussion so far has been of legal restraints on freedom of religious expression. In practice, though not by force of law, there are other restraints. It is of course well known that the B.B.C. rarely allows the expression of rationalist views and when it does the protest from the Churches is loud and long, as after the famous sound broadcast of Mrs Knight some years ago. We have seen that both the B.B.C. and the I.T.A. have religious advisory committees and it would seem that they both strike a fair balance between the various Christian sects in their quite extensive religious programmes. As we have also seen, what is frowned on is the introduction of religious themes in other programmes. Despite the large number of topical discussions now broadcast in such programmes as *Tonight*, *Panorama*, *This Week*, and *Ten O'Clock*, it is remarkable how rarely controversial religious matters are the subject of discussion. The I.T.A. is not allowed to broadcast religious advertisements. Both the B.B.C. and the I.T.A. are restrained from interfering with attendance at church services in that only adult programmes are permitted between 2 p.m. and 4 p.m. on Sundays, and that no home broadcasts other than religious ones are permitted between 6.15 p.m. and 7.25 p.m. on Sundays.

RELIGIOUS DISABILITIES

We have seen that the restrictions formerly imposed on Nonconformists, Roman Catholics, and Jews have successively been swept away. Nor will the Home Secretary in the exercise of his discretionary power to admit aliens apply religious tests, as he made clear in 1946 when a question was asked in the House of Commons about the entry into this country of members of the Oxford Group. A very few restrictions remain. The sovereign must be a member of the Church of England. A person who marries a Roman Catholic is excluded from succession to the Throne. A Roman Catholic probably cannot be Lord Chancellor.

Clergy of the Church of England, Church of Scotland, and the Roman Catholic Church are disqualified from sitting and voting as members of the House of Commons – Bishops of the Church of England have of course twenty-six seats in the House of Lords.

Although the law then does not generally discriminate against a person because of his religious beliefs, it often refuses to make special allowances for them. An accused's religious objection to the use of medicine will be ignored in deciding whether he is guilty of criminal neglect of somebody in his care.[10] Suppose the defendant has injured a Christian Scientist and contends that the plaintiff's recovery has been retarded through his failure to have surgical treatment: it is believed that the plaintiff (where he claims damages) would not be able to plead that it was reasonable for him as a Christian Scientist not to have such treatment if a reasonable non-Christian Scientist would have had it. Suppose, too, that where a doctor exercising reasonable skill would have advised a patient to have an abortion because the death of the patient is otherwise most likely to occur, and on moral grounds a Roman Catholic doctor neither performs this operation nor advises the patient to consult another doctor: the doctor's Roman Catholicism will not afford a defence either in an action of negligence, or, probably, in proceedings for manslaughter.

A certain intolerance towards non-Christian religions and customs persists in the law relating to divorce, which is really only equipped to deal with a Christian monogamous type of marriage. Consequently the Courts will not dissolve a polygamous marriage: they will not recognize such a marriage as one in respect of which they are willing to exercise jurisdiction in divorce. A man and a woman domiciled in Nigeria married there according to a customary law which permitted polygamy, although neither of them, being Christian, intended to take another spouse. After settling in England they went through a marriage ceremony at a register office. The Court held in subsequent divorce proceedings that it could dissolve the English marriage but not the Nigerian one. Presumably the parties remained married according to the law of their domicile.[11] The hardship of this rule is best illustrated by the fact that it prevents magistrates from entertaining proceedings for maintenance by a wife whose marriage was at least potentially polygamous.[12] A wife of a polygamous marriage whose husband has been killed may be severely handicapped if she wishes to claim damages under the Fatal Accidents Acts against those responsible for her husband's death.

Where a person wishes to create a trust, the objects must be consistent with the policy of the law – otherwise the trustee will be forbidden to carry out the trust at all. Before the passing of the Toleration Act trusts for nonconformist purposes were therefore void. It was not until the twentieth century that the House of Lords overruled earlier decisions and held that trusts for anti-Christian purposes[13] or for masses for the dead were valid.[14] Even if a trust is consistent with public policy it may still be necessary to prove that its purpose is charitable in the eyes of the law. If there is an element of uncertainty in the objects of the trust the trust will fail, unless it is charitable, when its funds will be applied for charitable purposes which correspond as nearly as possible with what appear to the Court to have been the testator's intentions. A trust cannot ordinarily be devoted to a particular purpose for ever where the effect would be to prevent alienation of the property – for this would infringe the rule against perpetuities – but gifts to charities are not subject to this rule. Moreover charities are exempt from income tax. The importance of a gift's being held to be charitable is obvious. Trusts for the advancement of the Christian religion are charitable, and so is a trust for any shade of Christian object. A trust for non-Christian religious purposes would probably also be charitable although the law is not clear on this point. On the other hand, a gift for the establishment of a college for training spiritualistic mediums was held not charitable, and in the circumstances the gift therefore failed.[15] With the high rates of contemporary taxation, the effective worth of a valid, though not charitable, gift is greatly curtailed.

EDUCATION

Traditionally, organized education throughout the Western world was religious education. It could hardly be otherwise when the education of children meant chiefly study of the word of God. Even in Protestant countries like England, where the identification of Church and State had, as we have seen, become less close, the basis of education was largely the Bible. Even as late as the Reform Act of 1832 the State did not regard the furnishing of education as a public duty. Elementary education was in the hands of two societies, the one desiring that religious teaching in the schools should be undenominational and the other seeking to teach the principles of the Church of England. Gradually the State started providing financial assistance, with increasing supervision, until by 1870 it was recognized that elementary education was a national responsibility.

Once the State supports schools out of public funds, controversy on the teaching of religion in them is inevitable. Some countries like the United States found the task of harmonizing multiform creeds impossible and prohibited religious teaching in schools altogether. Sharp though the conflict was between Anglican and Nonconformist, England was less heterogeneous religiously than countries like the United States, and a compromise was eventually worked out, which it is believed meets with the general satisfaction of all parties. The present arrangements, which are developed from the Education Act of 1870 and succeeding Acts, are found in the Education Act of 1944. Schools are divided into two main groups, the county schools established by local education authorities of every category, and the voluntary schools which were originally erected by the voluntary effort of persons usually associated with a particular religious sect, whether Church of England, Roman Catholic, or Nonconformist. The problem of welding the voluntary schools into the national system of education is complicated by the inability of the persons owning them to meet the increasing costs of education, both for capital improvement and maintenance, and by the existence of trusts governing the religious instruction to be given in them. Voluntary schools are of two main kinds. In 'aided schools' the managers or governors are responsible for the provision and equipment of the school buildings and for their repair, whereas the local educational authority is responsible for running expenses and inside repairs. The Minister of Education makes a direct grant to aided schools of one half the cost of alterations and repairs. 'Controlled schools' are those where all the expense of maintenance, alteration, and repair is borne by the local education authority, the managers or governors having merely provided the premises.

The Act requires in the case of both county and voluntary schools that the school day shall begin with collective worship and that religious instruction be given. No county or voluntary school can impose a condition that the pupil shall attend or abstain from attending any Sunday school or other place of religious worship. A parent retains the right to withdraw his child from either collective worship or religious instruction. The Act then deals with the situation where the parent wishes his child to have some religious instruction which he has arranged for him instead of that from which he has been excused. If the local authority cannot conveniently move him to another school which provides that instruction, they will allow his withdrawal during the necessary periods so long as they are at either the beginning or the end of the school day. In county schools the collective worship must be undenominational and the religious instruction must not include any catechism and must conform to an agreed syllabus. A conference of representatives of religious denominations, teachers, and the local education authority is charged under the Act with the task of settling this syllabus. The fact that the voluntary schools were built subject to trusts which regulated the religious instruction to be given naturally leads the Act to have different rules for them. Ordinarily religious instruction in controlled schools must still conform to the agreed syllabus, but, if the parents of any pupils so request, the managers are to arrange instruction in accordance with the trust deed or previous practice. The rule is reversed in aided schools where, as a general rule, religious instruction should conform to the trust deed or former practice. For example, when a Roman Catholic school continues to meet out of its own funds one half the cost of repairs and alterations, in return it is recognized that religious instruction will be in Roman Catholicism. Yet, if parents in these aided schools so require, their children must be taught in accordance with an agreed syllabus, unless they can conveniently arrange for them to attend another school where that syllabus is in use.

The regulations concerning appointment of teachers reflect these arrangements. No teacher at a county school is disqualified by reason of his religious opinions, or of his attending or omitting to attend public worship, and no such teacher shall be required to give religious instruction, nor shall his pay or promotion be affected by any of the above factors. Up to one fifth of teachers at controlled schools are to be 'reserved teachers', competent to give religious instruction in conformity with the trust deed or previous practice. Though these reserved teachers are also appointed and dismissed by the local education authority, the managers or governors have the right of veto over their appointment and can require that the local education authority dismiss a reserved teacher who has not given religious instruction satisfactorily. Once again the 'voluntary' school which is not content to provide the premises but also helps to maintain them has the greater power in matters affecting religious teaching. The managers or governors of these aided schools have the power to appoint and dismiss on religious grounds, free from any control by the local education authority, those who provide religious instruction in accordance with the trust deed or former practice.

Section 76 of the Education Act of 1944 provides:

In the exercise and performance of all powers and duties conferred and imposed on them by this Act the Minister and local education authorities shall have regard to the general principle that, so far as is compatible with the provision of efficient instruction and training and the avoidance of unreasonable public expenditure, pupils are to be educated in accordance with the wishes of their parents.

To what extent does this section give a parent a right to choose a school for his child? The matter was tested in *Watt* v. *Kesteven County Council* in 1955.[16] The plaintiff, a Roman Catholic, sent his two sons to a Roman Catholic boarding public school. There was no *local authority* grammar school in Stamford where the family lived, but the defendants, in accordance with their duties under the Act, had offered places for the boys at a suitable *independent* non-denominational grammar school in the town. The plaintiff sought to make the authority pay in full the tuition fees at the public school (which were in fact less than the fees at the Stamford School). The Court of Appeal held that the Act imposed no duty to provide free education at any independent school of the parent's choice. They held that Section 76

does not say that pupils must in all cases be educated in accordance with the wishes of their parents. It only lays down a general principle to which the county council must have regard. This leaves it open to the county council to have regard to other things as well, and also to make exceptions to the general principle if it thinks fit to do so. It cannot, therefore, be said that a county council is at fault simply because it does not see fit to comply with the parent's wishes.

There is no doubt that Section 76 was carefully drafted so as to prevent the authorities from being legally answerable should they fail to carry out the parent's wishes about his child's education, and that the Court interpreted the statute correctly. The Act contemplates that an aggrieved parent will forward his complaint to the Minister who will if he thinks it expedient issue an appropriate direction to the local education authority: this is the kind of administrative remedy normally provided where failure on the part of a local authority to perform its duties is in issue. But is it defensible that the aggrieved parent is not entitled to a hearing before the Minister of Education and has no means of knowing what evidence is before the Minister when he proceeds to make his decision?

SUNDAYS

Certain old Acts restricting activities on Sunday remain on the statute book. Of course these are no longer in harmony with contemporary attitudes, but they remain unrepealed because whatever party is in office, it always believes that, by tampering with a religious issue, it stands to lose some votes and can hope to gain none. Best known of these Acts is the Sunday Observance Act, 1780, which, as subsequently amended, makes it an offence to use a place for public entertainment or amusement on Sundays on admission for money, unless it is a licensed performance of films at a cinema or a musical entertainment falling within the scope of a music licence granted by a local authority or justices of the peace. In practice great ingenuity is shown in bringing entertainment within the ambit of a musical concert, and with the abolition of the system of common informers rather less use of the Act has been made recently. Another curious survival is the Sunday Observance Act, 1677, whereby contracts made by tradesmen and artificers on Sundays in the ordinary course of their business are unenforceable *by* them. The Courts do not approve of the conduct of those who invoke the Act in order to avoid payment, and construe the Act very narrowly. Such contracts are enforceable *against* the tradesman.

Much more modern and important restrictions, and yet also of an unusual character, are those on Sunday trading contained in the Shop Act, 1950. Under this Act every shop must be closed throughout Sunday unless it falls within one of the exceptions set out. There are detailed rules about the circumstances in which Jewish shopkeepers may trade on Sunday, and provision for a tribunal constituted after consultation with the London Committee of Deputies of the

British Jews to decide whether the shopkeeper is in fact a Jew. Shops are allowed to open for the sale of intoxicating liquors, meals (though fish and chip shops must not open), sweets, refreshments, flowers, fruit and fresh vegetables, fresh milk and cream, medicines, vehicle accessories, newspapers, periodicals, and tobacco. Post offices and undertakers may also be open. Local authorities may make orders allowing shops to open until not later than 10 a.m. for the sale of bread, fish, and groceries. Special orders may also be made allowing shops in holiday resorts to sell bathing, fishing, and photographic requisites, toys, souvenirs, books, stationery, postcards, and any article of food. No doubt these lists have been settled after consultation with the trade unions and employers' associations concerned, but they certainly strike the foreign visitor (and not a few Englishmen) as containing some oddities.

CONSCIENTIOUS OBJECTORS

A chapter on religious freedom ought not to end without a reference to the English attitude to conscientious objection to military service. Both in war and in peace a person who 'conscientiously objects' to military service is entitled to appear before a local tribunal. If the tribunal is satisfied that he 'conscientiously objects' it may grant him unconditional exemption from military service, or exempt him on condition that he undertakes prescribed civilian work, or make him liable to call up for non-combatant duties. The objector has an appeal to a central appellate tribunal where once again he is entitled to appear personally and to be legally represented. With the abolition of compulsory military service, these tribunals have been wound up.

CHAPTER 8

FREEDOM AND SECURITY

PROBLEMS of national security have never been greater than they are today. The conflict between cherished individual freedoms and security of the state is sharp. We have to see now how, both in criminal law and in its administrative practice, the United Kingdom attempts to resolve this conflict.

SEDITION

In the eighteenth century the Government made great use of prosecutions for sedition in an attempt to restrict criticism of its conduct in the Press and elsewhere. It turned to this weapon especially, because with the lapse of the Licensing Acts in 1694 it no longer had powers of censorship.

John Wilkes's *Essay on Woman* and his articles in the *North Briton* led to his prosecution for sedition in 1764. The most famous political commentator of the day, Junius, wrote in the *Public Advertiser* an open letter, which was also printed by one Miller in the *London Evening Post*, addressed to King George III which was very critical of the Government and its advice to the King. This is an extract; 'Sir, it is the misfortune of your life, and originally the cause of every reproach and distress which has attended your government, that you should never have been acquainted with the language of truth, until you heard it in the complaints of your subjects.' The Government could not identify Junius, and so it prosecuted the printer, Miller, for seditious libel. The judges of the day were determined not to let the jury acquit on the grounds that the writings were not seditious. Miller was tried by the leading judge of the day, Lord Mansfield, who told the jury that the writings were seditious, and that the jury had only to decide whether the paper was printed and published. The jury ignored what was virtually a direction to convict and promptly found Miller not guilty, to the great joy of the crowds outside waiting in the hope of celebrating Miller's acquittal.[1] Junius followed up with scathing attacks on Mansfield, supported by that judicial champion of freedom whom we met in *Entick* v. *Carrington*, Lord Camden, and by a newcomer, Erskine, soon to become the most famous advocate of his day, if not of all time. Erskine successfully defended the Dean of St Asaph in a famous case of sedition in 1779. Later the Government proceeded against Thomas Paine for his *Rights of Man*. Despite much pressure from judges, statesmen, and his fellow lawyers, and even though the Government stripped him of a Crown appointment for doing so, Erskine insisted on his right to defend Paine, regardless of whether he sympathized with or abhorred his views, and thereby firmly established that vital principle of the English legal profession: that a barrister will accept a brief on behalf of any client in a Court in which he holds himself out to practise. As Erskine said: 'From the moment that any advocate can be permitted to say that he will or will not stand between the Crown and the subject arraigned in the Court where he daily sits to practise, from that moment the liberties of England are at an end.' In 1791 Charles Fox proposed and Erskine seconded in the House of Commons a Bill establishing that it was the province of the jury, not the judge, finally to pronounce on whether a libel was seditious. Despite the opposition of the Lord Chancellor and other judges and their gloomy prediction of 'the confusion and destruction of the law of England', the Bill became the Libel Act of 1792.

The subsequent history of the law of sedition has merely confirmed how right the eighteenth-century juries were. No longer can Governments invoke this branch of the criminal law in order to secure the imprisonment of those who criticize their conduct. In 1886 John Burns, Hyndman, and other Socialists were prosecuted at the Old Bailey for their speeches at a meeting in Hyde Park.[2] The judge told the jury that 'a seditious intention is an intention to bring into hatred or contempt, or to excite disaffection against the person of Her Majesty, her heirs or successors, or the government and constitution of the United Kingdom, as by law established, or either House of Parliament, or the administration of justice, or to excite Her Majesty's subjects to attempt otherwise than by lawful means the alteration of any matter in Church or State by law established, or to raise discontent or disaffection amongst Her Majesty's subjects, or to promote feelings of ill-will and hostility between different classes of such subjects.' On the other hand, he told them: 'An intention to show that Her Majesty has been misled or mistaken in her measures, or to point out errors or defects in the government or constitution as by law established, with a view to their reformation, or to excite Her Majesty's subjects to attempt by lawful means the alteration of any matter in Church or State by law established, or to point out, in order to their removal [*sic*], matters which are producing, or have a tendency to produce, feelings of hatred and ill-will between classes of Her Majesty's subjects, is not a seditious intention.'³ Turning more particularly to the case before them, the judge added: '. . . if you trace from the whole matter laid before you that they had a seditious intention to incite the people to violence, to create public disturbances and disorder, then undoubtedly you ought to find them guilty . . . On the other hand, if you come to the conclusion that they were actuated by an honest desire to alleviate the misery of the unemployed – if they had a real *bona fide* desire to bring the misery before the public by constitutional and legal means – you should not be too swift to mark any hasty or ill-considered expression which they might utter in the excitement of the moment.' The jury returned a verdict of 'Not guilty'.

Look next at the prosecution in 1947 of Caunt, the editor of the *Morecambe and Heysham Visitor*.⁴ At the time when Palestinian Jews were attacking British soldiers in Palestine, the accused had written an article in his newspaper assailing the British Jews and complaining of their alleged blackmarket activities in strong terms. One paragraph stated:

If British Jewry is suffering from the righteous wrath of British citizens, then they have only themselves to blame for their passive inactivity. Violence may be the only way to bring them to the sense of their responsibility to the country in which they live.

He was tried at Liverpool Assizes by Mr Justice Birkett and a jury for publishing a seditious libel. Mr Justice Birkett told the jury that Caunt was guilty if he wrote the article with the intention of promoting violence by stirring up hostility and ill-will between Jews and non-Jews. It was not enough that hostility or ill-will was provoked; 'sedition has always had implicit in the word, public disorder, tumult, insurrections or matters of that kind'. He stressed that the prosecution had to prove that this was in fact Caunt's intention. If the natural consequence of his article was violence and ill-will between Jews and non-Jews, and no explanation or evidence was given by Caunt, then the jury could find him guilty of doing the act with the intent alleged; if, on the whole of the evidence, there was room for more than one view of the intent of the prisoner, and the jury were left in doubt, the prisoner was to be acquitted. He stressed also the great role which the jury had to play in protecting the freedom of the Press. Again, the jury acquitted.

In 1951 the Supreme Court of Canada had occasion to consider at length the common law of sedition.5 They reached the conclusion that the crime requires an intention to incite to violence or to create public disturbance and disorder against the sovereign or the institutions of government and that proof of an intention to promote feelings of ill-will and hostility between different classes of subjects does not alone establish a sufficient intention. There must be proof of an incitement to violence or retaliation or defiance for the purpose of disturbing constituted authority. This important case is in line with the progressive narrowing over the years of this offence and probably represents good English law.

The police must notify the Director of Public Prosecutions before they prosecute for sedition, and he always looks at the matter personally.[6] The crime of sedition is not, then, the means of oppression by Government which it used to be in the eighteenth century. Both judges and juries can be relied on to protect from conviction for sedition those who are devoting their energies to critizing the Government and its policies, or advocating those changes which they are convinced are necessary.

In 1936 the printers and publishers of a newspaper which contained statements reflecting on the Jewish community as a whole were found not guilty of a seditious libel, but guilty of a public mischief.[7] The next edition of the leading text book on criminal law accordingly stated that the crime of public mischief comprises 'such acts as making scurrilous attacks, whether oral or in writing, on a class of the community, or disseminating rumours calculated to cause widespread alarm' and that the judge, not the jury, was to decide whether the statements were a public mischief.[8] In a book written in 1949 Mr Justice Denning (as he then was) criticized this case and the text-book view just quoted. The case has never been followed, the latest edition of the text book omits the quoted passage, and the prevailing attitude is that the offence of public mischief is to be restricted. In 1954 the Judicial Committee of the Privy Council heard an appeal from the Court of Appeal for the Windward Islands and Leeward Islands by a man who had been charged with both sedition and effecting a public mischief.[9] He had been found guilty on the public mischief charge only. Quashing this conviction, the Privy Council held that the judge wrongly told the jury that it was for him to decide whether the speech amounted to a public mischief: the Privy Council stated that it was for the jury to decide whether the facts, in the light of the law explained to them by the judge, amounted to public mischief. They also condemned the practice resorted to in this case of trying a prisoner both for sedition and for causing a public mischief by making the seditious speech, and left open the question whether there was any separate crime of effecting a public mischief, apart from cases of conspiracy. Perhaps, therefore, there is no serious risk of the police again invoking the crime of public mischief for statements like that in the case of 1936 just mentioned. At the same time, in view of the broad view of the crime of conspiracy formed by the House of Lords in the *Ladies' Directory* case,[10] there is the danger of prosecutions for a conspiracy to create a public mischief arising out of publications of this kind; even so, it is believed that the last word on the essential element in the alleged crime would still be with the jury, and therein perhaps lies the greatest protection for the Press and other publishers.

INCITEMENT TO DISAFFECTION

In 1797 sailors of the Royal Navy mutinied at the Nore. Alarmed at the French Revolution which was in full spate across the Channel, Parliament resolved on legislation, and passed the Incitement to Mutiny Act, 1797. Rather surprisingly, inciting troops to mutiny had not been a crime at common law. This Act provided that it was a felony maliciously and advisedly to seduce any serviceman from his duty and allegiance or to incite him to commit any act of mutiny. The Act was originally only a temporary measure and was allowed to lapse in 1805 when it was seen that there was no danger. Indeed, it is now clear that the Nore mutiny was not a politically-motivated rising; the real grievance was inadequate messing and the withholding of pay. Yet the Act was revived in 1817 and remained in force substantially unchanged until the nineteen-thirties.

In 1934 the National Government announced in the King's Speech its intention to introduce a Bill concerning disaffection. It was widely expected that some wider powers for dealing with the Fascist Blackshirts were envisaged. The Bill itself, the Incitement to Disaffection Bill, was very different and created a major political storm. Moving its second reading, the Attorney-General, Sir Thomas Inskip, informed the House of Commons that subversive tracts had been circulated among members of the forces during the preceding few years, and that the object of the Bill was to facilitate the prosecution of those responsible. In fact, the Bill proposed to extend the existing law so much that its opponents could not accept that this was its only object, especially as no adequate evidence of increased attempts to cause disaffection among troops was adduced. Sir William Holdsworth, a Conservative and the leading jurist of the day, described the Bill as 'the most daring encroachment upon the liberty of the subject which the executive Government has yet attempted at a time which is not a time of emergency'. The Society of Friends thought that the object of the Bill was to put in prison their members who possessed pamphlets advocating pacifism. Others held that the Admiralty, in a panic at the Invergordon uprising of the Navy, had insisted on the Bill. Another view was that the Government was determined to muzzle the expression of what seemed to it revolutionary principles recently voiced by Cripps, Trevelyan, Laski, and other Socialists. A more extreme version which gained currency in Left Wing circles was that it was intended to prevent any criticism of the Government. Trade unionists discerned in it the determination of the Government to make troops fire on strikers.

Certainly, the National Government was disingenuous in presenting the Bill as a minor one making procedural changes. The Bill would have made several changes in the law. First, under the then existing legislation the prosecution had to prove, as is usually required in criminal law, that the accused had a guilty mind; for instance that he knew that the person to whom he was speaking was a soldier. Clause 1 of the Bill removed the words 'maliciously and advisedly' from the definition of the offence, so that a person could be found guilty even though the prosecution could not establish that he intended, say, to seduce a soldier from his allegiance. Secondly, not only did the Bill propose to create the new offence of being in possession of documents the dissemination of which would be a crime under Clause 1, but it provided that the mere possession of such documents was an offence unless the accused proved that he had lawful excuse for possessing them – and in practice it is often difficult for the accused to discharge this burden of proving his innocence. A pacifist might have some of his literature in a drawer at home: that would be enough for the prosecution to obtain a conviction unless he discharged the onus of showing lawful excuse. Thirdly, any magistrate, on the application of a policeman, could issue a warrant authorizing him to search the premises of the person named in the warrant and to seize any documents which the policeman reasonably believed to infringe the Bill. A policeman might seek out a magistrate who was a political opponent of the suspect, and without giving notice or hearing to the suspect, obtain the search warrant: the fears of pacifists, trade unionists, and other opponents of the Government were understandable. Fourthly, English law recognizes as of course that one who does not actually commit a crime may nonetheless be convicted of an *attempt* where he has done an act with intent to commit that offence, and where that act is a step towards the commission of that offence which is immediately connected with it. If, therefore, the Bill had been silent about attempts, they would still have constituted crimes as long as they fell within the definition in the previous sentence. But the Bill did not stop there. A person was to be guilty of an attempt if he did or attempted to do, or caused to be done or attempted, any act preparatory to the commission of an offence. The man who boarded a train to Portsmouth might find himself arrested on the train and he might be guilty of a crime under the Act unless he could prove that the object of his journey was innocent.

If all these provisions had passed into law, they would undoubtedly have curtailed civil liberties to a serious extent. In fact the Government bowed before the storm and none of these clauses survived. The words 'maliciously and advisedly' were put back into the Act so that a man would not be guilty unless he were shown to have a guilty mind. Possession of documents was to be no offence unless an intent to commit or help another to commit an offence under the Act were also proved. The power to issue search warrants was taken away from magistrates and was to be exercised by a High Court judge only, and the policeman applying for a warrant had to be at least of the rank of inspector. The clause which purported to extend the law of criminal attempts to merely preparatory acts was deleted altogether.

Nonetheless, in the form in which the Bill survived, there were some important extensions of the old law. The previous legislation restricted the offence to where the accused endeavoured to seduce a serviceman from his duty *and* allegiance; this Act replaced 'duty and allegiance' by 'duty *or* allegiance'. There can be no doubt that this is an important difference. Suppose that a wife persuaded her husband to take an illicit forty-eight hour leave, or not to return to barracks until the day after his leave expired. Such conduct is certainly not an interference with allegiance, but is is an interference with his duty, so that the Act for the first time would make such conduct a crime. Or take a more serious example: suppose that a soldier could not reconcile it with his conscience to obey an order to fire on strikers, and that he was persuaded to disobey such an order by his father, an active trade unionist. The father's conduct was now made criminal, but it is extremely doubtful whether he would be seducing his son from allegiance – the soldier's loyalty to the sovereign could have remained unaffected.

The new offence of being in possession of documents remained (although the prosecution must now establish that the possessor intended to bring about an offence within the preceding paragraph). This section has the desirable purpose of enabling the police to prosecute the man behind the scenes, for instance, the printer who has the documents stored in his warehouse; previously the pawn who was handing out the documents was the only one likely to be apprehended. It is a possible objection that no act by the possessor need be proved – once the police establish possession and intention the man is guilty. The effectiveness of this provision is ensured by the wide powers of search and seizure conferred on the police by the section: under the warrant of the High Court judge they may enter premises by force, if necessary, and seize anything which they have reasonable grounds for suspecting to be evidence of the commission of an offence under the Act.

The Act made it possible either to charge offenders before magistrates for a summary offence, or to indict them and have them tried by jury at Assizes or Quarter Sessions. Previously it had not been possible to proceed before magistrates. The change was a good one, in that it enabled the unimportant mere distributor to receive the summary trial and limited punishment that his offence merited. The Opposition found another aspect of this new alternative sinister and objectionable. They were particularly worried about politically prejudiced magistrates trying such cases. Under the Bill as originally drafted, there was nothing to prevent the police from denying an accused the opportunity of trial by jury and insisting on trial by magistrates in a particular area. Suppose that the offence charged was that of dissuading soldiers from putting down a strike; there was a feeling that a bench of Conservative local employers would not give such a case a fair hearing. The Government responded to this pressure by altering the Bill so as to give the accused the choice of trial by jury. Another objection was not met by the Act. A prosecution under the Act cannot be tried by magistrates without the consent of the Director of Public Prosecutions. Although his post is a permanent non-political one, he is subject to the directions of the Attorney-General, a member of the Government of the day. The objection was that whenever the accused was likely to be tried by a bench sympathetic to him or even composed of persons of his own class the Government would insist on his being tried at Assizes instead, and that such practices would be discriminatory.

The leading text book on constitutional law says that 'the Act goes a long way to arming the Executive with power to restrict the distribution of political propaganda and of pacifist literature'.[11] Is this a fair judgement on the Act in its final form? It must be remembered that there is no restriction on the distribution of any political propaganda unless intent to seduce servicemen from their allegiance or duty is proved. The Act does not restrict in any way the distribution of political propaganda to civilians – the one Act which does that is the Police Act, 1919, which makes it a crime to do an act calculated to cause disaffection amongst the members of a police force. In practice, prosecutions under the Act have been very few, although it is true that the Act appeared to be used harshly on one occasion in the nineteen-thirties. A young student, son of a parson, engaged in casual conversation with an airman in a railway refreshment room. Learning that the airman was a pilot, he asked him why he did not fly to Spain and help the Republicans. The trial judge sentenced him to a year's imprisonment for breach of the Act.

The conclusion must be that although the original Bill conferred unreasonably wide powers on the Executive to interfere with the citizen, the Act, despite some objectionable features, is not now a serious threat to liberty. Indeed, this account of the passage of the Bill through Parliament furnishes an excellent example of the way in which Parliament can operate effectively as a watchdog for freedom.

GOVERNMENT SECURITY

In this section no attempt will be made to deal with the special problem of security in time of war. The scope of the crime of treason, which is particularly concerned with assistance to an enemy, and the emergency rules concerning the detention of enemy aliens will therefore not be examined. The emphasis will be on the safeguarding of such information in the possession of the Government as would, by its unauthorized disclosure, harm the interests of the country.

Official Secrets Acts

In 1878 a temporary writer in the Foreign Office, by the name of Marvin, found himself dissatisfied with his employment: he particularly resented the short working day of his superiors. In August 1878 he had to copy in the course of his duties a secret treaty negotiated between England and Russia. At the end of his day's work he walked down to the office of the *Globe* newspaper and gave them particulars of the secret treaty. To the astonishment of the Government, these were published next day in the *Globe*. The leak was traced to Marvin and the decision made to prosecute him. But for what offence? The Government had the mortification of unsuccessfully prosecuting him for removing a State document.[12] The criminal law was not equipped for conduct like his, so long as no document was stolen. An attempt was made to fill the gap by passing the Official Secrets Act of 1889. This Act made it a crime (among other matters) for a person wrongfully to communicate information which he had obtained owing to his position as a civil servant. The Act could fairly be regarded as an orthodox enactment of criminal law: the burden of proving guilt was on the prosecution, the offences were defined with adequate particularity.

As tension between Britain and Germany developed in the early twentieth century the Government concluded that the Act of 1889 was not effective to stop German spying. In 1909 a German Secret Service officer came to London, for the purpose, as he announced, of interviewing 'suitable candidates' for a new and greatly enlarged espionage system to cover all England. Scotland Yard advised the Government that there was no offence for which they could arrest him. When the police prosecuted those who were using field glasses in the vicinity of harbour installations and the like, they had difficulty in securing convictions because they could not disprove the accuseds' assertions that they were merely bird-watching.

The upshot was the passing of the Official Secrets Act, 1911. Despite its innocuous title, 'An Act to re-enact the Official Secrets Act, 1889, with Amendments' this Act was a very different kettle of fish from its predecessor. In it were many provisions, weighted strongly against the accused, and of a kind most rare in English criminal law, especially at that time. Yet the astounding fact is that this extremely important Bill was given its second reading in late August in the House of Commons, the Attorney-General giving no proper explanation of its provisions and resisting successfully any discussion, and that in less than twenty-four hours from its introduction it passed through all its stages in the House. This Act made it a felony if any person for any purpose prejudicial to the safety or interests of the State approached any military or naval installation or other prohibited place, or obtained or communicated to others information which would help an enemy, or if he made a sketch or note which might help an enemy. The important new features were as follows. The onus was no longer on the prosecution to prove that the accused had a purpose prejudicial to the State. Moreover, if the accused denied that he had such a purpose, the prosecution was free to lead evidence of his bad character, including previous convictions, a course which is ordinarily prohibited in criminal cases. The Act also made it a misdemeanour for a person who has any information of the kind mentioned above, or information which has been entrusted in confidence to him by an officer of the Crown or which he obtained as a Crown servant or while employed in connexion with contracts with the Crown, to communicate that information to an unauthorized person or to retain a sketch or other document without any right to do so. Anyone receiving such a document or information was also guilty unless he proved that the communication to him was contrary to his desire.

In 1920 the Coalition Government announced its intention to strengthen the Official Secrets Act in the light of war-time experience. Introducing the Bill, Hewart, the Attorney-General, was at pains to allay the fears of those who thought the new Bill an attack on the freedom of the Press. This Act, the Official Secrets Act, 1920, made communication with foreign agents a felony under the Act of 1911. It also introduced an offence of a kind not previously found in the criminal law. Ordinarily, before a person may be convicted of an attempted crime he must have taken a step towards the commission of that crime which is immediately connected with it. This Act made it a felony to do any act preparatory to the commission of a felony under the Official Secrets Acts.

Do these Acts strike a fair balance between the security of the State and individual freedom? It may be argued that where the safety of the country is involved it is proper for the criminal law to be much harsher than usual. What must be realized, however, is that the Official Secrets Acts are deliberately framed in terms so wide as to go far beyond the protection of national safety and to cover all kinds of official information unrelated to security: in that extended area such extraordinary rules have no place. It may be retorted that even if the Acts are so extensive it is merely the usual technique of British Governments to assume wider powers than necessary on their reliable assurance that these will not be used except for the important and restricted purpose.

A few random illustrations will show that the Acts have been used for matters unconnected with national security. The *Empire News* had to drop its advertised plan of serializing the memoirs of Pierrepoint, the hangman, under threat of prosecution under the Official Secrets Acts – there would have been communication of information which Pierrepoint had obtained as an officer of the Crown. The systematic way in which the Act is used for matters unrelated to espionage is borne out by these observations of the proprietor of the *Daily Mirror*:[13]

... the Act is now used quite cynically to protect the reputations of ministers and, above all, of civil servants.

As the communication of any official document to an unauthorized person is a serious offence, any accusation against a government servant usually lacks documentary basis. Even if the document has been seen, it cannot be quoted from or paraphrased and a Minister can usually be put up to deny its existence. One of the last occasions of the use of this Act, as I recall, was to raise difficulties about a newspaper report of attacks on nurses by patients in Broadmoor. Thus far have we strayed from the original purpose of the Act.

Major Clayton Hutton invented, designed, and produced many of the escape devices used during the War: buttons containing compasses, silk maps of every country in Western Europe, flying boots with tops that could be ripped off to make a waistcoat leaving a non-military pair of shoes. What follows is his published version of his experiences after the War.[14] He believed that he would get permission to write a book about his war-time adventures but was eventually told that he would be prosecuted under the Acts if he carried out his plan. He heard this news while on an American lecture tour on the same subject, which the War Office had permitted him to make. On his return home he was met by two soldiers who required him to surrender all the documents borrowed from contractors in support of his claim for inventor's rewards from the Royal Commission on Awards, and all lecture notes relating to his service in the Forces. He did not comply and was charged under the Official Secrets Acts with failure to obey the directive and with unlawfully obtaining certain sketches, models, and documents. Hutton then produced letters from a senior officer at the War Office sending him in 1946 sets of the various inventions and a receipt from King George VI's secretary for a similar set of articles and asked whether he too was to be prosecuted. The police took a statement the next day but objected to including the reference to King George VI. Hutton stated that he would inform the Court that the police 'prevailed' on him to exclude these matters from his statement. Air Marshal Sir Basil Embry, despite warnings from the Air Ministry, intimated that he would give evidence for Hutton, whereupon the police asked that he should not appear in uniform. At the hearing the Crown offered no evidence and obtained permission to withdraw the charges.

In 1938 the *Daily Dispatch* published a statement that X was wanted by Southport police on some comparatively minor charge of false pretences. A Stockport police officer went to the home of the reporter responsible for this news item and demanded to know from whom he had got his information. The reporter refused to tell him. He was thereupon prosecuted under the Official Secrets Acts for failure to give information to a police inspector, and his conviction was upheld by the High Court.[15] This conviction led to a parliamentary debate. Obviously, no issue of State security was raised, but there was an official secret, the 'wanted notice' which Southport police had put out to other police authorities but had not handed to the Press. Parliament refused to be content with the Government's assurance that similar prosecutions would not recur. The Official Secrets Act, 1939, consequently amended the Acts, but only by requiring the police to obtain the Home Secretary's permission before exercising their powers under the Act: a journalist who refused a similar request today would still commit an offence under the Acts provided that the police officer had the Home Secretary's backing. Nothing has been done to confine 'official secrets' to matters affecting State security.

In 1962 the House of Lords ruled that members of the Committee of 100 who conspired to incite others to enter a R.A.F. station thereby committed the crimes of conspiring to commit and to incite a breach of the Act. The House held that the accused could give no evidence that their purpose was the peaceable one of protesting against nuclear weapons. Their conduct was for a purpose prejudicial to the safety or interests of the State if it interfered with dispositions of the armed forces. The Court would not listen to evidence that the purposes of the community would be benefited, not prejudiced, by the nuclear disarmament campaign.[16] The Court upheld the dangerous doctrine that whatever is Crown policy is necessarily in the interests of the State.

'D' Notices

It might be wondered how the intolerable restrictions on freedom in areas totally unconnected with national security which are implicit in this legislation have survived Press opposition. Obviously, if a statute so widely drawn were rigorously applied, the Press would continually be under the threat of prosecution for matters of no importance to security and would be afforded no defence. As is commonly the case, the explanation lies in unpublicized unofficial arrangements behind the scenes. It is not surprising that the Ratcliffe Committee on Security Procedures in the Public Service (1962) found that

the Official Secrets Acts are not an effective instrument for controlling Press publication of that kind of 'military' information of some though perhaps no great individual importance, which it is nevertheless most desirable to keep from hostile intelligence. ... [and that] it must often be impossible at the critical moment of publication for the editor himself to say whether he is within or without the provisions of the Acts.[17]

At the same time the Committee misinterpreted the Act in believing that it was confined to information about prohibited places, and information obtained through a wrongful communication by an official; the Committee wrongly inferred that an editor who published information falling outside these categories did not commit an offence under the Acts, although it rightly held that prosecution of the Press under the Acts was in any event unlikely. Almost as soon as the Act of 1911 reached the statute book the Government had to seek ways and means of clarifying and alleviating the position of the Press. Their solution was to set up in 1912 a Committee whose object was to let the Press know unofficially when they could commit an offence without risk of prosecution. This system has survived in essentials to the present day. The 'D' notice system was obviously important during the Second World War, when the Home Secretary had power by Defence Regulation 2 B (1940) to forbid the publication of any newspaper if he were satisfied that it was systematically publishing matter calculated in his opinion to foment opposition to the prosecution of the war to a successful issue (it will be noticed that the Home Secretary was given in law uncontrolled power to decide when a newspaper must cease publication). The existence of this Committee first came to the public notice in 1961 in connexion with the conviction under the Official Secrets Acts of

George Blake. To judge from the comments of members of the Royal Commission on the Press in 1948 when questioning witnesses such as Mr Michael Foot, M.P., they too were unaware of the peacetime operation of the Committee.

The Services, Press and Broadcasting Committee consists of sixteen members. There are eleven representatives of the Press and broadcasting, and the Permanent Secretaries of the Admiralty, the War Office, the Air Ministry, the Ministry of Defence, and the Ministry of Aviation. Its secretary is Sir George Thomson, who was Chief Press Censor in the Ministry of Information during the war: as with other unofficial organs of censorship which we have considered, the Secretary is the man who really counts in the working of the censorship. The Committee has no legal basis whatever. The aim of the arrangements is to make clear to the Press what the Government is willing that it should publish on security matters and what it does not wish it to publish. The Press and broadcasting bodies have the unofficial assurance that they will not be prosecuted under the Official Secrets Acts so long as they comply; the Government expects to prevent the disclosure of technical and strategic information – one may contrast the publication in American newspapers of missile sites under construction. The lists of permitted and forbidden matters are circulated in 'D' notices to the publications likely to be concerned: during the War 'D' notices circulated by the Press Censorship Division of the Ministry of Information contained lists of subjects which were considered detrimental to national security. In addition, 'D' notices were issued from time to time with special prohibitions: this explains, for instance, why, if one wanted to know during the War what was stated in propaganda leaflets dropped on Germany, one had to read American newspapers.

The Minister concerned with the particular subject matter initiates a 'D' notice (which must relate to 'naval, military, and air matters the publication of which would be prejudicial to the national interest'), the contents of which are approved by such members of the Committee as are available in London. The Committee meets only when there is an objection or a new issue of principle. It has, from time to time, sought modification or rejection of a Minister's proposed 'D' notice, although there would be nothing then to prevent the Minister from ignoring the Committee and circularizing the Press directly with a request not to publish certain material. In an emergency the Secretary may issue a 'D' notice on his own responsibility with the concurrence of only two Press members. Individual newspapers are under no obligation to conform to a 'D' notice which the Committee has approved. For instance, the Government issued a 'D' notice in 1956 on its project for a supersonic bomber. Some newspapers took the view that this project was, in the circumstances, beyond the Government's resources and deemed it in the national interest to discuss the matter in disregard of the 'D' notice: no prosecution followed and the project was ultimately abandoned. This case shows how a Government may be tempted to treat 'security' as a pretext for preventing discussion of controversial issues. Although a Minister has been held by the Prime Minister (Mr Macmillan) to be politically responsible for issuing a 'D' notice, this notion of ministerial responsibility has that mythical content which it so often has when national security is involved. Just as Sir Anthony Eden would not answer questions about underwater activities when Commander Crabb disappeared, so also Mr Macmillan has stated that the House of Commons cannot require a Minister to justify his decision to issue a 'D' notice.

In the case of Blake, after a preliminary hearing *in camera*, he was committed for trial on 24 April 1961. On 1 May the Services, Press and Broadcasting Committee issued a letter requesting newspapers not to publish certain facts, and pointed out that the lives of certain persons were in danger. On 3 May Blake was convicted after a trial partly *in camera*. On 4 May newspapers were asked not to reproduce stories from foreign newspapers; this ban was lifted on 8 May. The ban aroused much protest since these reports only contained two facts: that Blake was an agent for both the

British and the Russians, and that he had given away other agents in Berlin. It was not obvious how the reproduction of these facts from foreign newspapers would have affected national security, and the Prime Minister in the House of Commons did not clarify the matter.

Baldwin used other unofficial machinery in 1936 to persuade the British newspapers not to follow the American example of reporting the doings of Mrs Simpson and Edward VIII. Compare too the successful request from the Palace in 1946 to the newspapers not to publish Prince Philip's application for British nationality.

Service Clearance for Books

The Government imposes other unofficial brakes on freedom in the interests of security. Each service Ministry has recognized machinery for clearing books which touch on service matters. In January 1946 all publishers received a circular from the Services, Press and Broadcasting Committee asking them to refrain from publishing certain information about escapes by prisoners of war. Mr Selwyn Lloyd has explained in the House of Commons that service departments work to certain rules of scrutiny when deciding whether to 'clear' books submitted to them – in part these consist of a secret list of prohibited items. Copies of these rules are not available to the public, and they have no legal effect. Presumably these rules must be general in so far as they are not merely a secret list. When clearance is refused reasons will be given. But the author is given no opportunity to argue his case before those who decide; indeed their identity is concealed from him. This is yet another example of a matter which can closely affect a person's livelihood being decided by unknown civil servants according to undisclosed rules without the citizen having any opportunity to present argument or test the reasons on which his application is about to be refused. The usual Government apologia, ministerial responsibility for a collective departmental decision, accountability to Parliament, necessary anonymity of civil servants, decisions of policy, matters of security, are as unconvincing in this instance as they usually are in decisions of this kind.

The Government expects all books affecting security to be submitted to it, and has issued a 'D' notice to this effect about 'escape' books. Ordinarily, it has no legal means of securing compliance, other than the ever-present threat of prosecution for contravention of the Official Secrets Acts. It will be recalled from the Hutton case discussed earlier that the Air Ministry there issued a directive to him that he surrender immediately all the documents in his possession relating to his service in H.M. Forces and, upon his failure to comply, prosecuted him under the Acts for retaining information and documents contrary to his duty. It uses other methods to secure compliance. For example any employee or consultant of the United Kingdom Atomic Energy Authority is required to sign a declaration that he understands that any note made or acquired by him during the tenure of his appointment must be surrendered unless he has written sanction to retain it, and that he is liable to be prosecuted for retaining without that sanction. Yet the Official Secrets Acts merely make it an offence to retain a note 'which relates to or is used in a prohibited place ... when he has no right to retain it'. Plainly, the Act is much narrower than the terms of the declaration which the employees and consultants are given to sign, although the form gives the misleading impression that the signatory is merely declaring his understanding of the consequences of his violating the Act. At the same time the declaration gives the false idea that whether the consultant commits an offence by retaining a document depends on whether he has first obtained permission of the Authority to do so.

The publication by Lieutenant-Commander Lithgow of a book, *Mach One*, which contained information about military aircraft revealed one legal control sometimes available to the Government. Mr Lithgow had obtained this information in his capacity as an employee of Vickers-Armstrongs, and had not submitted the manuscript of his book for security clearance because he was under the mistaken impression that his employers had done so. In 1954 Mr Selwyn Lloyd, in reply to a parliamentary question, explained that all manufacturers of aircraft and other security weapons are under a contractual obligation to obtain security clearance for books published by them. The legal sanction behind that arrangement is obvious. What is far from clear is Mr Lloyd's further statement that the firms concerned were also made responsible for their employees. How can a contract between a Ministry and a firm impose liability on the firm if somebody who was an employee publishes a book without security clearance? Only if the firm were required to include in its contracts of employment with each employee a clause that the employee was not to publish a book without prior Service clearance. It is not the practice to have such terms in contracts of employment. Presumably the sanction is of an indirect kind only; there is no means of reaching the employee unless he is prosecuted under the Official Secrets Acts – he is not in contractual relation with the Ministry – but the Ministry could in future contracts prevent the firm (or any other firm) from employing in connexion with the work a person who had ignored the security clearance arrangements.

Those who have disclosed to foreign powers secrets about atomic energy obtained in the course of state employment, such as May and Fuchs, have been convicted under the Official Secrets Acts. The Government has decided, as a matter of policy, to conduct research into atomic energy, even for peaceful purposes, through its own agencies, especially the Atomic Energy Commission, rather than in universities. One consequence is that such work, and the knowledge acquired from it, is a state secret, so that those employed are subject to the Official Secrets Acts. Had such work been carried on in universities without any contractual relation between Government and university, even though with Government finance, university staff who mentioned to their scientific colleagues the results of their researches would not for that reason have been guilty of offences under the Acts.

When the impending publication of the Casement diaries by a crime reporter was announced in 1926 the author was promptly summoned to the Home Office, and informed by the Home Secretary and his chief legal adviser that he would be prosecuted under the Official Secrets Acts if he proceeded. The author has related how, in consequence, he had to abandon publication of the book.

Cabinet Secrets

A particularly important body of secret information is that derived from Cabinet meetings. Control over Cabinet secrets is effected first by the all-pervasive Official Secrets Acts. Any member of the Cabinet who reveals to others, however long after the event, any information obtained at a Cabinet meeting, is guilty of a criminal offence. In 1943, the son of Mr George Lansbury was convicted under the Official Secrets Acts for publishing verbatim in a biography of his father a memorandum prepared by his father for the Labour Cabinet of 1929–31 of which his father was a member. One upshot of this case was a change in practice which made the offence less easy to commit – for the first time Cabinet members were prevented from retaining Cabinet papers.

Cabinet members are subject to another more subtle form of control. They are always made Privy Councillors, all of whom are required to swear an ancient form of oath to keep the Queen's counsel secret. The disclosure of any information obtained as a member of the Cabinet would violate this oath. There is a recognized procedure when a present or former Cabinet minister wishes to act contrary to his oath. He applies to the Prime Minister of the day, who refers the matter to the Secretary to the Cabinet. The Secretary advises the Prime Minister whether publication would be detrimental to the public interest, and the Prime Minister advises the Queen accordingly. Thus, Sir Winston Churchill was permitted, under the Attlee administration, to include Cabinet material in his war memoirs, and Sir Anthony Eden included Cabinet secrets in his book on Suez with the approval of Mr Macmillan. There is a misconception, especially in the House of Commons, that there are many exceptions to this rule: Mr Bevan believed that he needed no permission to explain to the House why he had resigned from the Attlee administration. It is widely believed that the procedure applies only to publishing Cabinet papers, and does not prevent a Cabinet member from explaining his part in some decision of policy arrived at by a Cabinet of which he was a member. In fact, there are no exceptions to the requirement. What often happens in practice is that the Government turns a blind eye when former members disclose Cabinet secrets in violation of their oath of secrecy.

Government Papers

What of the disclosure of Governmental information by permitting scholars and others to have access to it for research purposes? The normal practice of the Government is to transfer to the Public Record Office, and thereby to make available to public inspection, documents fifty years old. Even then documents in certain classes, together with any other documents named by the Government of the day, are excluded. A typical expression of discontent with this rule was afforded by the repeated demand for access to the diaries of Sir Roger Casement. The rule is one typical facet of British public life. A British student of government will often learn more from a short period in Washington about the American administrative process than he can learn about his own from a lifetime in England. The Government and the senior members of the Opposition are agreed on one thing: that the less the public knows about the process of decision-making the better. Whether this is an understandable confusion of what is politically and administratively convenient with what is in the public interest may well be asked. One consequence of this, among many, is that the British citizen has less protection when decisions affecting his private rights are made than in many Western countries. Whether he be a playwright having his play banned by the Lord Chamberlain, an author being refused permission to publish a book, a householder being refused a telephone, he has no legal right to a hearing, or to know the reasons for refusal. Those who seek improvement of these procedures are met by a solid wall of resistance from the Government of the day, whatever its complexion. Civil servants themselves are usually helpful in discussions with outside experts and often appreciate exchange of views with them about their work, but when the time comes for permission to publish, they have to refer the decision to the top where the answer is only too likely to be 'No'. And American visiting scholars, accustomed to a more liberal order, to whom it never occurs to seek permission, are not popular with the British Treasury and other departments when they inform the British public for the first time of the processes by which they are governed. What is particularly irritating is that top people in Government have appeared quite willing to violate even the Official Secrets Acts in disclosing information to the appropriate other 'top people', like the editor of *The Times* – one has only to read memoirs and biographies of the thirties for proof of this. The 'leak' is no new Transatlantic phenomenon of the nineteen-sixties.

Security Tests on Employees

Although the Official Secrets Acts constitute a strong penal sanction against disclosure, they operate only to close the stable door after the horse has bolted. The British Government has also rightly concluded that the imposition of loyalty oaths on the American pattern would be ineffective. No doubt the test oath is of value against a Jesuit, a Presbyterian, or a Quaker, but to invoke it against those who accept lying as a legitimate political weapon is peculiarly naïve. For these reasons, it is accepted that the State as an employer is entitled to keep bad security risks out of employment involving security considerations. At the same time, as the Radcliffe Committee on Security Procedures in the Public Service pointed out in 1962 [18] when criticizing the Report of the Conference of Privy Councillors of 1956, the real threat to security is not from declared Communists who might have access to state documents, but from the Russian Intelligence Service.

In March 1948 the defections of scientists like May and the course of the cold war caused the Government to introduce special measures for the first time while we were at peace. Where a particular post involved some security risk, a special investigation was to be conducted to ascertain whether the civil servant selected to hold the position had any communist or fascist associations. A civil servant whom his Minister found to be unreliable was allowed to have his case reviewed by three Advisers, specially appointed for such purposes. Sir Hartley Shawcross stated that by the end of 1953 these security measures had been applied to about 17,000 out of over a million civil servants because the posts they occupied might involve some degree of security risk. As a result, 148 were suspended. Of those, 28 were reinstated after inquiry had shown that they were loyal and reliable; 69 were transferred to non-secret work; 19 resigned; and 9 were on special leave pending decisions in their cases; only 23 were dismissed, and these because their qualifications were such that they could be employed only in secret work. In the following two years three were transferred, one resigned, and none was dismissed.

The escape to Russia of Burgess and Maclean, senior civil servants in the Foreign Office who had access to vital information, caused the Government to set up in November 1955 a Conference of Privy Councillors to examine the security procedures applied in the public service and to consider whether any further precautions were called for and should be taken. The members were the Lord President of the Council, the Lord Chancellor, the Home Secretary, Lord Jowitt, Mr Herbert Morrison, and the Permanent Secretary to the Treasury. The Conference reported to the Government in 1956, but the Government stated that in the public interest neither the Report nor the recommendations could be published in full. All that was issued was the substance of the report, so far as the Government thought that it could be made public, and some of the recommendations.[19] This document pointed out that the chief risks were not professional agents for foreign powers but Communists and their sympathizers whose loyalty to their country was undermined by their political beliefs. It took the view that a serious character defect, such as drunkenness, homosexuality, or drug addiction might well be the determining factor in deciding whether to dismiss or transfer a civil servant.

The Government accepted the recommendations in principle and in 1957 announced revised procedures for dealing with security risks. A civil servant employed on work vital to the security of the State was to be regarded as in doubt on security grounds if he were, or had recently been, a member of the British Communist or Fascist parties, or, in such a way as to raise reasonable doubts about his reliability, was or had recently been sympathetic to Communism or Fascism, associated with Communists or Fascists or their sympathizers, or was susceptible to Communist or Fascist pressure. No further clarification of 'sympathy' or 'association' could be afforded: each case would be decided on its own merits.

The Minister first rules whether there is a prima facie case. There is perhaps an analogy with the ruling of magistrates whether to commit an accused for trial. The outstanding difference is that whereas the accused in the latter case is given notice of the charge, confronts the witnesses for the prosecution, and may cross-examine them and be legally represented and give evidence himself, here the first the civil servant learns of it is after the Minister has decided that there is a prima facie case against him. When he is told of his prima facie guilt, he will not be given any particulars which might involve the disclosure of the sources of the evidence against him. The Minister will reconsider his prima facie ruling in the light of any written representations sent to him by the civil servant. If he adheres to his ruling the civil servant may ask the Minister to refer the case to the three Advisers. None of these is a lawyer and in 1948 the Prime

Minister, Mr Attlee, said in reply to a parliamentary question that there was no need for them to be legally trained.

The terms of reference of the advisers were also revised. Mr Attlee had stated in 1948 that details of the charges would be available to the civil servant. This is no longer allowed in so far as the disclosure of sources of evidence might result. He is not allowed to be represented, whether by a lawyer or otherwise, except that in September 1962 the Prime Minister acceded to a request of the staff side of the Civil Service National Whitley Council that a friend, who might be a staff association official, could accompany him in presenting his opening statement, but would be prohibited from being present at the rest of the proceedings. He is not entitled to know of the evidence against him, and he is denied any opportunity to cross-examine witnesses. He is not allowed to bring witnesses to contradict whatever he might guess the evidence against him to be, except that he may ask third parties to testify as to his record, reliability, and character. He has no facilities by way of subpoena for ensuring the presence of witnesses. There is no machinery for having the evidence against him given on oath. No members of the public are allowed to be present.

The Advisers then advise the Minister whether his prima facie ruling has been substantiated. If they disagree or have no firm opinion they are to assess the evidence in detail. The civil servant knows nothing of the advice tendered. The Minister can still adhere to his original opinion even though the Advisers dissent.

The Government interferes not only with civil servants but also with employees of private firms engaged on secret work. It does so by always including in a contract for such work a provision for defining the secret matters on that contract. The Minister is empowered by the contract to call for a list of the employees who will have access to these secrets in the course of the work, and to direct the contractor that particular named persons on the list shall not have access. In short, the Government exercises a contractual right to bar named employees of contractors from access to secrets as defined in the contract. Upon breach by the contractor, the Government is empowered to terminate the contract. Up to 1956 this power had been formally exercised nine times, although there is no doubt that many more employees had been dismissed or transferred on Governmental suggestion, even though the firm had not resisted to the point of the Government having to issue a formal direction. An employee of a private firm was not entitled even to those minimal protections accorded to civil servants, nor could he have the case heard by the three Advisers.

In 1956 Imperial Chemical Industries had to dismiss their assistant solicitor, Mr Lang, because the Government announced that a condition of placing any further secret contracts with the firm was that he should have no access to the secrets. In fact, he could no longer be employed as assistant solicitor in view of this requirement. There was a debate in the House of Lords and the matter was raised at question time in the House of Commons. The Government refused to inform Lang of the charges against him or to state after the event why he was to be denied access to secrets. The Government refused to allow him to bring his case either before the three Advisers or a panel of independent legal advisers: he had previously been given the choice of being interviewed by the Second Permanent Secretary to the Ministry of Supply or of waiting to see whether eventually the Advisers would be empowered to deal with cases like his. He saw the civil servant, and came away with the impression that the reason for the action against him was that before marriage his wife had been a Communist. Although Lang was denied an appearance before the Advisers, the Government announced at the end of the debate on his case that in future employees of private firms would be allowed to go before them. These employees are denied representation at the proceedings.

Are these procedures fair? The Government's attitude is only understandable in the light of the policy declared by the Conference of Privy Councillors and accepted by the Government:

It is right to continue the practice of tilting the balance in favour of offering greater protection to the security of the State rather than in the direction of safeguarding the rights of the individual.

The procedures afford the maximum protection to State security and leave the citizen stripped of any rights which might, even remotely, militate against security.

Above all, the citizen has no legal rights whatever under these procedures. It is the consistent policy of British Governments to avoid putting themselves under judicial controls whenever possible. If a person is not accorded the protection, such as it is, allowed him by the arrangements already described, there is no Court to which he can complain. This defect is particularly important where one is dealing with vague words like 'security'. 'Security' is an abstraction, and the citizen is at the mercy of the administrators who will define it as they please. To tilt the scales against liberty in favour of security is serious enough – when security is undefined the threat to the citizen is manifest. Contrast a case in the United States, where a civil servant was liable to dismissal 'in the interest of the national security of the United States': he was able to take his case to the Supreme Court of the United States which reversed the Administration's dismissal of him on the ground that there had been no proper determination that 'national security' was affected.[20] Or take the decision in 1959 of the United States Supreme Court that the right to follow a chosen profession free from governmental interference is so important that in the absence of Congressional authorization it was unconstitutional to deny a worker access to classified materials essential to his job by proceedings in which he was denied the safeguard of confronting adverse witnesses.[21] The justification in the innumerable cases of Englishmen being denied access to the Courts in situations where judicial scrutiny is standard practice in the rest of the Western world is always the same: ministerial responsibility. In the words of Lord Kilmuir, then Lord Chancellor, the balance 'must be struck by a Minister who is responsible to Parliament;

whose decision it is; who can be questioned in Parliament;
... and who is there to be shot at.'[22] The value of this
protection can be measured by looking at the proceedings
of the House of Commons ten days previously. The Minister
of Supply was asked on what grounds he had denied access
on the part of Lang to secrets: he refused to answer, and no
doubt was within his constitutional rights in so refusing.
What is the point of stressing the right to ask a question on
matters of security when the Minister can be relied on never
to answer? The political accountability of a Minister is a
completely inadequate substitute for the right to take one's
case before the Courts.

Forgetting for the moment that the citizen, then, has no
legal 'rights' we must now appraise the effectiveness of the
unofficial safeguards afforded to him under the existing
procedures. It is obviously of the first importance that the
employee should have full details of the charges against him:
it is not enough that vague statements like association with
Communists be used; he should have the names and dates.
The rules laid down by the Government in 1957 make no
such specific references. There is no means of knowing
whether such details are given; one can only say that the
rules do not appear to envisage their being given. If the
employee does not know when and where he is supposed to
have been associating with Communists, how can he refute
the charge, or perhaps show that security officers are in
error? One's guess is that such details are not given, lest
the source of the evidence be revealed.

We have seen that the employee cannot be represented by
anybody throughout the hearing before the Advisers. To
deny him legal representation is absolutely inexcusable.
When the Society of Civil Servants protested at this the
Prime Minister told them that the Advisers were the employee's friend, and that the presence of yet another friend
might lead to the Advisers having to abandon or severely
curtail their attempts to give the individual the maximum
chance to clear himself. In short, the argument is: we have
decided to appoint the judges as your advocate; if you have

your own advocate the judges will cease to be your advocate. This argument is unconvincing and the objection remains in substance after the limited concession of September 1962 already referred to. Even if the Advisers really fear that a representative would glean intelligence from their questions which an unaided civil servant would not, why not put a security check on the representatives? Why not let the employee decide what will serve his interests best? The hearing itself bears no resemblance to a Court proceeding. None of the witnesses for the Government is there to be cross-examined. Why not? Because it would disclose their identity. But the evidence may be that of a neighbour, or a fellow-employee. Departments were requested by the Report of the Privy Councillors to inform on employees. The interests of security may demand that the identity of security agents be concealed. But why should a man whose whole livelihood is menaced be prevented from confronting his workmates or neighbours who have spied on him? The answer that they will be discouraged from informing in the future is inadequate, but it shows the consequences of the 'tilting' to which the Government is committed. When a man is charged with a specific offence, as in the George Blake case, none of these rights is withdrawn. The solution there is to hold the trial *in camera*. Why should a person charged with treason be allowed to confront his accusers, and yet a person about to be dismissed because he is likely to commit treason be denied these minimum judicial rights?

The task of the Advisers is a curious one. They do not see witnesses; they cannot elicit information beyond that supplied by the Minister. They are at one and the same time to help the employee and to evaluate the cogency of each strand of evidence. This seems a job for the most experienced judges in the land. But when the system was introduced in 1948 Mr Attlee announced that it would be better not to employ any lawyers: the task was given to a couple of superannuated civil servants and an octogenarian retired trade union official. And yet even at the height of the war, when large numbers of enemy aliens were being detained under the defence regulations, they were entitled to have their cases heard by a distinguished lawyer before the Home Secretary decided upon internment.

The position of the Minister is even more curious. He first of all decides whether the employee is prima facie guilty without ever seeing the employee, but presumably having seen the other witnesses. He then takes advice from three men who do not see the witnesses he has interviewed, but who can see any witnesses, whom he has not interviewed, called by the employee. Upon receiving advice from the three men he decides whether to adhere to his original view. After the Minister has decided to uphold his decision he gives the employee a further opportunity to make representations. What about? The employee gets no transcript of the record before the Advisers; he is shown nothing of the advice given by the Advisers to the Minister. The Minister's decision is final.

These procedures are a travesty of justice as Englishmen are accustomed to it. They are what is to be expected in an area where Government is in the saddle, and the senior Opposition politicians soon hope to be. That civil servants and privately employed citizens should have their careers ruined by procedures like this is inexcusable. One wonders whether the British Government is aware of how badly its procedures compare with those followed in other parts of the Western world, where it would be unthinkable, for instance, to deny a man a lawyer. It may be said: look how few dismissals and transfers there are. But does the Government publish regular lists of the cases heard by the Advisers? And the Institution of Professional Civil Servants sees something more sinister in this rarity of instances – transfers and denials of promotion for security reasons without the victims being told and without their being able to invoke such protections as there are. It is a further weakness of the arrangements described that the civil servant has no legal redress if he is by-passed completely. The Radcliffe Committee found that, rather than refer a case to the three Advisers where it was doubtful whether Communist associations could be proved, the establishment officer would be astute in seeing an opportunity to remove the suspect to a less sensitive post; the Committee found this to be a not altogether satisfactory state of affairs.

There is another big gap in the procedural arrangements. The Government has publicly stated that character defects, as distinct from Communist sympathies, might prejudicially affect promotion or posting, and might result in exclusion from a sensitive post. Such cases are outside the jurisdiction of the three Advisers. The Radcliffe Report stated that 'Departments appear to follow no consistent practice as regards intimating to him [the suspect] any formal finding or decision adverse to him or providing him with a right of appeal to the Head of the Department under normal departmental procedures.'[23]

Soldiers, too, are liable to be dismissed on security grounds: twenty-seven were dismissed in the five years to July 1956. Those engaged on secret work are also screened. Other countries recognize that their cases should be heard by procedures similar to those for civilians. Not so Britain. The soldier is challenged, given no information which would compromise the source from which it is obtained, and invited to make representations. He is given no opportunity of going before the three Advisers or any similar body. The War Office correctly points out that the Crown may lawfully discharge a man at any time in his own interests or to meet the requirements of the Service, and maintains that it would be contrary to the policy of the Department to disclose reasons for its decisions in this matter.

Screening also takes place of persons seeking secret employment. The Ministry of Supply expects university teachers to answer detailed questions about both their students and colleagues who seek employment on secret work. Information as to their political affiliations is particularly sought. Schoolmasters are expected to notify M.I.5 officials, upon request, of the political affiliations of their pupils, a practice which has had the support of the Minister of Education.

CHAPTER 9

FREEDOM TO WORK

ONE of man's most cherished freedoms is the right to earn his living. 'Freedom to work' is a slogan less familiar to the Englishman than say 'freedom of property'. Consequently, its legal basis is less secure. Yet one would conjecture that it is a freedom which is going to become more important and obtain more legal protection. Britain lags behind in its industrial charter; in its devising of solutions to problems of redundancy, movement of labour, automation, provisions for adequate notice. Chiefly because there is so little legal protection now, there is little to write about some of these aspects. But they will form part of the law's content in the future. 1963 has seen the passing of the Contracts of Employment Act, which, when it comes into force, will require employers to give a minimum period of notice of dismissal: four weeks for employees of five years' standing, and two weeks for those of two years' standing. Similarly, redundant railwaymen are to be offered compensation by the Railways Board.

We shall not deal again with restraints on that right imposed in the interests of security. Our concern here is with the protection afforded by the law to the worker against his employer and against his trade union, and with the obstacles in the way of his earning a living in the way he chooses.

CONTRACT OF EMPLOYMENT

If an employer dismisses his employee in breach of contract, the employee cannot ordinarily compel the employer to keep him in the job – the Courts will order the specific performance of many types of contract, contracts for sale of land, for instance, but they will not require an employer to carry out a promise to employ a man for a certain period.

In exceptional cases like the one we shall now describe, however, the Courts will treat a relationship as creating a status going beyond that of employee. All the dockers of the United Kingdom are employed by the National Dock Labour Board, which is responsible for allocating them to available work on the docks. In 1955 Vine, a docker, was summoned to appear before the disciplinary committee of the Southampton Dock Labour Board for an alleged refusal to obey an order to work for a particular stevedore. After inquiry, the committee struck him off the register of dockers. Vine was thrown out of work: once he was removed from the register he was unemployable as a docker. Vine took an action against the Board all the way to the House of Lords. The House of Lords found that the disciplinary committee acted illegally in removing him. The Board had no power to entrust to the disciplinary committee the power to remove for breaches of discipline: that was the responsibility of the Board alone. The House of Lords had no difficulty in deciding to award damages to Vine for wages lost between the removal and the trial. But Vine wanted more than that: he wanted his name to be put back on to the register of dockers and a declaration by the Court to that effect. The House of Lords declared him to be reinstated, so that it was as if he had never been off the register, distinguishing his case from the ordinary case of unlawful dismissal on the ground that Vine had more than an employment: he had the status of a docker, and this key to his employability had to be protected as such.[1]

Cases like that of Vine are exceptional. In the ordinary case no harm is done provided that the unlawfully dismissed man is fully compensated in damages, for he can seek elsewhere alternative employment in his trade. If, say, a man has a contract which has three years to run, the Courts will estimate how much earnings he has lost through the employer's breach. This does not mean that he will recover three years' loss of salary – from this figure there will be deducted everything that he will earn in some other job in the same period, or that he could reasonably earn if he took diligent steps to obtain other work. If, however, he is dismissible on a week's notice, his damages will not exceed the loss of a week's earnings. Frequently, a man may be dismissed in a totally unreasonable manner and in circumstances which expose him to public humiliation. The dismissal may even be made in such a way that it will be very difficult for him to obtain fresh employment. It is a serious defect in English law that the employee gets no compensation whatever on account of losses of that kind. He cannot recover any more than he would have earned during the period which he was legally entitled to stay in the employment – the law of contract gives no compensation for humiliation, distress, the reprehensible behaviour of the employer, or the harm to reputation and character which is suffered by the dismissed employee.[2] English law falls behind that of other Western countries in this matter.

An employer often requires an employee to agree that after leaving his present employment he will not compete against his employer, either by setting up in business on his own account or by entering the service of a rival trader. The law, however, does not allow the employer to impose such restrictions as he thinks fit on the employee. The employee is entitled to use his skill once he has left that employment, even if he acquired it there. Two matters only may the employer guard himself against: the use of trade secrets learned by the employee, and the risk of his customers being exploited. If the employment is such that customers will rely on this employee's skills or deal with him directly to the exclusion of the employer with the result that he may gain their business if he sets up on his own account, then the employer can protect himself by covenant. Even so, the agreement must be reasonable with respect to the interests of the parties, both in respect of area and duration. A contract by a junior reporter on a Sheffield newspaper not to be connected with any other newspaper business carried on within twenty miles of Sheffield was held to be void;[3] a lifetime's restraint imposed on a pathologist's assistant was also void.[4] In short, the Courts recognize that it would be contrary to public policy to allow a servant to deprive himself or the State of his labour, skill, or talent.

THE TRADES UNIONS AND THE WORKMAN

An important right, in both political and industrial spheres, is the freedom to associate with others in a common enterprise. Englishmen are great 'joiners', and they have been aided by the law in this. English law gives citizens remarkable freedom to join together in political associations – the Campaign for Nuclear Disarmament is a contemporary illustration. The trade union movement also benefits from this liberty. The Trade Disputes Act, 1906, put on a firm basis the unions' freedom of organization. The only category of employees to be denied this freedom of organization are the members of the police force, although civil servants were similarly restricted between 1927 and 1946. The trade unions have of course utilized this freedom to create the conditions in which a man is able to work for a fair wage in proper conditions. But along with this unrestricted freedom for trade unionism are attendant risks of abuse of power. In particular, there is a clash between freedom of union organization and the right to work.

It is a commonplace that in many factories there is now a closed shop: a man cannot be employed in a particular trade unless he is a member of a particular union. There is no law which lays this down – it is the practical expression of the power of the union – and, conversely, English law does not make 'closed shops' illegal. How and in what circumstances will the Courts aid a workman who is prejudiced by the 'closed shop' system?

The common case is of the man who has been expelled from the union, and is thereby effectively prevented from following his trade. Mr Spring, along with 10,000 other dockers, left the Transport and General Workers Union and joined the National Amalgamated Stevedores and Dockers Society. The Trade Union Congress had a Bridlington Agreement designed to prevent unions from poaching each other's members. Because they thought Spring had been poached, the Trade Union Congress ordered the National Amalgamated Stevedores and Dockers Society to expel him. Spring had never agreed to this condition about poaching, so that to exclude him on that account was illegal. He therefore obtained a declaration from the Court stating that his expulsion was void and an injunction restraining the union from denying his status as a member.5 As other trade unionists have found out, the sting in an injunction is that those who ignore it are liable to be imprisoned for contempt of Court. A decision of the House of Lords extends the protection.6 Mr Bonsor was expelled from the Musicians' Union: he could not obtain employment as a musician in consequence, and was driven to accept a job scraping rust off Brighton Pier. When he sued the union, the Court declared that the branch secretary acted in breach of the rules of the union in removing him. So far the case is simple: it merely confirms that the Court will not allow a union to disregard its own rules in punishing a member. But Mr Bonsor was not content to seek reinstatement – what he (and later his widow) sought was damages for loss of livelihood. The House of Lords laid down the important rule that when a union expels a member in breach of contract – the union rules form the contract – the member is entitled to damages for breach of contract, as well as reinstatement. Whatever reason the union may have for exclusion (or lesser deprivation such as denying him office in the union) – to take some actual incidents, the man may fall in with his employer's request to work overtime, he may refuse to join in an illegal strike, he may work too hard and upset the union's plans for piece work rates – the Courts will give him a remedy if the union violates its rules. Moreover, whatever the rules may say, he is entitled to notice of the complaint against him, to be heard by the union before he is punished, and to have a fair hearing not marred by the grosser forms of bias: these rights of natural justice the Courts will insist on.

We turn next to the case of Mr Huntley.7 His offence was

to refuse to join in a one-day strike at a Hartlepools ship-yard. He was summoned to appear before a branch meeting of the Amalgamated Engineering Union, then told that the matter was one for the district committee, although nobody mentioned what action against him was contemplated. When he left the room the meeting decided to recommend his expulsion. The district committee was informed of this recommendation, but not that it had been done behind his back. Huntley was summoned to the district committee, where, despite his objections, the chairman allowed a charge to be investigated which was totally different from the one intimated to him in the notice. This district committee also recommended expulsion. In consequence Huntley found difficulty in getting work. Meanwhile the general executive council of the union refused to carry out the recommendation to expel, although the district secretary sent a letter to them containing false reasons for the recommendation. The secretary did not tell Huntley of the executive council's decision: instead his committee purported to expel him behind his back. When Huntley eventually got work at a Tees-side power station, the Hartlepools district committee put pressure on Tees-side to have him sacked, pressure which succeeded with the aid of false accounts of what had happened at Hartlepools. Huntley sought to recover damages for what he had suffered through these actions. He was unable to prove breaches of contract, and so fell back on a civil action in tort. The union movement had exacted from the Liberal Government of 1906 an immunity from liability in tort. To this day, the Trade Disputes Act, 1906, provides the only example of an immunity in tort. Instead of suing the union Huntley sued the various officials concerned for the tort of conspiracy. If two or more persons combine together with the object of harming another and not for some legitimate object, they are liable for conspiracy. The Court held that Huntley had established such a conspiracy against the various unionists and awarded him £500 damages.

Matters were straightforward for Huntley because he

could prove a conspiracy. The next question is whether the trade unionist victim of industrial pressure can succeed even though he cannot prove a conspiracy.

Draughtsmen at London Airport had agreed with their employers, B.O.A.C., to settle disputes by arbitration and not to resort to strike action. Barnard and Fistal, branch chairman and shop steward respectively of the Association of Engineering and Shipbuilding Draughtsmen, resented the refusal of Rookes, a draughtsman there, to join their union. Under threat by Bernard and Fistal of strike action, B.O.A.C. had to dismiss Rookes, after giving him the notice to which he was entitled. Rookes sued Barnard and Fistal, and the trial judge held that if an individual illegally causes economic loss he is liable in damages, and that the threat of an illegal strike in breach of contract was such an illegality. Rookes was awarded £7,500 damages. The Court of Appeal reversed this decision. They agreed with the trial judge that the victim of unlawful conduct could sue even in the absence of conspiracy. They held, however, that the illegality must be something more than a threat to break a contract; it must be a threat or fraud of a criminal or tortious nature.[8] The difference between conspiracy and this other wrong, often called intimidation, is this. Conspirators are liable, even though there is no separate illegal act, provided their object is to harm; the individual is liable for intimidation only if his conduct is illegal – the illegality may be use of physical force or threat of it, or conduct which violates a statute, or libel, but illegality there must be. The Courts will not listen to vague words like coercion or industrial pressure, unless the plaintiff points to some specific act of an unlawful character: thus the House of Lords held that a union official who maliciously induced an employer not to engage employees from a rival union did not commit a tort against persons thereby deprived of a job.[9] Even if conspiracy is proved the defendant may still have a defence under the Trade Union Act, 1906. If the defendant proves that his act was done in contemplation or furtherance of a trade dispute, the plaintiff must then prove some wrong independent of the conspiracy; e.g. that violence or fraud was resorted to.

Despite the provisions of the Trade Union and Trade Disputes Act, 1906, and the reversal of the judgement in Rookes's favour, it can be claimed that the Courts do give at least some protection to the employee against the excesses of his union and its officials. The employee cannot be expelled except after a fair hearing in conformity with the union rules. He can obtain damages from the union if he proves a breach of contract. He can sue officials who either conspire to harm him or individually use certain illegal means in doing so. The Trade Union Acts exempt the union itself from liability in tort, but the official who has recourse to illegal threats of the kind described above has no defence under that legislation. The Courts have been vigilant to keep within reasonable bounds the extraordinary concessions to trade unionism made by the Liberal Government of 1906.

TRADES REGULATED BY STATUTE

Many professions, such as medicine and dentistry, are closely regulated by Act of Parliament. If a member of such a profession maintains that he has been removed from the register of qualified persons by proceedings which violate the Act or otherwise violate the rules of natural justice, he can take steps to have his name restored to the register by the Courts. Probably he will be able to sue for damages in tort – the question of breach of contract could not arise.

Many other occupations are controlled, not by Parliament, but by informal arrangements. For instance, Mr Lee was a showman and a member of the Showmen's Guild which had an elaborate set of rules. He was allocated a site at Bradford Moor Fair by Bradford Corporation. Another showman, Mr Shaw, also claimed this site, and maintained that he was entitled to it according to the rules of the Showmen's Guild. Lee insisted on using the site despite

Shaw's protest. Shaw complained to the guild which expelled Lee. Lee then sued the guild on the ground that he had not violated the following rule on which the guild had relied in expelling him: 'no member of the guild shall indulge in unfair competition with regard to the renting, taking, or letting of ground or position.'[10] The Court felt free to decide for itself whether Lee was guilty of 'unfair competition' within the rule, and, finding that he was not, issued a declaration that he was still a member and an injunction restraining the guild from interfering with his membership rights. The task of obtaining damages as well in such cases is harder. If the plaintiff can prove breach of contract, he will succeed. He will succeed if he can show intimidation. Whether he will recover damages by merely proving expulsion in breach of these 'non-legal rules' is doubtful. In principle, the answer should be 'Yes', but in an imperfectly argued case in 1952 the Court of Appeal issued a rather peremptory 'No'.[11] In practice nobody can be a cornporter in the Port of London unless he is on a register kept by a committee, which has no rules or constitution of any kind. Abbott was removed from this highly lucrative occupation register by the committee. When Abbott sued, the Court held that the committee had exceeded its powers in removing him for having committed an assault on a trade union official in the street, but refused to hold that there was a tort for which damages could be awarded.

Even more indirectly powerful are those bodies which control professional sport. No law authorizes the Football League to suspend players, the Jockey Club to ban racehorse trainers, the British Board of Boxing Control to license boxers and their managers. These bodies do not extend membership to those sportsmen but none the less they exercise great powers over them. Their powers are probably less than those concerned believe; it was a pity, for instance, that the threatened proceedings by Sunderland footballers, who had been suspended with consequential loss of pay, were settled before trial on terms whereby the Football Association officials submitted to an order giving the players all the damages which they could claim, for the Courts might well have exposed the flimsy basis of much of the control now exercised. Proceedings have been taken against the Jockey Club and the National Hunt Committee. The Courts have maintained that these self-appointed and self-perpetuating bodies, even if they have given no contractual rights to those whom they have deprived of their livelihood, must observe the rules of natural justice, and also the rules of their own organization. Any attempt to contract out of the obligation to give a fair hearing will be probably void as being contrary to public policy. If there is a breach of contract the deprived sportsman will obtain damages as well as an injunction. In the absence of contract, at the most he can recover damages in tort. The doubts about the availability of this remedy are the same as those expressed in the preceding paragraph.

LICENCES

Britain, like the rest of medieval Europe, had the guild system, whereby persons could practise particular trades only if they were members of the guild. As these guilds became more powerful, they became more openly monopolistic, restricting entry into the crafts, and imposing long apprenticeships. The decay of this guild system was heralded as a triumph for free enterprise and freedom of competition. The guild system of occupational control disappeared. Today, however, in its place we have many varied forms of occupational licensing which impose restraints of a not dissimilar kind.

Many professions have long possessed the power to regulate the entry into their ranks, and, subject only to appeal to the Courts, the power to remove from the register. Leading examples are medical practitioners and solicitors. More and more professions take the initiative in seeking this statutory self-regulation: dentists, architects, and opticians are twentieth-century examples. No doubt the object is said to be the public interest, but what of prestige and the financial benefit from a closed shop? In the United States hundreds of occupations, egg-graders, yacht salesmen, well-diggers, tile-layers, for example, have all obtained legislative protection. In the United Kingdom hairdressers have repeatedly sought a statutory system of registration under their own control. Veterinary surgeons complain that the People's Dispensaries for Sick Animals are allowed to function as they do. The effect of such self-controlled professions is, of course, to restrict the freedom of those outside to make their living as they choose.

Occupational licensing extends far beyond self-regulating professions. Local authorities have had wide powers conferred on them by general statutes. Pedlars, hawkers, street traders, pawnbrokers, taxi-drivers, animal trainers, nursery and child-minders, bookmakers, theatrical employers and agencies, game dealers, riding-stable proprietors, pleasure-boatmen, marine-store dealers: these are examples at random of trades which cannot be carried on unless the local authority in the area permits. In Scotland, a governmental commission reported that many trades were licensed unnecessarily: golf caddies and newsvendors, for instance. Local authorities are continually pressing for further powers to be given to them in Private Acts, a practice of which Mr Erroll, the present President of the Board of Trade, has complained in the Press. Licences to take photographs on the highway, to sell goods on the promenade, to be a masseur or provide heat or sun-ray treatment, to run a shop in which meat, fruit, or vegetables are stored, these are typical examples of powers which several local authorities have obtained for themselves from Parliament. And once one local authority has obtained a particular licensing power, other local authorities will request Parliament for the same power, pointing to the first granting of it as a precedent. It is easy to see that in many cases the interests of public safety, public health, and the like justify this interference. Yet it is difficult to understand the need for local variations in occupational control, and, whenever licensing of some occupation is introduced for the first time, the onus ought to be firmly on the Administration of proving that there are some considerations of public benefit which out-weigh the right of a man to pursue his employment.

Licensing is not merely at the level of local government. Pilots, airline operators, master mariners, public-service vehicle operators, aliens seeking any employment whatever, are examples of persons who are subject to forms of central licensing. Add to the above catalogue the restrictions of the apprenticeship system, the activities of unions, the unofficial bodies previously described, and the result is very consider-able restraint on freedom of work. So diffuse is this licensing that the general public fails to realize its scope and impact. We should be vigilant to see that mere sectional interests, whether a central or local bureaucratic urge for tidiness and power, or a profession's desire to up-grade its status and to protect its financial interest, do not masquerade as the public interest and needlessly restrict man's freedom to work.

CHAPTER 10

PROTECTION AGAINST
PRIVATE POWER

OUR concern so far has been mainly with the legal content
of liberty. We must also look at something else if we are to
have a balanced view of the state of freedom as a whole in the
country. We must round off the story by ascertaining what
in fact is done within the law to put a different gloss on the
practical scope of freedoms.

THE PRESS

We have seen already that English law endorses the
proposition that the Press is free. But does English law
enable the Press to abuse this freedom in an unwarrantable
way? By 'freedom of the Press' the law means freedom to
publish, no more, no less. Cynically and deliberately, the
Press distorts the maxim in order to justify freedom in
collecting news. The British Press gate-crashes into private
parties of Royalty, spies on them in their holiday retreats,
and uses concealed cameras to photograph them while
undressing for a bathe, cruises round in boats, cameras
clicking, if a royal parent wishes to instruct his son in sailing,
and so on. It regards itself as free to burst into hospital
wards in order to photograph those lying there seriously ill,
and to press them for interviews. Intruding on the grief of a
murdered person's relatives is justified by the Press because
they have 'a story'. To incite relatives to stop a wedding
dramatically at the last moment in order to have a photograph of the scene at the altar is conduct which a newspaper
will indulge in and defend against criticism. Freedom of
competition being what it is, the packs of rival newspapers
will hunt in droves for the same story. Photographs of the

dead, however lurid, are permissible if they feed the sacred cow of circulation.

Suppose that a newspaper reporter stumbles across an ex-convict who is struggling to adjust himself to society, and also is happily married to, employed by, and lives among, persons unaware of his past. What a good story to republish the account of the sensational crime of twenty years ago, to reveal what the criminal is now doing! What does it matter that it will cost him his marriage and his job if it titillates the Englishman in bed on Sunday morning? The Press may publish the story secure in the knowledge that the Courts will afford no remedy against it to the ruined victim. It is only doing its duty of publishing the truth, which of course cannot be libellous.

What is more sinister is that the privacy of certain persons only is invaded: we are told nothing of the private lives of newspaper proprietors; a Minister may have, to the general knowledge of Fleet Street, a mistress, but on this there will be silence. But let a Mrs Gilliatt expose the methods of the leading gossip columnists in an article in *Queen*, and she will be hounded by squads of reporters from the *Daily Telegraph* and other national 'dailies' who will report her minute-by-minute movements in the company of playwright John Osborne.

Why are such practices allowed to go on? Simply because English law does not make them unlawful and because the Press Council, even if it wishes, is powerless to control the offending newspapers. Once again the United Kingdom, mother of the common law, lags behind other countries which have developed that same common law to accord with changed circumstances.

Take the United States, for example. Under the lead of jurists writing articles in academic legal journals, and virtually unaided by legislatures, American Courts have moulded the common law so that it protects the victims of behaviour of the kind described. The aim of their Courts is to award damages whenever a person's interest in seclusion, or in his personal dignity and self-respect, or in being free from emotional upset, is interfered with by conduct which they regard as intolerably anti-social. They have therefore awarded damages in the following situations: installing tape-recorders secretly in hospital wards in order to have the account given by the victim of an accident to her relatives; tapping another's telephone call; publishing lurid photographs of the victim of a car accident; publishing X-ray photographs of the deformed pelvis of a woman celebrity; photographing the body of the plaintiff's dead husband; photographing a plaintiff mother's Siamese twins and publishing it. In none of these cases would the English Courts afford any remedy to the victim; the freedom of the British Press is intact.

Both Courts and Government share the blame for this gap in English law, a gap which is the more serious when new electronic devices make eavesdropping so easy. The Courts are as free as the American ones to develop a law of privacy. But there is no spirit of adventure or progress, either in judges or counsel, in England today. Today's English judges are not the innovators that some of their distinguished predecessors were; in the hands of modern judges the common law has lost its capacity to expand. They have not been helped by counsel. Cases are argued and tried by a narrow circle of men who seldom look beyond the decided cases for guidance. The entire development of the American law of privacy can be traced to an article in a law periodical published by Harvard Law School. It is inconceivable that the views of an academic journal would exercise similar influence in Britain. This inward- and backward-looking attitude of the English Bar only serves to increase the likelihood that the Courts will fail to make the law fit the needs of the time.

A Government committee sat for many years in order to consider reform of the law of libel. Its attention was directed to this problem of invasion of privacy by the Press. Characteristically, it found this problem to be outside its terms of reference and reported in 1948 that it had no proposals on it to make. In 1961 Lord Mancroft attempted to make up for the omissions of Courts and committees by introducing a private Bill which would have reformed the law along American lines. The House of Lords, including two distinguished judges who supported the Bill in debate (Lord Goddard and Lord Denning), gave it a second reading, but the predictable opposition of the Lord Chancellor, Lord Kilmuir, caused Lord Mancroft to drop it.

English law affords no protection against commercially exploiting another's personality. In each of the following cases the newspaper or advertiser has no legal obligation to pay for the use of the other person's name. A newspaper may freely say that Sir Blank Blank reads and enjoys it; an advertiser may promote the sale of his football boots by saying that Jimmy Greaves wears them; he may reproduce another's photograph for instance to lend tone to an advertisement, or on postcards offered for sale, or on cigarette cards. Untrue statements may be made. Statements may be made without permission, they may deprive the affected party of the opportunity to exploit for his own profit a valuable asset of his: none of these considerations counts with our Courts, which leave him remediless. In contrast, in States like New York there is a cause of action for damages against those who so misappropriate without permission the name or likeness of another; for instance a model whose picture was used for an advertisement without permission recovered damages; whereas in England she would have no remedy.

The influence of the Press may be discerned in other ways. As a casual reading of many newspapers shows, and as complaints to the Press Council have confirmed, many newspapers review only those entertainments which are advertised in their columns. Or, as a typical example, take the *Sunday Times* and *Observer* of 16 September 1962. The *Observer* contained one advertisement for investment in a unit trust and the paper's investment adviser recommended investment in that unit trust and mentioned no other. The *Sunday Times* contained an advertisement for another unit trust; the adjoining investment editorial column mentioned that other unit trust and no others. One may contrast, too, the readiness with which the sins of the B.B.C. are commented on, with the reluctance with which organs of the Press are criticized in newspapers. More unhelpful still to the reader is the attitude of the Press to consumer durables. Descriptions of goods which purport to aid the shopper are regular features in newspapers. Damaging criticism and invidious comparison with competing products are almost never found, presumably out of deference to advertisers or potential advertisers. The intelligent shopper, of course, is not taken in by the fulsome praise of products which is habitually in the Press, but he is denied the advice which he needs. As we have seen, the excuse that the Press is scared of having to pay damages for libel if it subjects products to honest and well-grounded criticism is without legal foundation. These deficiencies of the Press have made possible the success of *Which?*, a periodical which is devoted to objective analyses and comparisons of consumer products and services.

The Press may discriminate in exercise of their power to refuse advertisements. They may refuse advertisements for temperance because their important advertisers from the brewing industry would object. Some will refuse advertisements because they conflict with their moral views – advertisements on birth control or for football pools, for instance. They refuse any advertisement which 'knocks' some other product.

OTHER INFLUENCES ON FREEDOM OF EXPRESSION

Private power may detract from freedom of expression in less obvious ways. The Hulton Press was unable in 1956 to launch a new newspaper, the *Sunday Star*, because the Newsagents' Federation refused to handle it on the same discount terms as other Sunday newspapers, and the Newspaper Proprietors' Association refused to allow it to use the special newspaper trains and distribution facilities controlled by the association if the Hulton Press gave better terms. On another occasion Mr Randolph Churchill published a pamphlet critical of the British Press. W. H. Smith and Son Ltd refused to distribute it as wholesalers or to sell it from its own bookstalls. Mr Churchill complained to the Press Council about what seemed to him to be a hindrance on free expression designed to insulate the Press from criticism. The Press Council refused to interfere, and thought that W. H. Smith and Son Ltd had no moral obligation to accept the pamphlet. A comparable example is the refusal of shipping companies to include in the libraries of ships on the South Africa run books favouring the rights of African Negroes. We have previously mentioned the B.B.C's practice of dispensing with the services of those like the Muggeridges and Altrinchams, who elsewhere criticize untouchable topics like the monarchy. More subtle but no less restrictive is the play-safe approach – the avoidance of adult controversial films by the cinema industry, or the rootless mid-Atlantic film of television which sacrifices artistic standards in the interests of a double market.

ECONOMIC POWER

On the whole the United Kingdom has been successful in adjusting developing concepts of a Welfare State to an existing free-enterprise structure. The Restrictive Practices Court set up by the Act of 1956 has successfully restrained many formal monopolistic and restrictive arrangements which were contrary to the public interest. The worst evils of the earlier period have been largely eliminated: collective enforcement of price-fixing arrangements by stop lists, restrictions on distribution, private Courts fining those who defied the rigid rules. There was urgent need for drastic reform, and the Act has been as successful as could reasonably be hoped, although no doubt in some trades dominated by a few large companies uniform price observance, or what the Americans call 'conscious parallelism', still prevails.

The biggest single blot on the economic scene is the

legality of resale price maintenance which seems to have been the price exacted by industry from the Government for the other privileges forfeited: under the 1956 Act for the first time the manufacturer can enforce price maintenance, even against traders who have no contractual relation with the manufacturer and who have not undertaken to observe any fixed price. The general public does not support manufacturers' being entitled to prevent by injunction (with the accompanying threat of imprisonment) a retailer from selling below a price fixed by the manufacturers. Vociferous though the press relations officers of the interested manufacturers are, resale price maintenance is crumbling. In groceries the super-markets have forced it into the limbo, and perhaps the discount houses will have similar success in respect of the lower-priced durable goods. Some manufacturers are too well aware of the public condemnation of price maintenance to risk the harmful publicity of enforcing price maintenance by legal proceedings.

Another evil against which the public has to contend is the commercial practice of foisting on to them contracts in fine type full of conditions unfair to the buyer and calculated to exempt the manufacturer as much as possible from liability for his defective goods. Under the guise of a 'guarantee' the buyer of a motor car is lured into buying a car with less rights, in the event of its being defective, than if he had bought it without the benefit of any express contractual terms. The Courts have strained the existing law to the utmost in an attempt to protect the innocent buyer from this kind of dealing, and the consumer organizations have done what the Press has failed to do hitherto, namely, draw attention to the liability-evading character of the 'guarantees' of particular firms. It would be rash, however, to expect the average unsophisticated buyer to guard against these pitfalls. There are enough votes in 'consumer protection' to make it likely that these unfair trade practices, or at least the most heinous of them, will be outlawed by Parliament sooner or later.

Our system of credit is also closely affected by private

financial powers. Decisions by banks about the purposes for which they will lend money are legally unregulated. Finance houses are free from controls (other than on the size of deposits) in their hire-purchase dealings. The whole structure of hire-purchase law calls for overhaul. It has suited the finance house to take up the legal status of seller-hirer instead of the dealer – a fact of which the hire-purchaser is usually unaware – and yet the finance house strives by its one-sided forms of never-to-be-altered printed contracts to opt out of the responsibilities for the condition and quality of the goods which the law would ordinarily impose on the seller and to assume the limited responsibilities of banker instead. It has been found convenient for the finance house to save the expense of working a credit-rating system as in countries like the U.S.A. and Canada, and then to justify its own contracting out of liability and imposition of harsh terms on the hire-purchaser on the ground that otherwise the house would suffer losses from disreputable dealers foisting expensive (often worthless) cars at grossly inflated prices on persons of limited and uninvestigated financial resources. The country cannot endure indefinitely a system in which the finance house demands for itself the privileges of a seller but insists on casting off the liabilities which the law impliedly attaches to a seller.

SOCIAL POWER

Ordinarily, manipulation of social power will be seen as less important. Perhaps it is of no great moment that certain golf clubs will not allow Jews to be members, and that Coventry public houses will not allow Indians in certain public rooms, a practice with which Coventry licensing magistrates refuse to interfere. When one passes to the educational sphere, the problem becomes more serious. There is the educational institution which requires a photograph from each applicant because (it is thought) it restricts its intake of Jews and Negroes. If there is any substance in the often-voiced complaint that some Oxford and Cambridge colleges will more readily admit the product of a leading public school than the similarly qualified candidate from a State grammar school, this would be a serious grievance – the more so as such institutions are dependent in practice on the State's financial support for their survival in their present form.

CONTRACT

A contract enables a dominant party to it to exercise power. No law prohibits employers from denying union membership to employees. Yet no Government department will hand out a Government contract unless the firm accepts the Fair Wages Resolution of the House of Commons – a resolution without legal effect. One of the clauses in this Resolution is that the employer must recognize the freedom of all his workpeople to be members of trade unions. We have seen, too, how Government uses the contract device as a means of ensuring that firms do not employ security risks on defence contracts. This was the weapon which it threatened to use in the case of Lang and the Imperial Chemical Industries, Ltd.

The attempts made by the royal family to maintain privacy furnish another example. Large sums are offered by the Press to the Queen's nannies and other servants in the hope that they will reveal the intimacies of the royal family. Appeals to the sense of loyalty of such employees not having succeeded in stopping the flow, contract had to be resorted to. Now all royal servants, upon entering their employment, must accept the following clause in their contracts:

Communications to the press. You are not permitted to publish any incident or conversation which may be within your knowledge by reason of your employment in the royal service, nor may you give to any person, either verbally or in writing, any information regarding her Majesty or any member of the Royal Family, which might be communicated to the press.

None the less, several royal employees have not been deterred from publishing, whereupon the Treasury Solicitor has applied to the Courts in the ordinary way for an injunction restraining this breach of contract. To disobey the injunction is a contempt of Court, punishable by imprisonment. Henceforth, royal servants will be lucky if they manage to publish more than one instalment of their intimate revelations before the Palace and the Courts catch up with them. On the other hand, the Palace remains powerless, to cite one actual instance, to prevent advertisements showing a photograph of the Queen going down a mine in overalls, safety boots, and helmet: the indirect advertisement value to the manufacturer of the equipment is obvious, but the dislike of the royal family for such practices is equally understandable.

PRESSURE GROUPS

Many members of Parliament on both sides of the House are paid by outside organizations to look after the interests of these organizations when matters affecting them come up for parliamentary discussion. Likewise, organizations employ other persons as 'contact men' with government departments. These pressure groups (as well as the more familiar lobby groups like the F.B.I., the T.U.C., and the Lord's Day Observance Society) are a commonplace of public life. One well-known recent example is the pressure group of members of Parliament with large financial interests in advertising, entertainment, and television which was able to convince an unenthusiastic Prime Minister of the country's need for commercial television. English law is lax on these matters in contrast with that of many other countries. Members of Parliament are not bound to publish details of the organizations which they are paid to represent. Other contact men are not bound to register themselves. Members of Parliament, Ministers even, are legally free to retain large shareholdings in companies which enjoy lucrative government contracts. The only *legal* restriction is contained in an Act of 1792 denying a vote to a member with an interest in a government contract, but the provision is useless today because 'interest' does not cover shareholdings, however large, in companies. There is, however, a parliamentary *practice* whereby a member who has a financial interest, direct or indirect, in the matter on which he is speaking in the House discloses the fact in his speech: enforcement of the practice is spotty because of the vagueness in defining what is an 'interest' in the issue being debated. By parliamentary practice, too, Ministers must resign directorships, other than those in certain family businesses, and must declare their financial interest in matters affecting public business – the case of Mr Marples, Minister of Transport, in 1960, as a director of a public works company engaged in government work was one where this practice was followed. There is a corresponding absence of law, and vagueness of practice about the financial interests, postservice employment, and gift receiving, within the civil service.

All this is in contrast, not only with the comparative precision of United States law on all these matters, but, more surprisingly, also with our local government law. Legislation requires local government officers and members to declare all pecuniary interests, direct or indirect, and prohibits voting on matters in which there is such an interest. The Courts interpret this local government legislation in such a way as effectively to maintain high standards of integrity in this part of local government.

The freedom to associate, which English law allows, also serves to facilitate pressure groups. In the typical statute, when the Minister is required to consult before he promulgates delegated legislation, it is obvious that he will consult the trade association more fully than the general public. Decisions of the Courts have aided this process. The restrictions on the sums spent on advertising at a parliamentary election do not prevent a company from spending money to advertise one political party.[1] A sugar company which launched a big advertising campaign against the plans of the Socialists to nationalize the sugar industry was entitled to set off for income tax purposes the expenses of this campaign against its profits.[2]

There is no space here to evaluate pressure groups in British politics. Suffice it to say that their ramifications are deeper and more extensive than many recognize, that they are virtually free from legal control, and that in consequence they are able to function concealed from the public gaze.

LOCAL AUTHORITIES

English law allows local authorities to take many decisions affecting individuals without giving them a hearing. Local authorities have also resisted pressures for legislation making it compulsory for meetings of the authority and committees always to be held in the presence of the public and the Press. This absence of publicity makes it easier for members of local authorities to wield private power. Take the controversial matter of allocating local authority houses to tenants: a local authority is under no compulsion to allow an applicant to put his case before its committee, it need give no reasons why that applicant has not been given a house, it need not disclose the principles if any, by which it, its committee, or its staff, decides upon individual allocation.

Local authorities take many decisions which impinge upon freedom. One may decide to ban a procession, another, as the Middlesex County Council used to do, may refuse to employ Communists as head teachers (compare the dilemma of Coventry Education Committee over Jordan, the National Socialist leader and Coventry teacher), another, like Flintshire Education Committee formerly, may insist on children being educated at a school where Welsh is the medium of instruction for half the subjects in the curriculum in face of the parents' desire to send their children to another English school also run by that education authority in the same town. Or take Caithness library sub-committee, whose librarian was willing to let his own children read Bruce Marshall's novel of the Spanish civil war, *A Fair Bride*. In 1954 the committee banned the book after the member introducing the motion to do had said: 'The book is foul, filthy, and obscene. But are you surprised when the heroine is a harlot and the hero a renegade Catholic priest?

254

And are you surprised that it should be admitted to a Protestant Caithness library? There is an insidious sneaking Roman Catholic propaganda in it which I detest. I move that this book is not fit to be taken into the family circle and should not be allowed to lie on the shelves of a Protestant Caithness library.' We have seen that many local authorities have unofficial approved lists of comic postcards which will not be the subject of prosecutions for obscenity.

LEGAL AID

However extensive the freedoms conferred by the law, they are of little value unless the citizen may have free access to the Courts in order to have them defended there. One of the great triumphs of post-war English judicial administration has been its development of legal aid, for which both Governments and the legal profession take credit. A committee of lawyers investigates the merits of litigants who are contemplating civil proceedings and decides whether the cause has merit before issuing a legal aid certificate. A means test is applied in a precise manner to determine the amount of legal aid. The system works well, and has greatly increased the accessibility of justice. It is particularly necessary that Britain should have a generous legal aid system in civil cases because of the peculiar rules about costs of legal proceedings. In many countries, each litigant pays his own costs regardless of the outcome of the suit. In the United States, the poor litigant who is, say, the victim of a car accident will usually employ a lawyer on the terms that he pays nothing if the action fails, and that he hands to the lawyer an agreed percentage of the damages (say a third) if the action succeeds. In Britain the loser pays the winner's costs as well as his own. Suppose that a suitor wins at the trial, the other party unsuccessfully appeals to the Court of Appeal, but then by a majority of three to two secures a reversal in the House of Lords. In short, six of the nine judges who have tried the case have found for the loser, yet he has to pay all his own legal costs and those of his opponent also, an amount which might well total £10,000. Without legal aid, the private person in this kind of legal system is unfavourably placed when his opponent is, say, a public body or commercial organization. He would often be deterred from embarking on litigation at all. Some gaps in civil legal aid remain and need to be filled as soon as financially feasible. A few actions like libel are not covered, and no proceedings before administrative tribunals, which transact an increasingly large slice of judicial business affecting the citizen, are legally aided. Perhaps, too, the financial ceiling for those seeking aid ought to be raised. There is also excellent provision for obtaining legal advice under the legal aid scheme. Further, nobody accused of serious criminal offences will be denied legal assistance in presenting his case owing to a lack of financial resources.

CHAPTER II

FREEDOM OF MOVEMENT AND
RACIAL DISCRIMINATION

WHAT we are concerned with here is the freedom with which people can enter and leave Britain. We encounter a tangled mass of legislation, decided cases, and, above all, practice of the Executive. The best way through the morass is to understand that there are three separate categories: aliens, citizens of the United Kingdom, and citizens of the British Commonwealth.

ALIENS

Until the emergency of 1914, restrictions on aliens in Great Britain were few. Those which were introduced solely because of that emergency have been allowed to survive ever since in substantially the same form. Their 'temporary emergency' character is still nominally recognized in that the legal provisions outlined in the next paragraph, most of which are now contained in an item of subordinate legislation, the Aliens Order of 1953, have to be renewed annually by Parliament in the Expiring Laws Continuance Act.

An alien is not entitled to enter the United Kingdom: he may land if and when he obtains the leave of an immigration officer, but not otherwise. That officer will not give him leave unless the alien is able to support himself and any dependants and, where he proposes to enter the employment of a particular employer in the United Kingdom, he produces a permit issued to that employer by the Ministry of Labour. The officer may attach other conditions to the leave to land, for example, about his place of residence and reporting to the police. Criminals, mental defectives, and those whom a medical inspector certifies as undesirable immigrants for medical reasons will be refused leave. The immigration officer is entitled to demand a passport, or other document of identity, and a landing card. When he refuses leave he may direct those in charge of the ship or aircraft which brought the alien to remove him from the country in their ship or aircraft. He may arrest without warrant anybody whom he suspects to have committed an offence under the Order. He has to act in accordance with the instructions of the Home Secretary in the discharge of all these tasks.

So much for the legal rules. What happens in practice? Immigration officers may well be men in their mid-twenties who are earning rather above £1,000 a year after serving a two-year probationary period. The Home Office exercises its legal powers to give them further instructions, beyond the requirements already set out, about the conditions of landing: these are not published. Each immigration officer is armed both with an alphabetical list of individuals who must not be allowed to land and with a further set of general instructions. It is the policy to admit tourists, businessmen, students, those who have already obtained a work permit, and certain categories of relatives of British residents. Recent relaxations permit writers, artists, and the like to enter without work permits. Before granting a work permit the Ministry of Labour must be satisfied that there is essential work to be done, that British labour will not be displaced or excluded, and that there will be no under-cutting of British wage standards. In practice trade union opposition to permits in highly organized trades is enough to prevent them from being issued for work in those occupations – the difficulty experienced by the Government after the Second World War in persuading the mining unions to allow the entry of Italian miners in order to make good the shortage of coal miners is an example. Fewer than 40,000 permits a year are ordinarily granted. Permits are normally for twelve months, but may be renewed, and after four years the Home Office may accept the alien as a resident, and allow him to take any form of employment.

The Home Office is concerned to prevent the admission of security risks, of those who will become a charge on national assistance, of those who will put a British subject out of work, and of those who are really intending to emigrate here. There are no literacy tests, and no quota restrictions in respect of particular countries. No reasons for refusal will be given and there is no appeal either to the Courts or to an administrative tribunal. The influential may pull strings to reverse a decision or to have a case ventilated by parliamentary question. In practice, any alien who insists on questioning the immigration officer's ruling can have his case referred to the Home Office for further consideration.

The alien may well complain that these provisions lack definiteness. Yet it is not easy to see how the procedure could be completely judicialized. Immigration officers have to make difficult on-the-spot decisions and cannot work to precise rules throughout. Perhaps more should be done in the way of publishing the directions given to immigration officers on the manner in which they are to operate the Aliens Order; perhaps reasons for refusal should always be given, and some formal machinery introduced for obtaining a decision in advance of an intended visit when an alien requests it. It does no credit to Britain summarily to turn back men like Pastor Niemöller and Dr Pauling, a Nobel prize winner, who had come to England in order to address a meeting – even if they are pacifists. Perhaps Parliament should have some say in the formulating of the list of reasons for discretionary exclusion – it has none at present. When pressed on this, the stock answer of the Home Office is that to formulate the grounds of refusal would inevitably cause entry to be restricted even more than at present: the logic of this is obscure and unexplained. There must also be many cases where it is difficult, without detailed investigation, to ascertain the real motives of the alien who wishes to land: there is much to be said for enabling an alien to appear before a tribunal to argue his case for entry and to be cross-examined. In these matters the procedure in the United Kingdom compares unfavourably with that of other countries in the West. In the United States, for instance, the alien is entitled to a fair hearing before he is refused permission to land, and to a review by the Courts of any decision to refuse it.

Treaties making visas unnecessary have been concluded with most European countries, but they are still required for aliens from eastern countries. This is another important practical restraint on freedom of entry: 1,700 aliens were refused visas in 1954. No reasons are given for these refusals, and, if challenged in Parliament, the Government declares that it is contrary to the public interest to disclose reasons for refusing visas. In any event, the grant of a visa in no way ensures that the immigration officer will allow the alien to land.

In an average year, two or three thousand aliens out of over a million alien visitors will be turned back on arrival in Britain. The main groups will be: those intending to work, but having no labour permit; those having a concealed intention to immigrate; those who, arriving in circumstances requiring a visa, have not applied for one; those without means of financial support; stowaways. There will also be a few mental and health cases.

Although there is no control at British ports over travellers from Ireland, this is probably not a back-door means of entry into Britain for aliens because Ireland has legislation control over aliens similar in pattern to the British one and is believed to work closely with Britain in its operation.

CONTROL OF AN ALIEN IN THE UNITED KINGDOM

Obviously, one important power of the immigration officer is to define the period of stay allowed to the alien. The tourist or other short-term visitor will ordinarily be given a three-months permit: the Aliens Order normally exempts an alien from registering his movements when he enters in such circumstances. Consequently the tourist is free from restrictions. One would like to think that the power to permit entry for a limited period would be exercised in those cases where detailed inquiry is needed to check whether the alien is really going to stay with his uncle, or whether she is a genuine domestic servant or a prostitute, or whether his enrolment for a course at a recognized institution of learning proves him to be truly a student.

Aliens who are staying for more than three months but who are subject to a landing condition that they shall leave after a specified period have to register with the local police and to notify them of all changes of address. All aliens have to inform hotel keepers of their name, nationality, passport number, and next destination. They must produce registration certificates or passports on demand at any time by an immigration officer or by a policeman, and may be detained upon failure to do so. When a permitted period of stay expires, there is power to apply for an extension. All these provisions concerning control of the alien while in the United Kingdom are reasonable.

EXPULSION

An immigration officer may order the removal, not only of a person whom he has refused leave to land, but also of somebody who is found in the United Kingdom to have landed without leave in contravention of this Order. In terms, this Order seems to give the immigration officer unlimited discretion, but perhaps an alien who could prove that in fact he had not landed unlawfully could obtain the aid of the Court to prevent the officer from removing him.

The Home Secretary also has wide powers to order the deportation of an alien. He may deport him whenever the Court has recommended deportation following upon conviction for an offence for which there was power to imprison or of an offence connected with prostitution. The precision of this power is misleading in view of the next provision that the Home Secretary may deport if he 'deems it to be conducive to the public good to make a deportation order against the alien'. This is a power without limit. The Courts could only interfere if the deportee proved that he was not an alien. The alien cannot seek to persuade the Court that the public good does not call for his deportation: by using the expression 'if he deems' the Order gives the Secretary uncontrolled discretion in deciding the issue of 'public good'.

By an administrative concession made in 1956, which does not have the force of law, the following proceedings are open to an alien about to be deported otherwise than on a Court's recommendation. He may ask to have any representations which he wishes to make heard by a metropolitan magistrate at Bow Street, and for this purpose he may be represented by a lawyer. The magistrate would then make an advisory recommendation to the Home Secretary on whether the order should be carried out. This concession does not apply where the order was made on grounds of public security or on the grounds that the alien had landed without permission or that, having been in the country for less than two years, he had failed to observe the conditions attaching to his stay. This opportunity to challenge is most restricted. Once again we see the Administration making a concession which cannot bind them in law – there is no valid reason for not according legal rights of challenge to the alien. But beyond that the procedures on this concession are unfair to the alien. He is not told why he is to be deported; he has no opportunity to confront those who may testify against him and cross-examine them; he is not entitled to bring witnesses on his behalf; the magistrate does not reveal to him his recommendation; the Home Secretary does not reveal it, and, for all the alien knows, he may be deported although the magistrate recommends the contrary.[1] In contrast with those he enjoys in countries like the United States, the alien's rights in Britain are inadequate. In such other western countries, aliens are entitled to a full hearing, the ordinary Courts will quash a deportation order if the alien is denied a fair hearing, or if the Government has not established substantial evidence to support the deportation order.

It might perhaps be thought a hopeful sign that the

Government made that extra-legal concession in 1956. The facts provide no ground for such optimism. When the United Kingdom became a party to the Convention between member countries of the Council of Europe on Establishment, it was found that she did not afford aliens those minimum rights required by the Convention. This 1956 arrangement is merely a grudging concession of the least possible facility for an alien consistent with the Convention. It may safely be assumed that, but for this international pressure, not even this slight concession to the claims of justice would have been made.

RIGHT OF ASYLUM

An associated topic is the so-called right of asylum. When an alien's life or liberty is in danger or he has a well-founded fear of persecution of such a kind as to render life insupportable (e.g. denying him ration or employment cards) on account of his race, religion, nationality, or political opinion, it is the practice of the British Government to allow him to stay in Britain. He may have no visa, he may not fall within the usual categories of admitted aliens, but nonetheless he may be allowed to stay. Obvious examples are the sailors from behind the Iron Curtain who from time to time desert their ships in British ports and seek refuge here. No such alien has a *right* of asylum, either by international law or English law. All that is meant is that the state will *in practice* allow such aliens to stay in Britain; other states have a similar practice. The Home Office makes the decisions and will first interview the alien, who will not be allowed to retain residence here under the guise of a claim for sanctuary.

The case of Dr Cort in 1954 illustrates the limits of this practice. Dr Cort, an American citizen, was a qualified doctor of medicine employed by Birmingham University. Before leaving the United States he had been rejected for military service because of a tubercular condition. He was approached in England by the American authorities with a view to his reporting for a medical examination in connexion with military service. Dr Cort was convinced that the object of the American Government was to make him give evidence before the McCarthy Committee of Senate on Government Operations in Washington – he had at one time been a Communist, and his former associates had been subpoenaed before the Committee and had their reputations besmirched by the Committee. Accordingly, he refused the American request. Britain then informed him that it would not renew his alien permit and that he would have to leave the country. The Government was pressed in the House of Commons on several occasions to grant Cort political asylum, but the Government refused on the ground that the facts fell outside the scope of asylum. The Government maintained (erroneously[2]) that Cort's refusal, which amounted to evasion of military service, was a ground, according to American law, for depriving Cort of his citizenship, and that it was not the practice, except in 'asylum' cases, to allow an alien to remain in England when there was no country which would be required to accept him as its national when he finally left Britain. There was, in the Government's view, no evidence that the United States would threaten his life or liberty for his political opinions – Cort's apprehensions were not supported by the known facts. Cort left England, and, fearing to return to the United States, emigrated to Czechoslovakia.

EXTRADITION

Closely linked with asylum is the law of extradition. The United Kingdom has entered into many treaties with other states agreeing to hand over any person who has committed a crime in one of these countries, on the condition that the other country will hand over to the United Kingdom criminals wanted by it. These treaties apply to nationals as well as to aliens but not to political crimes. The Bow Street magistrate decides whether there is sufficient evidence that the person whose extradition is sought has committed an extraditable crime – there is an appeal to the Divisional

Court of the Queen's Bench Division from the magistrate's extradition order. Extradition for a political crime is forbidden. Thus, in 1954, the members of a Polish trawler took charge of the ship, imprisoned the captain, and steered her into Whitby because they feared that they would be punished for their political opinions if they returned to Poland. Their purpose was to escape from political tyranny. Poland applied for an extradition order: although the Court found that there was a prima facie case of revolt on the high seas and of unlawful wounding, the extradition order was refused and the men set free because the offences were of a political character.[3] The House of Lords has recently held that the idea behind 'political offences' is that the fugitive is at odds with the state that has applied for his extradition on some issue connected with the political control or government of the country.[4]

There is a separate statute, the Fugitive Offenders Act, 1881, enabling one member of the Commonwealth to have handed over a man located in another part of the Commonwealth. Curiously enough, this Act does not except political offences from its scope. Consequently the House of Lords found itself unable to prevent the making of an extradition order in 1962 relating to two Cypriots who had helped the British authorities in the Cyprus riots and who maintained that their lives would be in danger on that account should they be handed over.[5] The Act, however, did empower the Home Secretary to refuse a warrant if he were not satisfied that it was just to sign it. In this case Mr Butler refused the Cyprus Government's request for the return of the men. The outcome was satisfactory, but it seems a flaw in the Act that the Home Secretary could not act until the appeal of the men to the Courts against the order for their return had been dismissed. Meanwhile the men had languished in prison for nine months.

The case of Dr Soblen in 1962 illustrates the interrelationship of extradition, deportation, and the right of asylum. Dr Soblen was found guilty in the U.S.A. of delivering defence information to aid the Soviet Union and was sentenced to life imprisonment. He was released on bail pending appeal. As soon as he learned that his appeal had failed he flew to Israel on his brother's passport. He was forcibly removed from Israel and put under American escort on an El Al airline plane bound for the U.S.A. via London. While on the plane he inflicted such severe wounds on himself that at London he was removed unconscious from the plane to hospital. A notice of refusal to land could not be served on him until two days later; the following day he was served with a notice detaining him as a person refused leave to land, pending the giving of directions on the means by which he was to leave. By *habeas corpus* Soblen challenged the validity of the detention order: both the trial judge and the Court of Appeal ruled that the circumstances of his arrival in England amounted to a refusal by the immigration authorities of leave to land, and that his subsequent detention was valid.[6] Thereupon the Home Office directed El Al airline to remove Soblen: this they failed to do by the specified time.

The Government maintained that the facts fell outside the scope of political asylum because political offences for that purpose were restricted to situations where two or more political parties within the State were engaged in a contest in which they were seeking to impose the government of their choice on the State. The ideological struggle between East and West was not a political issue in the U.S.A. for this purpose. The Government therefore refused an application for political asylum.

The Home Secretary then issued a deportation order, on the ground that he deemed his deportation to be conducive to the public good, which Soblen again challenged by *habeas corpus*. On appeal to the Court of Appeal against the trial judge's refusal to grant him his freedom Soblen made two main points.[7] He alleged that the Home Secretary had refused to let him give evidence or to argue through counsel before the Home Secretary that his deportation was not conducive to the public good, and that this failure to give him a hearing was a breach of the rules of natural justice which invalidated the deportation order. The Court of Appeal ruled that in the interests of security an alien was not entitled to any hearing before he was deported. Secondly, he argued that the Home Secretary was abusing his power to deport, that under the guise of deportation he was really surrendering a fugitive criminal to the United States at the request of the American authorities. He was doing this because extradition was impossible here; the offence was espionage, for which extradition is not allowed. The Court of Appeal found that the offence was one for which extradition was not available, and that the United States had asked the British Government to return Soblen. The Court further held that the power to deport included a power to place him on a particular ship or aircraft making for his own country. The Court found no evidence that the deportation order was a sham; on the contrary there was evidence that the Home Secretary had made up his mind to deport Soblen by an aircraft bound for the United States before the United States Government intervened. Had there been evidence that the Home Secretary made the order in order to achieve the same result as an extradition order, and at the request of the United States, the Court would have required the Home Secretary to give an explanation; had he then refused to do so, or claimed (as he would be entitled) privilege for the communications from the United States Government so that neither Soblen nor the Court would be allowed to see them, the Court of Appeal would have set Soblen free.

There can be no doubt that the *Soblen* case was correctly decided. It is merely an illustration of the injustice which two firmly-established rules of English law produce. First, that the Executive in many areas affecting human freedom does not need to give a fair hearing. Secondly, that the Government is at liberty in any litigation to conceal from the Court any documentary evidence damaging to its case by saying that it refuses to produce the evidence because to do so would be contrary to the public interest. Both these rules are a blot on English law, but it is important to understand that they are of general application, in no way limited to problems of deportation such as those raised in *Soblen's* case.

IMMIGRANTS OTHER THAN ALIENS

The Commonwealth Immigrants Act, 1962, introduced for the first time restrictions on the entry into the United Kingdom of Commonwealth citizens: these restrictions cease to operate on 31 December 1963 unless Parliament otherwise determines. Paradoxically, citizens of the Republic of Ireland are not only free from the restrictions imposed on aliens but are also exempt from the restrictions on entry laid down in this Act. A person born in the United Kingdom or who holds a United Kingdom passport and is a citizen of the United Kingdom and Colonies, or who is ordinarily resident in the United Kingdom or was so resident any time within the past two years, continues to be entitled to enter the country – there are exemptions, too, for wives and children of persons who are themselves exempt. There are restrictions on all other Commonwealth citizens: none of them is entitled to enter if he is a criminal, or a security risk, or a mentally defective, or if he ought not to be admitted for medical reasons. Subject to those exceptions, Commonwealth citizens wishing to work in the United Kingdom and having a voucher issued for the purpose by the Minister of Labour are entitled to enter. Also entitled to enter, subject to the same exceptions, are, first, students who will attend a substantially full-time course at an educational institution, and, secondly, those able to support themselves and their dependants without taking up employment. When citizens in these last two categories are admitted, conditions restricting the period for which they may remain, or restricting their employment, may be imposed. The Act vests the administration of its provisions in immigration officers.

The Government has stated in a White Paper that immigration officers will carry out their duties without regard to the race, colour, or religion of citizens who seek to enter the country. Besides the stated objects of preventing the admission of criminals, the unfit, security risks, and the indigent, the aim is to control immigration in the light of employment and housing conditions. The Act is silent on the procedure relating to labour vouchers. In fact there are three categories: A, issued on demand to those with a prearranged job to come to; B, to those having useful professional qualifications or being skilled craftsmen; C, to the unskilled without prearranged jobs, issued on a first come first served basis subject to no country being allowed more than one quarter of the quota for any period. In the first year 7,000 out of 10,000 A vouchers applied for, 8,700 of some 11,000 B, and 29,000 of 145,000 C, were granted. Even though immigration officers are not to discriminate, there is clearly a risk that the uncontrolled decisions of unspecified officials of the Ministry of Labour on granting labour vouchers will have the effect of bearing most harshly on coloured applicants.

The Act itself is, then, much more specific than that relating to aliens. Moreover, in contrast to the lack of information available to aliens, the instructions of the Home Secretary to immigration officers on the exercise of their functions under this Act are published. Examination of these instructions only emphasizes those inadequacies with regard to aliens on which we have previously commented. Commonwealth citizens can obtain rulings before they leave their own country; reasons for refusal are to be stated, where practicable – one still deplores the Government's refusal to incorporate this in the Act. Only a chief immigration officer or an immigration inspector is authorized to refuse admission. Unfortunately, no appeal against refusal is allowed either by the Act or by the instructions, despite the persistent attempts made by the Opposition in Parliament to persuade the Government to allow a right of appeal.

The Act confers a power (which does not lapse at the end of 1963) to deport a restricted class of Commonwealth citizens and citizens of the Republic of Ireland. Naturalized, adopted or registered United Kingdom citizens, those born there, or whose fathers were born there, those resident there for the last five years, or whose parents resided there at the time of birth are not liable to be deported. The Home Secretary is empowered to deport any other Commonwealth citizen who has been convicted of an offence punishable with imprisonment, where the Court has recommended his deportation. Notice the odd situation of the Irish: they can be deported but there is nothing to stop them catching the next boat back to Britain, for there is no immigration check on ships entering British ports from Ireland. Although this power of deportation is, in contrast with the power to deport aliens, closely regulated by legal safeguards, its operation has given rise to disquiet. This came to a head over the case of Miss Carmen Bryan. This Jamaican girl was given a conditional discharge on a charge of shoplifting. Nonetheless, on the magistrate's recommendation, the Home Secretary ordered deportation, until parliamentary pressure forced him to revoke that order. The Home Secretary refused to appoint a panel of advisers to help him in these cases, and declined to circularize magistrates about the Government's repeated undertaking not to deport for trivial offences. Plainly, magistrates have been recommending deportation in breach of the Government's undertaking. It now seems to have been a mistake ever to have conferred on magistrates this power to recommend deportation. It should have been confined to High Court judges and Quarter Sessions; the victims cannot be expected to know that they have a right of appeal against the recommendation to deport from the magistrates to a higher Court. In the first three months of the Act's operation there were 310 recommendations for deportation of which more than half were persons from the Irish Republic; 123 were deported, all after conviction,

FREEDOM OF TRAVEL

In early common law a British citizen was prohibited from leaving the realm, without leave of the Crown, since to do so would deprive the king of the subject's military or other feudal services. Magna Carta subsequently gave every free man the right to leave the realm at his pleasure in time of peace. Writing in the eighteenth century, the great English legal author, Blackstone, said that the Englishman had a common law right to leave the realm subject to the prerogative right of the Crown to restrain him by writ of *ne exeat regno*. Originally that prerogative writ was issued to assure the carrying out of the military obligation to defend the King and the realm; later it became limited to preventing the evasion of legal liabilities. Now it is obsolete.

Before we go on to conclude that the subject must then be free to leave the realm at his will, we must consider the passport. It was not until the nineteenth century that the passport emerged in its modern form as a personal document to be carried on foreign travels. In essence a passport is a document which identifies the holder and provides evidence of his nationality. Whatever rights of protection the British citizen has abroad, he does not enjoy them because he has a British passport; he enjoys them because he is a British citizen. The passport is merely prima facie evidence of his nationality. May a British citizen enter and leave the country at will without a passport? There is a restriction, surprisingly enough, in the Aliens Order, 1953: that is not an Act of Parliament, but an item of delegated legislation which will have the force of law so long as it is within the powers conferred by its parent Act, the Aliens Restrictions Act, 1914, as amended. Article 7(1) of this Order provides that 'every person of or over the age of 16 years who lands or embarks in the United Kingdom shall, if so required by an immigration officer, produce to that officer ... either a valid passport furnished with a photograph of himself or some other document satisfactorily establishing his identity and nationality'. This does not apply to journeys between the United Kingdom and the Isle of Man, Ireland, or the Channel Isles. Where it does apply, the immigration officer may, by virtue of paragraph (2), examine the traveller 'for the purpose of ascertaining whether that person is or is not an alien ... and it shall be the duty of every such person to furnish to an immigration officer such information as that officer may require for the purpose of his functions under this paragraph'. It is clear then that under the Order a British citizen can still leave and enter the country without a passport, so long as he produces alternative evidence of identity and nationality. But suppose that he does not produce satisfactory evidence, although he is in fact a British citizen. Despite the Aliens Order, it is believed that the subject remains free to leave and enter. It is, of course, proper for an airline or shipping company to insert in the contract of carriage a requirement that he shall possess a passport, for they might otherwise have the expense of transporting him whence he came. Whereas the Order confers express powers on an immigration officer to detain an alien until he permits him to land, it is significantly silent about any power to detain a British citizen. It is believed that the Order gives the immigration officer no power to detain a British citizen, and that an immigration officer who mistakenly detains one does so at his peril provided that the subject has duly answered the questions put to him by the officer in the course of his examination.

The Commonwealth Immigrants Act, 1962, confers similar powers to detain those citizens of the Commonwealth to whom the Act applies, but only when they are seeking to enter the country, and not when they are leaving it. We have seen that the Act does not extend to those born in the United Kingdom, or holding a United Kingdom passport and being a citizen of the United Kingdom and Colonies. Its impact, then, on this class of citizens, is like that of the Aliens Order on all British subjects: an immigration officer detains them at his peril, although they must furnish to him such information in their possession as he may reasonably require.

So far we have concluded that a citizen of the United Kingdom is free to leave and enter his country without passport. It is when we consider his freedom to enter other countries that the passport becomes significant. Each country is free to demand such documents as it pleases of foreigners wishing to enter. If it will not admit without a passport, then a British subject has no legal right to enter that country without one. What has in fact happened is that when visa requirements were widely abolished after the war, the United Kingdom secured this abolition by a series of treaties on a reciprocal basis with the various other countries. It is standard form in these treaties to stipulate that the countries party to them will admit British citizens without visa on production of a British passport. The legal consequence is that a British citizen without a passport cannot enter foreign countries.

At this point, it is of the first importance to consider whether a British citizen is entitled to a passport. The answer is that no British citizen is so entitled, even though his British nationality is beyond doubt – he may even have obtained a declaration of the High Court that he is a British national. Granting a passport is entirely a matter of royal prerogative which is exercised on behalf of the Queen by the Foreign Office. The subject has no legal right to a passport, the Crown can refuse him one without giving any reasons, he is not entitled to a hearing in order to argue his case for the grant of one, there is no Court to which he can appeal if he is refused one, he is not entitled to compensation for any loss suffered because of the refusal.

The freedom to travel is of course an important freedom: men want to travel abroad on business, for family visits, to consult with experts in their profession, for educational and recreational purposes. It is startling that the citizen should seem so rightless. Contrast the United States where, when the Government refused a passport to a physicist on the ground that they believed him to have Communist associations, the Supreme Court held that the Secretary of State had acted without authority in withholding a passport because of a person's beliefs or associations.[8] As one might have expected, it is not by some carefully thought-out decision that the present rules operate. The Crown has had prerogatives in foreign affairs and retains those which Parliament has not taken away. Passports are treated as falling within that prerogative domain of foreign affairs, and have been left untouched. This is, moreover, a real problem, for from time to time British citizens are denied passports; for example, scientists who have wished to attend conferences in Russia have been refused passports.

Nor do the Crown's arbitrary powers stop there. In other parts of the Commonwealth it has been held that a Minister was not entitled to insist on a subject's handing back his passport. The passport issued in Britain is worded so that it remains the property of the Crown who can demand its return at any time for any reason. Its withdrawal may be insisted upon whenever it suits the whim of the Crown – for instance, to restrain the movements of a former member of the royal household who may wish to enjoy in the United States the fruits of his articles in American newspapers on the doings of the royal family.

Racial Discrimination

Britain has no laws which discriminate against persons on account of their race and colour. A Jew, a Chinese, a Negro, for example, all enjoy the same voting rights: they must merely comply with the same rules about nationality and residence as everybody else. They are equally entitled to the facilities for education and to the benefit of the social services. The law does not order segregation in public transport or anywhere else. We have already discussed the circumstances in which incitement to racial prejudice is an offence. In these respects Britain is free from the legal restraints which have agitated the United States so much. In this sense, there is equality before the law.

An equally important practical question is the effectiveness with which the law takes positive steps to ensure that persons are not discriminated against on account of race or colour. To say that the law does not discriminate is one thing, but does the law compel persons not to discriminate, or otherwise protect those who are liable to be discriminated against?

In 1943 the West Indian cricketer, Constantine, booked accommodation at the Imperial Hotel, London, for himself and his wife and child. Upon their arrival, the manageress refused them accommodation because they were Negroes, and allegedly used contemptuous and insulting words to them, saying that 'they would not have niggers in the hotel because of the Americans staying there'. Mr Justice Birkett found that Constantine suffered much unjustifiable humiliation and distress in being turned away in the presence of other hotel guests, and held that he had a cause of action in damages, because it is a tort for an inn to refuse available accommodation to travellers. He awarded him only nominal damages of £5.9 It is believed that he was in error in holding that he could not grant substantial damages. Just as for other wrongs – for example – libel, a judge can award large damages for the humiliation and distress which he has suffered, so here also he could have given Constantine a four-figure sum to atone for the humiliation which he had undergone. Constantine won his action although there was no law affording particular protection to Negroes. He won because there is a law of long standing, framed centuries before the colour bar was ever thought of, that an inn has a duty to provide accommodation for all travellers. This rule is only available in a restricted number of cases. If a Negro were turned away at a guest house or at any hotel which is not an inn he would have no remedy: an inn is an enterprise which holds itself out as willing to provide accommodation for travellers and other casual visitors, a definition so vague that it is difficult to apply sometimes. If he were refused a meal at an inn he could win on the authority of *Constantine*'s case, but not if he were refused a meal at a café or restaurant, or an alehouse which provides drink but not food and sleeping accommodation. Nor does the rule give any remedy against somebody who will not take in a Negro as a lodger or rent him a flat. Suppose that a Negro booked accommodation at an hotel or boarding house for himself and his family, to be turned away on arrival when the manager saw the colour of their skins. Even though the hotel was not an inn, the Negro would have an action for damages for breach of contract. He could not, however, recover any damages for humiliation or injured feelings: the law of contract will not award damages of that kind. His damages would be restricted to his cash loss through the breach of contract. To sum up, so long as Mr Justice Birkett's rule is applied, and in view of the restricted amount of damages awarded for breach of contract, the law is not vigorous enough to ensure that hotels will carry out their legal duties – the sums they will have to pay for law-breaking are so small that it will be scarcely worth the while of the aggrieved Negro to claim them in litigation.

There is a limited number of other circumstances where a person discriminated against on account of race or colour could take advantage of a general law requiring a service to be provided for those who require it. A common carrier of goods must carry the goods of all who ask, a ferryman operating under a ferry franchise must transport all who desire to use the service. An action for damages could be brought by anybody who did not receive the service which the other was compelled to give. In no other circumstances does English law provide any compensation for a person who is discriminated against.

Scala Ballroom (Wolverhampton) Ltd v. *Ratcliffe*[10] is another of the extremely rare cases where an incident concerning colour bar reached the Courts. The owners of a ballroom in Wolverhampton would not admit coloured people. Officials of the Musicians' Union told the ballroom owners that they would not allow members of the union to play there while the ban was in force. The owners then sued the officials for damages and for an injunction restraining them from conspiring to cause musicians to break their contracts. The Court of Appeal found that the union contained many coloured members, and that it would have caused bitterness among members had musicians played in the ballroom.

They held that even though the union's material interests were not at stake, it was lawful for the officials to take these steps to protect their legitimate, non-financial interests. The ballroom owners accordingly lost the action.

Many occupations can only be carried on at particular premises if a statutory licence is in force: public houses are licensed to serve intoxicants, cinemas and dance halls are licensed to provide their respective entertainments. Some of these occupations function in circumstances in which racial discrimination may be practised. From time to time objectors have appeared before the licensing magistrates – in Huddersfield and Coventry, for instance – to oppose the renewal of a liquor licence on the ground that the public house refused to serve Negroes. No case where the renewal of a licence was refused on this ground is known. The magistrates have discretionary powers so wide that they would be legally entitled to refuse the renewal of a liquor licence for this reason; on the other hand a higher Court would not interfere with their discretion if they ignored the objection, however clearly it was substantiated. Wolverhampton magistrates renewed the licence of a dance hall, although objectors appeared before them to oppose it on the ground that a colour bar was practised. According to a statement in the House of Commons made by one of the objectors, the magistrates were advised that they had no power to refuse the renewal for this reason. That advice, if given, is believed to be unsound: their discretion is wide enough to enable them either to refuse to renew for this reason or to renew the licence subject to a 'no colour-bar' condition. None the less, leading dance hall companies which have imposed colour bars in some of their halls are no doubt safe in assuming that they will forfeit none of their licences on this account. The position with regard to cinema licences is similar: the licensing bodies could lawfully make 'no colour bar' a condition of a licence if they thought fit.

It is increasingly common to practise discrimination with regard to dwelling-houses. A landlord can let his premises furnished or unfurnished, to those whom he chooses, and he is free to deny Negroes, Jews, or any other class. If he did enter into a lease or tenancy agreement, and then wished to back out on later discovering that his tenant was coloured, the Courts might enforce specific performance of the lease against him: that is, if the tenant requested, the Courts might not be content to compensate the tenant in damages, but instead they might order the landlord to carry out the terms of the lease. If a landlord prohibits his tenant from assigning or sub-letting then his prohibition is legally effective. If, however, he merely forbids assignment or sub-letting of the premises without his consent, the law requires that his consent must not be unreasonably withheld. Ordinarily, one would expect the Courts to declare unreasonable the refusal of the landlord on the ground that the proposed sub-tenant was of a particular race or colour. A local authority may effectively exclude coloured tenants from its houses by restricting them to natives of the area or by imposing a long residential qualification. Restrictions of this kind are in fact often made.

A landowner may wish to impose restrictions, for the benefit of the building estate as a whole, on all the plots of freehold land which he sells off. If he is developing the area for residential purposes, he may wish to ensure that all houses built on these plots shall be of a certain value. He may feel that the value of the remainder of the estate will decline should Negroes buy houses, and may therefore wish to insert covenants on sale which prevent them from doing so. Restrictive covenants of this kind are only effective when they bind not only the original parties to the sale, but also subsequent purchasers. Ordinarily, those who subsequently buy the plots are just as much bound by these covenants as those who first entered into them – as the lawyers say, the benefit and burden of restrictive covenants run with the land. Are restrictive covenants concerning racial discrimination valid? In the United States they have been held void on the ground that they violate the American constitution.[11] The Canadian Supreme Court was called upon to decide whether a covenant by the purchaser of land not to sell it to 'any person of the Jewish, Hebrew, Semitic, Negro or coloured race or blood' could be enforced by the vendor against subsequent purchasers.[12] The Court held the covenant to be unenforceable on two counts. First, it applied the rule that those covenants must touch and concern the land, as distinct from the persons who buy the land, and held that this covenant did not touch and concern the land. Secondly, it held that the covenant was too uncertain: it would be impossible to know whether a particular person had Negro or Semitic blood, in view of the inter-marriages which take place, and there is no specified standard to determine what degree of impurity of blood would fall within the covenant. Decisions of the Supreme Court of Canada are not binding in England, but are considered with respect, and it is quite likely that English Courts would follow the Canadian example and hold such covenants unenforceable for similar reasons.

This prediction is the more likely in view of the pronouncements of the English Courts on one analogous problem. Those who make gifts by will sometimes attach conditions designed to exclude racial classes. Where a testator prohibited the legatee from marrying a person 'not of Jewish parents and of the Jewish faith' the House of Lords held that the legacy was valid, but that the condition was void for uncertainty.[13] Another testator made a gift to a Cambridge college for medical research, but expressed in the will a particular desire that no coloured person or Jew should participate in the gift: the Court held that there was a valid charitable gift, but that the condition imposed was void for uncertainty.[14] Another straw in the wind was the opinion of Sir Hartley Shawcross as Attorney-General when answering a parliamentary question in the House of Commons in 1949. He expressed the view that if hotels were being leased subject to covenants restricting the admission of coloured travellers, those covenants would be void as being contrary to public policy.

Some countries, notably the U.S.A. and Canada, have

codes of fair labour practices designed to prevent discrimination against coloured labour. New York State is a good illustration. The opportunity to obtain employment without discrimination because of race, creed, colour, or national origin is declared to be a civil right, and for any employer or trade union to discriminate on any of those grounds is an unlawful practice. Any person may complain of an unlawful practice to a Fair Employment Practices Commission set up for the purpose. The Commission is empowered, after a hearing, to fine or imprison anybody who is guilty of an unlawful discriminatory practice. Britain has no comparable legal provision.

Complaints are made from time to time that doctors employed under the National Health Service refuse to accept coloured patients, allegedly because their presence in the waiting room would drive away some white patients. It is typical of the one-sided nature of the provisions of the National Health Service Act, 1946 (explained of course by the fact that the medical profession is a very powerful pressure group) that whereas a doctor is given full legal protection for all his rights under the scheme, a coloured person (or any other patient) is denied any legal remedy against a doctor who refuses to have him on his list, even though the local executive council has assigned him to that doctor.

This survey shows that English law is far from affording complete protection for the victims of racial discrimination. It is not surprising, therefore, that frequent attempts are made by private members of Parliament to introduce Bills designed to make various forms of racial discrimination illegal. These Bills have usually defined discrimination as that based on colour, race, or religion, and have made it an offence to deny facilities or advantages on that account: they have been specially directed at keepers of lodging houses, restaurants, and public houses, and places of entertainment. They have also attempted to prevent discrimination with regard to houses. Some earlier versions, but not recent ones, have also covered discriminatory employment practices. Recent ones would make it a separate offence to publish matter inciting contempt or hatred of persons because of their colour, race or religion. None of these Bills has survived a second reading in the House of Commons. The main Governmental objection has been the difficulty in enforcing provisions of this type, especially because of the difficulties of proof, and the belief that educating public opinion is the best solution. Perhaps no reform should be attempted until there has been close study of the methods by which other common-law countries regulate these matters. There has for instance been no serious consideration of the American control of discriminatory practices with respect to labour, public transport and other facilities, and housing, by some administrative agency which might be more effective than merely declaring punishable certain kinds of discrimination. It would remove some of the colour bars which management and unions practise in some areas of employment – for instance the unwillingness of branches of the Transport and General Workers Union to agree to coloured bus conductors in Bristol, Coventry, and other Midland cities. Unfortunately, the Royal Commission and the Departmental Committee seldom seem to be an effective instrument for making this type of comparative study of a legal system in operation. Normally, all that happens is that the Commission remains in London, and invites some visiting professor to attend before it and give evidence. The person chosen is often not the most expert, but the one who enjoys this kind of trip. The conclusion on such meagre investigation can easily be anticipated: the Commission is not satisfied that we should copy the foreign example.

It would be over-optimistic to expect any great reinforcement upon the transatlantic model of our present legal controls of discriminatory practices. Of course, the Courts can often use their present powers so as to further the cause of those who oppose racial prejudice. A good example was the very severe prison sentences imposed by Mr Justice Salmon in 1958 on persons committing offences in the course of the Notting Hill racial disturbances: these were remarkably effective in stopping hooliganism. None the less, it would not be fair to expect the Courts to do much more than they have so far managed, unless their powers are increased by statute.

CHAPTER 12

CONCLUSION

CIVIL liberties in Britain have been shown to be a patchwork. Some of them rest on the chance that citizens have sued each other and given the Courts the opportunity to declare some isolated legal rule. Some rest on sporadic legislation, often passed to meet some specific emergency, real or imaginary. The extent of inroads on certain freedoms rests on the subtleties of ministerial responsibility and the muted insistence of Whitehall to be allowed to govern unhindered.

Attempts have none the less been made to construct a general theory of civil liberties in Britain. Best known is the principle of the Rule of Law, expounded by the nineteenth-century Whig, Dicey, who said:

The general principles of our constitution (as for example the right to personal liberty, or the right of public meeting) are with us the result of judicial decisions determining the rights of private persons in particular cases brought before the Courts; whereas under many foreign constitutions the security (such as it is) given to the rights of individuals results, or appears to result, from the general principles of the constitution. ... Our constitution, in short, is a judge-made constitution. ... There is in the English constitution an absence of those declarations or definitions of rights so dear to foreign constitutionalists. ... Thus the constitution is the result of the ordinary law of the land.[1]

We know that this statement is inexact: for instance, a study, however comprehensive, of decided cases would give the reader a most incomplete picture of the state of British freedom. At the same time it does reveal an important difference of approach between Britain and many other countries. Britain has no one document which can be spoken of as the Constitution – Parliament has never attempted to list our freedoms. In sharp contrast is the

United States, for example. Here is an extract from its Constitution:

Congress shall make no law respecting an establishment of religion, or prohibiting the free exercise thereof; or abridging the freedom of speech, or of the press; or the right of the people peaceably to assemble and to petition the Government for a redress of grievances.

Dicey, successive British governments, and many judges point with pride to this distinguishing characteristic of British liberty and speak disparagingly of written constitutions. They maintain that it is useless to have documents which are merely high-sounding catalogues of freedoms phrased in language so inescapably vague that the little man who finds himself in the hands of the police derives no benefit from them. What counts is whether the judges can give a man a fair trial, whether procedures like *habeas corpus* are readily available to him. These arguments are cogent but not conclusive. The jurisprudential notion of liberty is the same, whether we have the Dicey Rule of Law or a Bill of Rights. For example, freedom of speech can never be a positive power to do something. Every legal system prescribes that you cannot do this and this: you must not defame another, you must not be seditious, you must not be obscene, and so on. The legal concept of liberty is that there are residual areas of great importance where man is free to act as he likes without being regulated by law. Both in Britain and the U.S.A. what is not forbidden is permitted. If a country enshrines its freedoms in a constitutional document, its citizens respond emotionally: the American cherishes many of his liberties the more because they are in the Bill of Rights – public opinion is effectively mobilized in their defence. More than that, in a system like the American, the Constitution is a special law, one that cannot be changed except by a special procedure different from that for ordinary laws. Was it a good thing that all the restraints on freedom contained in the Official Secrets Act of 1911 were rushed through the House of Commons in one day in time of peace as if they were matters of no moment, the citizen no doubt unaware of that curtailment of his liberty which was thereby being effected? Parliamentary sovereignty in Britain ensures that Parliament can change any law, however fundamental, by the same process as, say, a law which increases the amount which a local authority may charge for dustbins.

Even more important is the power given to Courts like the Supreme Court of the United States to intervene if laws inconsistent with the Constitution are passed. Judicial review of administrative interference with civil liberties is much more frequent and effective there than in Britain. Here is the explanation why so many of the British administration's interferences with liberty are beyond the Courts' control in circumstances where it is inconceivable that the Courts in America would stand aside. This has more subtle consequences. Because English lawyers have comparatively few chances to participate in cases affecting civil liberties, there is little interest in the subject professionally – there is no money in it for lawyers – and the dearth of case law makes the universities also inactive in research. This explains, but does not excuse, the fact that this is the first book ever to attempt a detailed survey of the content of British civil liberties, whereas in the United States there are dozens of such books, ranging from the highly specialized monograph to the survey for the general reader.

The British stand on this matter is having unfortunate consequences in the Commonwealth. One of the great unifying strands of the Commonwealth has been the common law. Many members of the Commonwealth are, however, being attracted to constitutions which embody human rights. They maintain that to do so is not inconsistent with the common-law system. They accept the British argument that judicial independence and procedural safeguards are essential for liberty. But they add: why are these inconsistent with a Bill of Rights? Law is not merely a matter of coercion and punishment; is not one of its tasks to set standards of justice acceptable to society? So regarded, a Bill of Rights can provide leadership and set standards. India, Ceylon, and Malaya have guaranteed human rights in the new constitutions which they have formulated since obtaining independence. Most important of all, Canada has recently amended its constitution so as to have a new Bill of Rights. Linked with this issue is the role of the Judicial Committee of the Privy Council which used to be a general Court of appeal from the Commonwealth and Empire. This is a Court composed largely of English senior judges. It could have made a magnificent contribution to Commonwealth relations by aiding the progressive development and unification of the common law. Instead, the measure of its failure is that one member of the Commonwealth after another has dispensed with appeals to it. One of the causes of its failure has been its inability sympathetically to interpret written constitutions, especially the Canadian one. This is a side-effect of our not having a written constitution. American experience shows that judges become much more important where there is a written constitution; they have to immerse themselves in major political questions; they see law as a positive instrument of national policy – the part played by the Supreme Court on racial desegregation over the years is an obvious example. On the contrary the British judge has trained himself as an umpire, avoiding clashes with the Government of the day, cutting himself off from politics whenever possible, and divesting his judgements of social, economic, and political references to the utmost. This outlook has made him unable to provide the kind of interpretation necessary for the written constitutions of other parts of the Commonwealth: hence the by-passing of the Privy Council.

This is a book about liberties in Britain, and not one about international affairs. Yet a quick glance at the international scene may be useful. After the Second World War, the United Nations eventually formulated a Declaration of Human Rights which embodied many of the fundamental freedoms which we have been examining. It was hoped to reinforce this by a Convention which would impose on states a binding obligation to respect these rights. Attempts to produce that Convention failed. Europe has had more success in its European Convention of Human Rights of 1950. This Convention is not content to spell out in detail the content of these freedoms: it sets up machinery for investigation and decision. A citizen who complains that a signatory has violated the Convention may take that state before the European Court of Human Rights, which is empowered to award satisfaction to a citizen who establishes the violation. To save the Court from being swamped, all complaints are screened first by a Commission, which decides whether there is a prima facie breach and ensures that all other remedies have been tried in vain. It is in line with British official attitudes to constitutional arrangements of this kind that, although it is a party to the Convention and has recognized the Commission, the United Kingdom has refused to accept the jurisdiction of the Court and to allow individual citizens to bring matters before the Commission: it is unfortunate that we should lag behind Austria, Belgium, Denmark, Germany, the Netherlands, and Ireland. Our excuse is the unjustified one that the Englishman would receive no more protection than that furnished by the English common law. An Irish citizen who complained of detention without trial has already had his case against the Government of Ireland adjudicated upon by the Court.

The reader will now be able to make up his own mind about the adequacy of the protection of an Englishman's liberties in any particular area. One or two other general matters which we have not stressed are always relevant in making such an assessment: especially the independence of the judges and their quality. Our judges may be relied on strenuously to defend some kinds of freedom. Their emotions will be aroused where personal freedom is menaced by some politically unimportant area of the executive: a case of unlawful arrest by a policeman, for example. Their integrity is, of course, beyond criticism. Yet there are obvious limits to what they can be expected to do in moulding the law of civil liberties. Two factors stand in their way: first, their reluctance to have clashes with senior members of the Government, their desire not to have a repetition of the nineteenth-century strife between Parliament and the Courts; and secondly, their unwillingness to immerse themselves in problems of policy, which of course loom large in many of the issues examined here. M.P.s too, play an important part, especially at question time, in keeping Ministers on their toes with regard to encroachments on the liberty of citizens; but, given the strength of the party system, it would be rash to expect them to safeguard liberty more thoroughly than they are able to do at present.

We are more complacent about our system than we ought to be. One possible way to improve it would be to set up a Civil Rights Commission. This body would be charged with the task of systematically reviewing the law and practice in the various spheres affecting civil liberty. Citizens would bring grievances to its attention, so that it would become a storehouse of information. It would be empowered to do what Royal Commissions conspicuously fail to do: to go into the departments and learn at first hand what is their practice by examination of the files. The deep-seated British reluctance to learn by direct on-the-spot investigation how administration works must be overcome. Just as the evidence before the Franks Committee showed that senior departmental heads knew little from personal experience of how the administrative tribunals under their control performed their tasks, so also English lawyers seldom reach beyond what the Courts have said in their inquiry into legal problems. Such a commission would need full-time expert direction and research staffs to report from first-hand investigation how other countries protect liberty: in short, its organization would have to be free from the obvious defects in personnel of Royal Commissions.

There is much in the history of our freedoms of which we

can be proud. They have not been won without much effort. Englishmen should neglect no available means of preserving and increasing their liberties.

Notes

NOTES

1. PERSONAL FREEDOM AND POLICE POWERS

1. [1914] 1 King's Bench, 595.
2. *Christie* v. *Leachinsky*, [1947] Appeal Cases, 573.
3. Hansard 5th series H.C. vol. 613, col. 1251.
4. 5 February 1954, p. 9.
5. (1765) 19 State Trials, 1029.
6. (1763) 19 State Trials, 1153.
7. [1934] 2 King's Bench, 164.
8. Cmd 3297, para. 33.
9. Hansard 5th Series H.C. vol. 274, cols. 341–2.
10. *Glinski* v. *McIver*, [1962] Appeal Cases 726.
11. *Davis* v. *Lisle*, [1936] 2 King's Bench, 434.
12. *R.* v. *Bass* (1953), 37 Criminal Appeal Reports, 5.
13. [1918] 1 King's Bench, 531.
14. *R.* v. *Podola*, [1960] 1 Queen's Bench, 325.
15. Hansard 5th series H.C. vol. 548, cols. 31–4.
16. *Rochin* v. *California* (1952), 352 United States Reports 165.
17. *Sommersett's* Case (1772), 20 State Trials 1.
18. *R.* v. *Governor of Wormwood Scrubs Prison ex parte Boydell*, [1948] 2 King's Bench 193.
19. *R.* v. *Governor of Brixton Prison ex parte Kolczynski*, [1955] 1 Queen's Bench 540.
20. *In re Castioni*, [1891] 1 Queen's Bench 149.
21. *R.* v. *Board of Control ex parte Rutty*, [1956] 2 Queen's Bench 109.
22. *Ex parte Daisy Hopkins* (1891), 61 Law Journal Queen's Bench 240.
23. Report of the Committee of Privy Councillors appointed to inquire into the interception of Communications (Cmnd 283).

2. PUBLIC MEETINGS

1. *Hickman* v. *Maisey*, [1900] 1 Queen's Bench 752.
2. *Harrison* v. *Duke of Rutland*, [1893] 1 Queen's Bench 142.
3. (1882) 9 Queen's Bench 308.
4. [1902] 1 King's Bench 167.

5. *Lansbury* v. *Riley*, [1914] 3 King's Bench 229.
6. [1936] 1 King's Bench 218.
7. *Jordan* v. *Burgoyne*, [1963] Weekly Law Reports 1043.
8. [1935] 2 King's Bench 249.

3. THEATRE, CINEMA, RADIO, AND TELEVISION

1. *L.C.C.* v. *Bermondsey Bioscope, Ltd*, [1911] 1 King's Bench 44.
   Stott v. *Gamble*, [1916] 2 King's Bench 504.
2. *Ellis* v. *Dubowski*, [1921] 3 King's Bench 621.
3. *Mills* v. *L.C.C.*, [1925] 1 King's Bench 213.
4. Hansard, 5th series, H.C., vol. 494, col. 170.
5. 24 April 1955. 'Coping with British Movie Censorship'.
6. Cmd 8579, as supplemented by Cmnd 80, Cmnd 1066, Cmnd 1537.
7. For post-1964 arrangements about contracts, see the Television Act, 1963.
8. Cmd 8117, Minutes of Evidence of the Committee, Appendix H, Paper 8, para. 2.
9. Television Act, 1954, Section 3 (1) (g).
10. Section 16 (1).
11. Section 16 (2).
12. 62 H.L. Deb. col. 1099–1101.
13. Section 3 (1) of the Television Act, 1954, as amended by Section 16 of the Television Act, 1963.
14. *New Statesman and Nation*, 13 August 1955, p. 187.
15. E.g. Annual Report, 1959–60, Cmnd 1174, p. 12.
16. *R.* v. *Hailwood*, [1928] 2 King's Bench 277.
17. Set out in the Report of the Committee on Broadcasting, Cmnd 1753 (1962), pp. 48–50.
18. Mary Scrutton, *New Statesman and Nation*, 13 October 1956.
19. Changes in the structure of advisory committees from August 1964 are made by para. 12 of the 2nd Schedule to the 1963 Act.
20. Section 2 (2).
21. Section 3 (3). Section 14 of the 1963 Act authorizes I.T.A. to control the amounts of prizes and the rules governing the conduct of the programmes in which the prizes are offered.
22. This is made clear beyond doubt by the Television Act, 1963, Section 16.

4. THE PRINTED WORD AND ADVERTISING

1. Blackstone's Commentaries, vol. 4, 151–2.
2. Cmd 7700.
3. Para. 553.
4. Paras. 413–14.
5. Para. 479.
6. Cmnd 1811 (1962), para. 325.
7. *Carlill* v. *Carbolic Smoke Ball Co.*, [1893] 1 Queen's Bench 256.
8. *Hedley Byrne & Co. Ltd* v. *Heller*, [1963] 3 Weekly Law Reports, 101.
9. Cmnd 1781 (1962), para. 746.
10. Certain detailed changes in the law of television advertising, to come into force after August 1964, are contained in the Television Act, 1963; the text sets out the present law.
11. Section 19 reads: 'It shall be the duty of the Authority to satisfy themselves that the programmes broadcast by the Authority do not include, whether in advertisement or otherwise, any technical device which, by using images of very brief duration or by any other means, exploits the possibility of conveying a message to or otherwise influencing the minds of, members of an audience without their being aware, or fully aware, of what has been done.'
12. And in the Memorandum of Evidence before the Pilkington Committee on Broadcasting in Vol. I, Appendix E, Cmnd 1819 (1962).
13. Set out in full in Appendix E, n. 12 above.
14. *Ward Labs Inc.* v. *Federal Trade Commission* (1960), 276 F. 2d 952.
15. Para. 794.

5. OBSCENITY AND DEFAMATION

1. 11 Siderfin 168.
2. (1727) 2 Strange 788.
3. Hansard 3rd series H.C. vol. 146, p. 327.
4. *R.* v. *Hicklin* (1868), Law Reports 3 Queen's Bench 360 at 371.
5. *R.* v. *Secker & Warburg*, [1954] 2 All England Law Reports 683 at p. 686.
6. *Manchester Guardian*, 18 September 1954.

7. See *The Trial of Lady Chatterley*, ed. C. H. Rolph.

8. *Shaw* v. *Director of Public Prosecutions*, [1962] Appeal Cases 220.

9. Rolph, 121–2.

10. *Censors* (Rede Lecture 1961), 17.

11. Rolph, 232–3.

12. Rolph, 227–30.

13. *Mella* v. *Monanhan* (1961), *Times*, 20 January.

14. [1962] Appeal Cases, 226.

15. At 227.

16. Lord Radcliffe, *Censors* (Rede Lecture, 1961) 15.

17. *R.* v. *Clayton and Halsey*, [1963] 1 Queen's Bench 163.

18. It is unfortunate that H.M. Customs is so secretive about its black list, for most of its titles are such as 'Bottoms Up', 'How To Do It', 'Lascivious Abbot', 'There's a Whip in My Valise', and officers are instructed no longer to detain *Lolita*, Genet's *Journal*, *Ulysses*, *The Well of Loneliness*.

19. *Youssoupoff* v. *Metro-Goldwyn-Mayer Pictures, Ltd* (1934), 50 Times Law Reports 581.

20. *Byrne* v. *Deane* (1937), 1 King's Bench 818.

21. *Russell* v. *Notcutt* (1896), 12 Times Law Reports, 195.

22. *Cassidy* v. *Daily Mirror Newspapers, Ltd* (1929), 2 King's Bench 331.

23. *Tolley* v. *J. S. Fry & Sons*, [1931] Appeal Cases 333.

24. *Monson* v. *Tussauds, Ltd*, [1894] 1 Queen's Bench 671.

25. *Chapman* v. *Ellesmere*, [1932] 2 King's Bench 431.

26. *Kemsley* v. *Foot*, [1952] Appeal Cases 345.

27. *Lyon* v. *Daily Telegraph*, [1943] 1 King's Bench 746.

28. *Hulton* v. *Jones*, [1910] Appeal Cases 20.

29. *Newstead* v. *London Express Newspaper, Ltd*, [1940] 1 King's Bench 377.

6. CONTEMPT OF COURT AND CONTEMPT OF PARLIAMENT

1. *R.* v. *Almon*, reported in Wilmot's Judgments and Opinions (1802).

2. *R.* v. *Evening Standard* (1924), 40 Times Law Reports 833.

3. *In re Labouchère* (1901), 17 Times Law Reports 578.

4. *R.* v. *Evening Standard Co. Ltd*, [1954] 1 Queen's Bench 578.

5. *R.* v. *Griffiths*, [1957] 2 Queen's Bench 192.

6. *R.* v. *Bolam* (1949), 93 Solicitor's Journal 220.

7. *R.* v. *Odhams Press Ltd*, [1957] 1 Queen's Bench 73. The com-

ments of the Court of Appeal in *Attorney-General* v. *Butterworth*, [1963] 1 Queen's Bench 696, on the case also evince a trend away from the imposition of strict liability for contempt.

8. *Stirling* v. *Associated Newspapers, Ltd*, [1960] Scots Law Times 5.
9. *R.* v. *Beaverbrook Newspapers Ltd*, [1962] Northern Ireland Reports, 15.
10. *Manchester Guardian*, 13 February.
11. *R.* v. *Duffy*, [1960] 2 Queen's Bench 188.
12. Hansard 5th series H.C. vol. 640, col. 35, 8 May 1961.
13. *Williams* v. *Settle*, [1960] 2 All England Law Reports 806 at p. 812 (*per* Sellers, L.J.).
14. Hansard 5th series vol. 226, cols. 1238–9 House of Lords.
15. Op. cit. col. 191. Of course, after the week-end Press had exposed the error, the Lord Chancellor had to withdraw his advice the following week.
16. *R.* v. *Gray*, [1900] 2 Queen's Bench 36.
17. *R.* v. *New Statesman (Editor)* (1928), 44 Times Law Reports, 301.
18. A Report by Justice, *Contempt of Court*, (1959) p. 15.
19. *Ambard* v. *Attorney-General for Trinidad and Tobago*, [1936] Appeal Cases 322.
20. At 335.
21. *R.* v. *Colsey*, *Times*, 9 May 1931.
22. Slesser, *Judgment Reserved*, 256.
23. Mr Cecil H. King, at the Annual General Meeting of Sunday Pictorial Newspapers, Ltd, 4 June 1962.
24. Cmnd 479, 1958.
25. Hansard 5th series H.C. vol. 443, col. 1100 et seq.
26. 2nd Report from Committee of Privileges 1956–7. 20 December 1956.
27. Report of Press Council, 30 April 1957.
28. 4th Report from the Committee of Privileges, 1956–7, 5 February 1957.
29. May's Parliamentary Practice, 16th ed. 1957, p. 92.
30. See page 147.
31. See page 197.
32. *Stockdale* v. *Hansard* (1839), 9 Adolphus and Ellis 1.
33. *Howard* v. *Gossett* (1845), 10 Queen's Bench 359.

7. FREEDOM OF RELIGION

1. *Atwood's Case*, Cro. Jac. 421.

2. 11 Ventris 293.
3. *R. v. Ramsay and Foote* (1883), 15 Cox's Criminal Cases. 231 at 238.
4. *Bowman* v. *Secular Society Ltd,* [1917] Appeal Cases 406.
5. At p. 466.
6. (1921) 16 Criminal Appeal Reports 87.
7. Private member's bills were thrown out in the eighteen-eighties. When in 1921 the Home Secretary rejected Gott's petition for remission of sentence he supported the punishment of those venting coarse and scurrilous ridicule on subjects which are sacred to most people in this country.
8. *In re Gathercole* (1838), 2 Lewin 237.
9. At p. 254.
10. *R. v. Senior,* [1899] 1 Queen's Bench 283.
11. *Ohuchuku* v. *Ohuchuku,* [1960] 1 All England Law Reports 253.
12. *Sowa* v. *Sowa,* [1961] Probate 70.
13. *Bowman* v. *Secular Society Ltd,* [1917] Appeal Cases 406.
14. *Bourne* v. *Keane,* [1919] Appeal Cases 815.
15. *In re Hummeltenberg,* [1923] 1 Chancery 237.
16. [1955] 1 Queen's Bench 408.

8. FREEDOM AND SECURITY

1. (1770) 20 State Trials, 870.
2. *R. v. Burns* (1886), 16 Cox's Criminal Cases 355.
3. These were quotations from Digest of the Criminal Law, arts. 91 and 93, a book by the leading criminal lawyer of the time, Mr Justice Stephen.
4. *An Editor on Trial,* 1947.
5. *Boucher* v. *R.,* [1951] 2 Dominion Law Reports 369.
6. Evidence of the Director before the Select Committee on Obscene Publications, para. 367.
7. *R. v. Leese, Times,* 19 and 22 September 1936.
8. Archbold, p. 1209.
9. *Joshua* v. *R.,* [1955] 1 All England Law Reports 22.
10. [1962] Appeal Cases, 220, and see p. 140 *ante*.
11. Wade and Phillips 4th ed., 361.
12. Charles Marvin, *Our Public Officers,* 2nd ed. 1880.
13. Mr Cecil H. King, Annual General Meeting of Sunday Pictorial Newspapers, Ltd, 4 June 1962.
14. Clayton Hutton, *Official Secret.*

15. *Lewis* v. *Cattle*, [1938] 2 King's Bench 454.
16. *Chandler* v. *Director of Public Prosecutions*, [1962] 3 Weekly Law Reports, 694.
17. Para. 134.
18. Cmnd 1681.
19. Cmd 9715.
20. *Cole* v. *Young* (1956), 351 United States Reports 536.
21. *Greene* v. *McElroy* (1959), 360 United States Reports 474.
22. 197 House of Lords Debates, col. 1275, 21 June 1956.
23. Para. 52.

9. FREEDOM TO WORK

1. *Vine* v. *National Dock Labour Board*, [1957] Appeal Cases 488.
2. *Addis* v. *Gramophone Co., Ltd*, [1909] Appeal Cases 488.
3. *Leng & Co., Ltd* v. *Andrews*, [1909] 1 Chancery 763.
4. *Eastes* v. *Russ*, [1914] 1 Chancery 468.
5. *Spring* v. *National Amalgamated Stevedores and Dockers Society*, [1956] 2 All England Law Reports 221.
6. *Bonsor* v. *Musicians' Union*, [1956] Appeal Cases 104.
7. *Huntley* v. *Thornton*, [1957] 1 All England Law Reports 234.
8. *Rookes* v. *Barnard*, [1963] 1 Queen's Bench 623.
9. *Allen* v. *Flood*, [1898] Appeal Cases.
10. *Lee* v. *Showmen's Guild*, [1952] 2 Queen's Bench 329.
11. *Abbott* v. *Sullivan*, [1952] 1 King's Bench 189.

10. PROTECTION AGAINST PRIVATE POWER

1. *R.* v. *Tronoh Mines, Ltd*, [1952] 1 All England Law Reports 697.
2. *Morgan* v. *Tate & Lyle, Ltd*, [1955] Appeal Cases 21.

11. FREEDOM OF MOVEMENT AND RACIAL DISCRIMINATION

1. The Home Secretary stated on 20 November 1958 that in the three cases thus far when the magistrate did not concur in the recommendation to deport, deportation had not been proceeded with: Hansard, vol. 595, col. 1349.
2. The United States Supreme Court in fact held that the

United States had no power, without a hearing, to deprive Cort of his nationality for remaining outside its borders in order to evade military service.

3. *R.* v. *Governor of Brixton Prison, ex parte Kolczynski,* [1955] 1 Queen's Bench 540.

4. *R* v. *Governor of Brixton Prison, ex parte Schtraks,* [1962] 3 Weekly Law Reports 1013.

5. *Zacharia* v. *Republic of Cyprus,* [1962] 2 Weekly Law Reports 1163.

6. *R.* v. *Secretary of State for Home Affairs, ex parte Soblen,* [1962] 3 Weekly Law Reports 1145.

7. *R.* v. *Governor of Brixton Prison, ex parte Soblen,* [1962] 3 Weekly Law Reports 1154.

8. *Kent* v. *Dulles* (1958), 357 United States Reports 116.

9. [1944] King's Bench 693.

10. [1958] 3 All England Law Reports 220.

11. *Shelley* v. *Kraemer,* (1948), 334 United States Reports 1.

12. *Noble & Wolf* v. *Alley,* [1951] 1 Dominion Law Reports 321.

13. *Clayton* v. *Ramsden,* [1943] Appeal Cases 320.

14. *Re Meres Will Trusts, Times,* 4 May 1957.

12. CONCLUSION

1. Dicey, *Law of the Constitution* (10th ed.) 203.

Table of Statutes

TABLE OF STATUTES

TABLE OF STATUTES

Table of Cases

TABLE OF CASES

TABLE OF CASES

Index

INDEX

*Some more books published by Penguins
on the law are described on the
following pages*

JOHN CITIZEN AND THE LAW
Ronald Rubinstein

'The best "popular" account of everyday law that has ever appeared at the price ... will delight and instruct John Citizens in their thousands' – *New Statesman*

This fifth edition of *John Citizen and the Law* has been thoroughly revised and enlarged to over four hundred pages by the author's son, Christopher Rubinstein. There are new chapters on Civil Liberties and ownership of land, and major changes in the chapter on betting and gaming. Information on hire-purchase, the Rent Act of 1957, and many other important adjustments in English law are included to bring the book right up-to-date.

THE CRIMINAL LAW
F. T. Giles

The object of this book is to give a short, readable account of the English criminal law. The first part is devoted to a detailed account of a trial for murder as seen from the legal point of view. An outline of the powers and procedure of the criminal courts is given in the second section. The last part deals with the offences most commonly occupying the attention of the courts, such as murder, manslaughter, theft, and fraud.

This third edition of *The Criminal Law* had been brought completely up-to-date.

THE QUEEN'S COURTS
Peter Archer

English law embodies generations of experience, but it is constantly adapting itself to new situations, and the twentieth century has witnessed the birth of numerous tribunals which have taken their place alongside the ancient courts.

Of all these, their work, and their place in English life, *The Queen's Courts*, now completely revised and brought up to date, sets out to tell. It concludes with a comparison between the legal institutions of this country and those which function in different settings for different ways of life.

THE LAW IN PELICANS

Considering how often the ordinary citizen, as householder, parent, businessman, or traveller, is involved in the law, it is remarkable how little has been done to explain to him what the law is; how it has come to be what it is; and how it might be improved.

Pelicans have embarked, therefore, on a bold, new attempt to explore for the general reader a variety of legal topics of wide public interest.

This volume is one of the first three titles. The other two, published simultaneously, are:

THE CONSUMER, SOCIETY, AND THE LAW
Gordon Borrie and Aubrey L. Diamond

THE FAMILY AND THE LAW
Margaret Puxton

Future titles will include:

THE ART OF THE ADVOCATE
Richard du Cann

THE IDEA OF THE LAW
Dennis Lloyd

A SHORT HISTORY OF ENGLISH LAW
Alan Harding

THE WORKER AND THE LAW
K. W. Wedderburn